Daughters of Eve

Daughters of Eve
Women's Writing from the
German Democratic Republic

TRANSLATED AND EDITED BY

NANCY LUKENS AND

DOROTHY ROSENBERG

UNIVERSITY OF NEBRASKA PRESS

Lincoln and London

Acknowledgments for the use of
copyrighted material appear on pp. 327–29.

© 1993 by the University of Nebraska Press

Manufactured in the United States of America
The paper in this book meets the minimum requirements
of American National Standard for Information Sciences—
Permanence of Paper for Printed Library Materials,
ANSI Z39.48-1984.

Publication of this book was assisted by a grant
from the Andrew W. Mellon Foundation.

Library of Congress Cataloging-in-Publication Data

Daughters of eve : women's writing from the German Democratic Republic
/ translated and edited by Nancy Lukens and Dorothy Rosenberg.
    p.   cm. — (European women writers series)
  Includes bibliographical references.
  ISBN 0-8032-2892-9 (alk. paper) ISBN 0-8032-7942-6 (pbk.)
    1. German prose literature—20th century—Translations into English.   2. English
prose literature—Translations from German.   3. German prose literature—Women
authors.   4. German prose literature—Germany (East)   I. Lukens, Nancy.
II. Rosenberg, Dorothy, 1948–   .   III. Series.
PT1308.D38   1993
838'.914080809287—dc20   92-31238
                                                                              CIP

Contents

Translators' Preface

THIS ANTHOLOGY emerged from our common perception that East German women's writing is vitally interesting and our shared frustration that it is virtually inaccessible to English-speaking readers. Although a few major works by Anna Seghers and Christa Wolf have been translated and published in the West, the general ignorance of what has been written and widely discussed in Eastern Europe in recent years certainly includes the literature produced by women in the former German Democratic Republic. Considering a population of only 16.5 million prior to 1989 and the complications of publishing in a centrally planned economy, the volume and diversity of novels, short stories, nonfiction, and poetry published in the short history of the GDR is an indication of the vital role that literature played as a seismograph of social consciousness. The proportion of women writers is significant: for example, of approximately 250 new literary titles published in the GDR in 1984[1] (one title for every sixty-six hundred citizens), 30 percent were written by women.[2]

Our decision to create this book was a response to the 1983 Boston conference of the Coalition of Women in German. In making our selection, we considered more than one hundred single- and multiple-author anthologies, novels, and volumes of interviews published in the 1970s and 1980s which focused on issues relating to women. We chose to limit ourselves to the generation of women whose first publications appeared after the GDR was founded, whose adult experience was shaped primarily in that society. The twenty-five women represented in this collection span a quarter-century in age difference: the oldest, Christa Wolf, was born in 1929; the youngest, Gabriele Eckart, in 1954. The stories, novel excerpts, essays, and autobiographical narratives included were published between 1970 and 1986; some are first publications, and others are more mature writings. One indicator of the literary visibility of women writers is the list of published titles that accompanies the biographical sketch of each author in our collection preceding her text.

Our title deserves some explanation. It is borrowed from Renate Apitz's anthology *Evastöchter*, whose title is a tongue-in-cheek reference to an uncomplimentary German term for a stereotypical female and, in the GDR context, clearly ironic. We intend it to suggest both the diversity and the universality of women's experience articulated in this collection, as well as the thirst for knowledge associated with the Eve of biblical tradition.

Any attempt to transfer works of literature from one culture to another involves the risk of lost meanings and intentions, of misunderstood or missed inferences. We have taken a number of factors into account in making our editorial and translation decisions. First, we have chosen to paraphrase acronyms specific to the GDR and terms whose meaning in that context was so different as to be misleading in English—for example materialism, ideology, brigade, cooperative—rather than interrupt the narratives with extensive notes. Where a common term carries a different connotation in the East German context or situations specific to the GDR are alluded to or ironized, we have included explanatory comments in the text introductions or the Afterword.

With such a diverse group of authors, we have attempted to do justice to the wide variety of stylistic and linguistic features of the texts in our renderings of the tone and rhetorical style of each piece. Whereas Irmtraud Morgner consciously uses archaic terms as well as the highly technical vocabulary of nuclear physics to cause a sense of linguistic alienation, the narrator on Katja Lange-Müller's geriatric ward speaks the down-to-earth idiom of the working class, and Maxie Wander reproduces an unusually authentic slice of life in the Berlin dialect of her "Ute G." We have attempted to remain as literal as possible while reproducing the tone and style of the original or, in the case of regional dialect, creating an eye dialect to approximate it.

We have retained all original formating: paragraph divisions and space breaks, the use of italics and ellipsis points. One feature frequently encountered in German is the series of short utterances joined by commas into a single sentence or fragmented by periods to indicate a colloquial tone, indirect speech, or interior monologue. Another is the narration of dialogue or interior monologue without the use of quotation marks. In both cases we have generally followed the originals rather than imposing strict American conventions, since we feel that these features are an integral part of the authors' voices and the culture they represent.

Invariably, even women's linguistic usage still reflects gender bias. In the interest of accuracy, we have not tried to eradicate that when, for example, Ilse—the agricultural cooperative's chairperson in Eckart's documentary text—mentions that her successor will have to be "a strong man." In some cases, gender-exclusive language is used in conscious irony, as in Apitz's reference to the biblical creation myth in the sentence "It is not good for man to be alone, saith the Lord." There we have consciously chosen to let the exclusive connotation in English stand, despite the unmistakably inclusive German *der Mensch,* in order to suggest that the author is undercutting the prevailing gender-biased reading of the Genesis narrative. The reflections of Christa Wolf's tomcat narrator contain male-biased language that is an integral part of the created persona and therefore consciously retained in translation.

Concerning gender and pronoun choice, German usage applies the neuter pronoun *es* to a young girl, a baby, or a young child of either sex, unless the child's name or sex has just been mentioned. We have followed this usage in translation to retain the tone of the original.

We have not significantly altered or abridged any original texts, since omissions in effect create a different text. In presenting excerpts from longer works, we chose narrative portions that can stand alone. One story has appeared previously in an abridged English version under a different title;[3] one was translated earlier, also under a different title;[4] otherwise, we have included only previously untranslated works. In all cases, translations are our own and are the product of our collaborative effort.

Finally, a word about the collaborative process itself. Our backgrounds and scholarly experience are quite different. The project would have been unthinkable without Dorothy's research and travel in the GDR over the years and her firsthand knowledge of women writers of the 1970s and 1980s, complemented by Nancy's experience in editing and administration. As scholars and teachers of literature, we have both benefited from the feedback we have received when using some of these texts in courses on women writers and when doing public readings and presentations of our research. Although each text bears the name of its primary translator, we worked together on every part of the book. Each of us translated half the German material; we read and critiqued each others' drafts, read our revised versions aloud, and discussed them until we arrived at a "Third Way" that we felt approached the level of readability in English, accuracy, and stylistic faithfulness we aimed for.

Notes

1. Dieter Schlenstedt, former GDR Academy of Sciences, public lecture, March 27, 1989, University of New Hampshire.

2. Professor Eva Kaufmann, Humboldt University (East Berlin), correspondence with Dorothy Rosenberg.

3. Irmtraud Morgner, "The Rope," trans. Karen Achberger, in *German Feminism: Readings in Politics and Literature*, ed. Edith Hoshino Altbach, Jeanette Clausen, Dagmar Schultz, and Naomi Stephan (Albany: SUNY Press, 1984).

4. Christa Wolf, "A Tomcat's New Philosophy of Life," trans. Joan Becker, in *Thinking It Over: Thirty Stories from the GDR*, ed. Hubert Witt (Berlin: Seven Seas, 1976). As we go to press, this text has become available as "The New Life and Opinions of a Tomcat," trans. Rick Takvorian and Helke Schwarzbauer, in Christa Wolf, *What Remains and Other Stories* (New York: Farrar, Straus & Giroux, 1993).

Acknowledgments

WE ARE GRATEFUL to the National Endowment for the Humanities, a federal agency, for the 1988–89 translation grant that enabled us to devote a major portion of our time to research and translation. The project was also assisted by a travel grant from the International Research and Exchanges Board, with funds provided by the National Endowment for the Humanities, the Andrew W. Mellon Foundation, and the Department of State. None of these organizations is responsible for the views expressed in this volume.

The University of New Hampshire contributed cost-sharing and support services. Its Center for the Humanities and Research Office provided administrative assistance, enabled us to host one of the anthology authors in October 1989, and contributed to publication costs. Dean Stuart Palmer of the College of Liberal Arts granted additional release time and funds toward copyright permissions. The Nuclear Physics Group offered helpful advice on electron scattering terminology. The Computing and Information Services staff provided facilities and expertise. Jean Pietrowicz assisted in one stage of manuscript production.

Wolfgang Mueller of Dickinson College served as a reader of the manuscript.

We thank Patricia Herminghouse of the University of Rochester and Sara Lennox of the University of Massachusetts at Amherst for their advice and critical support of the project since its inception. Rochelle Lieber, Mary Beth Rhiel, and Cathy Turnbull of the University of New Hampshire and Robert McIntyre of Smith College offered helpful suggestions at various draft stages.

We also acknowledge our debt to Eva Kaufmann and Irene Dölling of the Humboldt University of Berlin and Ingrid Hammer of the Academy of Arts, Leipzig, for facilitating our access to texts and secondary materials, as well as to the former Ministry of Education and Culture and the Copyright Office of the German Democratic Republic for their cooperation and assistance.

Finally, we want to express our gratitude to the Coalition of Women in German for its consistent interest in and support of this project.

Nancy Lukens   Dorothy Rosenberg
Durham, New Hampshire   Northampton, Massachusetts

Introduction

Women, Social Policy, and Literature in the German Democratic Republic

Dorothy Rosenberg

THE EUPHORIA that greeted the political upheavals of 1989 has turned out to be extremely short-lived as the collapse of the Soviet bloc has turned from a triumph for Western democracy into a threat to Western stability and prosperity. In the midst of this geopolitical upheaval, the status of women and more generally of gender relations—among the most sensitive indicators of social and economic development—has not received significant attention in the discussions regarding the transformation of Eastern Europe. Even though the process of German unification offers the most radical example of a rapid transition from a planned to a market economy, the experience of women in the former German Democratic Republic has hardly been addressed, despite the fact that it provides us with important keys to understanding both the recent past and the probable near future of European women in both East and West.

The texts that follow take a first step toward filling in that gap.[1] As noted in the Translators' Preface, we were deeply affected by the universality of the issues addressed in the stories collected here. The wit, humor, stoic resignation, dignity, or despair with which these writers face familiar contradictions sends the same message to American readers as to the original GDR audience: We're not alone, we're not crazy, there is a problem and it isn't us. Our common experience as women in a postindustrial society far outweighs the cultural or political-economic differences among us. Still, the specificity of women's lives in the GDR offers a new and oddly unexpected dimension to Western discussions of gender and social policy issues. Long familiar in the West, unemployment, deskilling, and the feminization of poverty are shocking new experiences for women in the five new states.

The social and historical conditions under which the GDR was founded and developed led to a level of state attention to women's issues unparalleled in any other socialist society. In fact, the system of measures addressing women and family issues compared favorably with the social welfare systems of the Nordic countries, the wealthiest and most socially progressive of the advanced capitalist states, which explains the strongly declared interest of West German women in adopting these measures for themselves. Looking beneath the surface, we find that the GDR social welfare system was able to mitigate but not resolve the conflicts experienced by women struggling to cope with the demands of work and family. Although the GDR example cannot provide us with a solution to the contradictions inherent within women's lives in postindustrial society, it does offer a vivid illustration of the positive effects of social legislation and the limits of state intervention.

The Economic Effects of Unification

Germany, regarded as the economic engine that would pull Eastern Europe into the market system, quickly began to look less robust as the costs of the economic "shock therapy" program in the five new eastern states became visible. The drastic changes that followed German unification on October 3, 1990, are now costing the German government well over $100 billion a year.[2] In response to what has been described as a "budget hemorrhage," the German government has pledged to cut increases in federal, state, and local expenditures through 1995. Even using extremely optimistic growth projections, this planned moratorium would mean severe cuts in the social welfare system.[3]

By the spring of 1992, industrial production in the former GDR had fallen to 29 percent of its 1989 level,[4] and the labor force had shrunk from about 9.8 million to 6 million.[5] Of those, some 1.4 million were officially unemployed, another million were working shortened hours, and nearly a million more were in federally financed job-creation or retraining programs.[6] In other words, within two and a half years of unification, nearly 40 percent of the pre-1989 East German labor force had been removed, and half of those left were not fully employed.

Women, 48.8 percent of the labor force in September 1989, made up 63.2 percent of the unemployed in the five new states by June 1992.[7] Not only were women unemployed more often than men, but their prospects for reemployment were significantly worse: despite equal opportunity laws, only 36 percent of the positions in federally funded job creation programs (ABM) had gone to women.[8] The private labor market was even less hospitable.[9]

East German women's initial responses were pragmatic: the birth rate in eastern Germany declined 50 percent between 1989 and December 1991.[10] Women made up 56 percent of those enrolled in training and retraining courses (the majority for administrative and clerical tasks), although with massive reductions in the service sector, there was little chance of newly trained persons reentering employment quickly.[11] Price increases,[12] cut-backs and closures of child-care facilities, job losses, and economic uncertainty were also reflected in a growing number of sterilizations and abortions.[13]

For the majority of East German women, transition to the West German market system offers insecurity, deskilling and downward mobility, but unification with West Germany also provides unemployment benefits or welfare—that is, indignity, but not destitution. Now that the GDR is a part of history, it is even more important to place it in context, to determine current trends, and to compare the values and advantages or disadvantages of its former system. The foregoing statistics show that the problems and contradictions in women's lives described in the texts below not only did not go away on October 3, 1990, but have been joined or exacerbated by the social and economic dislocation of transition.

The popular rejection of the German "real socialist" state became visible with a wave of mass emigration in the summer and fall of 1989 following the opening of the Hungarian-Austrian border. One little-emphasized factor stands out: three out of four of the emigrés were young men. In contrast, women were equally represented in the crowd that gathered in the main square of Leipzig on October 9, 1989, to defy the police and march through the city chanting, "We are the people." Women were prominent in the GDR opposition and were present in large numbers in the demonstrations of October and November 1989 and in the organizations demanding democratic reform which sprang up in their wake. In December 1989, as the slogans turned from "We are the people" to "We are one people" and finally to "Germany, united Fatherland," and the agenda of the streets shifted from political reform to reunification, so did the composition of the crowd. Men once again dominated the scene.

Negotiations to form a confederation between the two German states in the spring of 1990 were initially impeded by West German demands that the GDR system be completely reorganized and reshaped to conform to the legal, political, and economic practices of the Federal Republic of Germany. Though these demands generally met with little resistance from the established political parties in either East or West, "Women and Family" policy stands out as a major and significant exception. Women's organizations and women's caucuses within existing parties and newly formed independent political movements, East and West, joined to demand that the extensive system of East German legislation addressing the social, legal, and economic status of women be not only retained within the territory of the GDR but extended to the FRG. Their concerns were brushed aside in the rush to unification.[14]

A Brief History of Women's Policy in the German Democratic Republic

The living and working conditions of women in the GDR were to a large degree determined by state policies that were motivated by a mixture of economic, ideological, and pragmatic considerations. The GDR was founded in 1949 as a socialist state within the territory of the Soviet Occupation Zone, the remnant of a culturally homogeneous central European society that had been dislocated and institutionally delegitimized by fascism and military defeat. The new leadership, largely returned from exile in the Soviet Union or imprisonment in Nazi concentration camps, was both ideologically committed to and politically and economically heavily dependent on the support and labor of women.

Measures to achieve the legal and economic equality of women were first instituted by the Soviet Military Administration in May 1945 and steadily expanded with the emergence of an autonomous civil administration. Special efforts were made to help reduce the economic burden of child raising and to encourage fertility. These financial support programs and social institutions, reorganized to facilitate simultaneous career advancement and motherhood, must be seen in light of the status of German women before May 1945. The National Socialist regime had systematically excluded women from higher education, the professions, the skilled trades, and the civil service; it had outlawed equal pay for women and attempted to force "eugenically sound" women into full-time and prolific motherhood.

The efforts undertaken by the GDR administration to reintegrate women into the public sphere included a comprehensive revision of the legal code to guarantee full legal equality and a series of special laws and policies promoting the education and training of women. Further legislation assured maternity leave and benefits with guaranteed reemployment, sick leave, and paid time off for child care and housework. The economic measures included the institution and enforcement of equal pay for equal work, the integration of women into the professions and skilled trades, and the full integration of women into higher education.[15] The legalization of abortion in 1972 was accompanied by an expansion of pronatalist measures, including maternity leaves, job guarantees, and child welfare transfer payments.

These efforts were motivated by a combination of ideological commitment to the emancipation of women and the immediate necessity of drawing the relatively untapped pool of female labor power into the depleted workforce for the reconstruction of postwar Germany. With an expanding economy and a continuing loss of population to the West, the female labor force continued to be vital to the GDR economy. By the 1980s about 92 percent of the female population was either in training or employed outside the home.[16] At the same time, 90 percent of GDR women had at least one child.[17] Faced by the simultaneous need to keep women in the labor force and to maintain and expand its population, the government responded with an array of parental leaves, affordable child care, and affirmative action measures resulting in an exemplary program of parent and child support.

In 1989, after forty years of active practical efforts to facilitate the emancipation and full social equality of women, the GDR was a society in which the structural details of emancipation were largely in place and, to a degree somewhat breathtaking to the outsider, taken for granted by the vast majority of the population. Yet these measures, which must be seen as a form of positive discrimination toward women, are now being rolled back in many areas to conform with the far weaker set of social guarantees and supports in the Federal Republic.[18]

Women in the Labor Force

FRG (1988)[19]

Of women aged 15–65, 55 percent were in the labor force: single, 61.4 percent; married, 47.5 percent; widowed, 32.0 percent; divorced, 75 percent.

Of all employed women, 32.2 percent worked part time (less than 34 hours per week); of these, 44 percent worked more than half time (21–34 hours), 54 percent less than 21 hours.

GDR (1989)[20]

Of women aged 15–60, 91.1 percent were in the labor force (including apprentices and students; without these categories the figure falls to 78.1 percent).

Of all employed women, 27.1 percent worked part time (less than 40 hours per week); of these, 80 percent worked more than half time (60 percent, 25–35 hours; 20 percent, more than 35 hours); the number working less than 25 hours steadily declined.

Unemployment

FRG (1988)[21]

Male unemployment was 7.7 percent; female, 12.3 percent. In 1986, more than 30 percent of unemployed women had been without work for more than a year, and the number unemployed for more than two years had tripled. In 1985, nearly twice as many women (41.2 percent) as men (22 percent) were denied unemployment benefits because of failure to meet employment insurance requirements. Women with children who cannot prove that they have day care are not eligible for unemployment benefits or job referral services because they are considered unable to work.[22]

GDR (1988)

Unemployment was 0 percent; all citizens were guaranteed employment. Unemployment has risen rapidly since February 1990. Women are currently over-represented among the unemployed and underrepresented among those being rehired. As of June 1992, women constituted 63 percent of the total unemployed,[23] with significantly worse chances of reemployment than men.[24] Single mothers are disproportionately represented among the unemployed (10 percent of total), and an extreme drop in living standard presents special difficulties for this group, as does reemployment. Women with college degrees are over-represented among the unemployed, compared with men who have the same qualifications. Women over the age of fifty-five now have an unemployment rate 250 percent higher than that of men over sixty.[25]

Education and Training

In the FRG, students accepted to university programs are eligible for state-subsidized (BAFÖG) loans.[26] In the GDR, education and technical training were free. Tuition, fees, and stipends were guaranteed to all students accepted into postsecondary, vocational training, or further education programs, regardless of parental income.

FRG (1987)[27]

25 percent of both men and women 20–24 years old have a high school diploma. Women as a percentage of student population:

High school/gymnasium	50.5%
Technical school	52.8%
Factory apprentices	42%
University	38%

Nearly 80 percent of all women with university degrees are either teachers, pharmacists, or doctors. In 1985 women held 3.8 percent of the 52,000 top executive positions in West German industry.[28] By 1990, women held only 2.3 percent of professorships and 5 percent of non-tenured teaching positions at West German universities.[29] The figure of 11 percent of academic employees sometimes used is achieved by including nonteaching staff.[30]

GDR (1989)[31]

Women as a percentage of student population:

High school/oberschule	56.8%
Technical school	70.3%
Trade apprenticeships	41.25%
University	48.6%

The 1978 figures show that 65.8 percent of teachers, 20 percent of school principals, 8.5 percent of tenured university professors, 49 percent of doctors, 52 percent of dentists, 64 percent of pharmacists, and 45.1 percent of judges were women.[32] By 1988, entry-level skilled trade or professional qualifications had reached gender balance in age cohorts up to forty.[33] Women were 35 percent of assistant professors and lecturers and 9 percent of full professors at East German universities.[34] In 1989 women held nearly 66 percent of the administrative positions in education, health care, and trade; 40–50 percent of the administrative positions in light industry, service industry, and local administration, and slightly more in the post office and telephone service; 25 percent in transportation and state administration; 20 percent in heavy industry and agriculture. Even so, overall representation at the upper levels remained very low: 1 to 3 percent. Women reached about 5 percent in trade and surpassed 20 percent representation only at the highest levels in education.[35]

Income: Male-Female Differentials

	Wage Workers	Salaried Employees
FRG (1987)[36]	women earned 70%	women earned 64% (all salaried)
GDR (1988)[37]	women earned 83.2%	women earned 84% (college grads)

Birth and Divorce Rates

	Birth Rate	Fertility Rate
FRG (1987)[38]	10.5/1,000	48
GDR (1988)[39]	12.0/1,000	54.7

Although the GDR birth rate was higher, neither German state has achieved simple reproduction of the population since 1971, and the trend is downward: the birth rate in the former GDR dropped 40 percent in the first seven months of 1991, compared with the same period in 1990.[40]

The GDR had the world's fifth highest divorce rate (after the United States, the Soviet Union, Cuba, and Great Britain). In 1988, 38 percent of all GDR marriages ended in divorce,[41] compared with 31 percent in the FRG in 1987.[42] As of 1989, the proportion of single-parent families (mostly mothers with children) was approximately 18 percent in both East and West. The GDR had 340,000 single mothers raising minor children;[43] the FRG, 821,000.[44] Nearly half of all single-parent families in West Germany were at or below the poverty line. Statistics assembled since unification show that 77 percent of all single-parent families in Germany have incomes below the welfare level.[45]

Maternity Leave

GDR

Women were given six weeks of leave before the birth and twenty weeks afterward (twenty-two if there were complications), during which the mother received a social insurance payment equal to her average monthly net earnings, followed by paid parental leave (for which a spouse or grandmother was also eligible) at 70–90 percent of average net pay until the child reached one year of age. Leave was extended to eighteen months for the second or subsequent child, two years for twins, three years for triplets.

As of 1989, 33.6 percent of all live births in the GDR were to single mothers.[46] In addition to the "baby year," single mothers received a support payment if no day care was available or if the child was unable to attend because of health problems.[47]

All new mothers received 1,000M per child, issued in seven installments by pre- and postnatal clinics. All parents also received monthly state child support payments depending on the number of children (250M for one child, 300M for two, 350M for three), until the child completed the tenth grade, regardless of family income level.[48] Children in the eleventh and twelfth grades received the same financial support as did those in apprenticeship programs. Students and apprentices who became parents received an extra 60M per month per child.[49] Single mothers who were students or in training and were unable to find public day-care space received a further monthly payment of at least 150M per month to finance private day care.[50] All these measures had been canceled by January 1, 1991, and replaced by the FRG system.

FRG

Mothers receive maternity leave six weeks before and eight weeks after birth at average net pay. Since July 1, 1990, a woman has been able to take child-care leave (which can be shared with her spouse) until the child reaches eighteen months at a flat payment of 600DM per month for twelve months (family maximum income limits apply after the seventh month), followed by regular state child support payments of 100DM per child (single mothers without outside income can receive a higher level of state support for a maximum of three years).[51] All new mothers receive 100DM per child at birth.[52] All other forms of support are subject to means testing, which includes examination of the income and assets of all first-degree relatives (parents, siblings, children).

Day Care

GDR

Day care was state subsidized and in fact universally available through a broad network of state- and factory-supported day-care centers, kindergartens, after-school child care, and school-lunch programs. As of 1989, 80.2 percent of children aged one to three were in day care, 89.1 percent of children aged three to six were in kindergarten, and 83.3 percent of children aged six to ten were in after-school care.[53] Spaces in these centers were available free of charge. Parents made a token copayment of approximately 0.35M per day toward the cost of milk and meals.[54] Since the economic union of July 1, 1990, day-care costs have risen rapidly to the 250–300DM a month (or more) per child paid in the West, and the school lunch program is now charging 35–75DM monthly per child.

FRG

Only 3 percent of children under the age of three are in public day care.[55] In 1989, West Berlin—one of the most liberal and well-funded administrations—was able to provide day care to only 18 percent of the children registered on waiting lists.[56] The need for day care is generally solved through private arrangements with "day mothers," grandmothers, *au pair*, and so on. A limited portion of day-care costs can be taken as a tax credit on a means-tested basis. In 1988 approximately 62.3 percent of children between three and six were in kindergartens.[57] The FRG does not have a hot-lunch program (although some schools do provide school lunches) or an organized after-school program.

Care of Sick Children

Parents in the GDR were guaranteed forty days per child per year in paid time off from work to care for sick children up to the age of fourteen. (In addition, married women, mothers of children under sixteen, and single women over thirty received one paid day off per month for housework.) West German parents may take a flat five paid days per year to care for sick children up to age eight.[58]

Housing

GDR citizens had a right to housing space on the basis of family size and were guaranteed a maximum rent of 5 percent of net household income. In addition, the prices of basic foodstuffs, water, power, garbage collection, public transportation, children's clothing, and so on, were heavily subsidized. The FRG sets no cap on housing prices, and rent subsidies are provided on a means-tested basis to social welfare recipients.

Health Care and Reproductive Rights

GDR

All health care services, including prophylactic and preventive care, were provided free of charge by a state-subsidized health insurance system. Marriage and childbirth were encouraged by support payments and subsidized loans. Even though the state strongly wished to maintain or raise its birth rate,[59] abortion on demand during the first trimester was legalized in 1972. Abortion, reproductive counseling, and contraceptives were free of charge and easily available throughout the country. The effective abortion rate in the two Germanies was virtually identical.[60]

FRG

Abortion was available only if medically indicated or if the woman could convince a physician other than her own doctor and a review panel that sufficient "social indications" justified terminating the pregnancy. Under the reunification agreement, abortion in the first trimester continued to be legal in the territory of the former GDR for two years (all other transitional regulations are for five years). A new law allowing women to choose to terminate a pregnancy during the first trimester, but still requiring mandatory counseling, was passed by the German Bundestag in July 1992. At this writing it had not yet been approved by the Bundesrat (upper house) or accepted as constitutional by the Constitutional Court.

The West German health care system relies on employee and union health plans and private physicians. Benefits and coverage vary widely, insurers charge different rates, fees and copayments depend on plan and eligibility. This system is now being introduced in the former GDR, and the prices of insurance and medications have already risen significantly. The GDR polyclinics (health care cooperatives emphasizing preventive care) and community health clinics for diabetics, lung diseases, prenatal care, and so on, have been closed and are to be replaced with private practices. Because few private practices have been established, however, significant numbers of people are being left without provision for health care during the transition period.

Policy Efforts and Real Outcomes

Despite the extensive structural framework to support the emancipation of women in the GDR, there were continuing contradictions within this generally positive picture. An overview of the economy revealed a pronounced gender-specific division of labor, which in some cases amounted to a gender classification of entire trades and in others suggested a pattern of assigning equally qualified women to tasks requiring lower qualifications. Although equal pay for equal work was fully established, pay differentials between traditionally male and female occupations and the greater tendency of women to work in part-time positions because of family responsibilities, to accept less qualified work to be near home, or to postpone career advancement because of small children, left the average female income at approximately 80 percent of male earnings. In addition, time-budget studies and sociological surveys showed that housework and child care continued to be seen as primarily female responsibilities.[61]

Although there were significant and progressive changes in women's social status and condition throughout the forty years of GDR society, it clearly exhibited the continuing influence of traditional culture. Increasing female participation does not appear to have affected the status of the professions,[62] but "female" roles and behaviors and qualities continued to be culturally less valued. This affected both the level of female participation and the public acceptance and support of women at higher levels of authority in the economic and especially in the political sphere. The GDR consistently displayed a significant underrepresentation of women at the highest levels of social, political, and economic power. Women constituted 52.8 percent of college and university students in 1980, for example, but received only 30.1 percent of the doctorates and 13.7 percent of the tenured positions awarded that year.[63] Among judges (an appointive position), 52 percent were women but only 27.2 percent of mayors and 32.2 percent of members of parliament (both elective).[64]

This small contrast between appointive and elective positions crystallizes the problem of a centrally administered attempt to revise the gender-specific division of labor in a society still largely dominated by traditional role models and gender definitions. The radical changes of 1989 had even more negative consequences for women. In 1989, before the social upheaval, women held 38 percent of the seats in parliament and the district councils. After the highly touted "first free elections" of March 18, 1990, women retained only a 20.2 percent representation in parliament. Their numbers have fallen with each successive election and are now at or below western levels in the eastern states.[65]

The "double burden" (full-time participation in the paid labor force followed by a "second shift" of unpaid labor in the home) and its practical as well as social-psychological effects became a focus of concern among Western feminists and scholars in the early 1970s. The GDR leadership defined it as a pragmatic problem and committed itself to palliative measures without reopening the question of the male-female division of reproductive labor, thus avoiding a tangle of theoretical complications. Women were better integrated into social and cultural activities. But as has historically been the case, however, there remained significant and often startling contradictions between the behaviors expected of women in the public (work) and the private (family) spheres. The double burden was extensively discussed in the

GDR, but the discussion took place in literature rather than in political or social theory. The subjective literary reflection of these conditions is an illustration of the complexity of social change and of how the process of social transformation developed its own momentum in the GDR.

The Role of Literature in a Changing Society

The period between 1976 and 1986 can be characterized as the Women's Decade in GDR literature. In the mid-1970s women stopped appearing only as "the other" described by men and started to be and to describe themselves. This new phase began with the publication in 1974 of three important novels written by women about women: *Leben und Abenteuer der Trobadora Beatriz nach Zeugnissen ihrer Spielfrau Laura* by Irmtraud Morgner, *Franziska Linkerhand* by Brigitte Reimann, and *Karen W.* by Gerti Tetzner. Along with *The Quest for Christa T.* by Christa Wolf (1968), these works were the first to question the role of women in both GDR literature and GDR society. The literary and literary-critical discussion of their depiction of women torn between the contradictory demands of career and family set off a public debate about the traditional role of women and their status in socialist society.

By the end of the 1970s, Morgner, Reimann, Tetzner, and Wolf had been joined by a large number of younger writers focused on "women's issues" such as equal rights, marriage and sexuality, career training and development, and the problems of single mothers with children. In these works, men either appear as secondary figures or are simply absent. In contrast to most of their male colleagues, who often use female characters as props equipped with purely stereotypical qualities, these writers frequently leave male roles unoccupied. Male characters may sometimes be satirically overdrawn, but paragons of prescriptive male virtue are rare indeed. The women authors appeared not to want to dictate to men how they were to behave and preferred to leave positive male role models empty, perhaps to encourage the men to rethink themselves for themselves.

These writers took full advantage of the acknowledged function of literature as a catalyst for social change. They used it as a forum to probe the question of whether the emancipated socialist woman was in fact living a fully human life. The consensus was that although economic equality is necessary, it is not sufficient, that the contradictions and conflicting demands of modern life are too complex to be contained within a simplistic positive role model. One of the significant functions of this literature was to provide a space within which to experiment with the creation of new intellectual and social models for women as alternatives to the traditional socialist model of rational, goal-oriented behavior in work, family, and personal relationships.

These women wrote about themselves with a strong sense of self-possession in accord with their objective circumstances. Women in the GDR were well educated, sophisticated, and economically independent. They had no reason to fear poverty or unemployment. They took for granted that they were needed by their society, that they would hold responsible positions, that they could support themselves (and, if necessary, their children) with their own earnings. This historically unusual and perhaps unique experience had an obvious effect on their self-image. The self-confidence women developed under such conditions was clearly reflected in the literature written by and about them.

The most striking quality of the body of literature they produced is its probing honesty: the good-natured but authentic and independent tone in which these writers criticized themselves and their social system. There is an extraordinary absence of the bitterness, isolation, alienation, and hopelessness characteristic of much contemporary West German feminist writing. GDR women's experience made the contradictions in their lives clearly visible but not inevitable. The system in which they lived had obviously not resolved these contradictions, but it did treat them as legitimate social questions rather than dismissing them as individual conflicts arising out of freely taken private decisions.

The sense of a social compact, of a supportive rather than antagonistic social environment, and the experience of entitlement rather than dependency gave women writers a unique perspective on what it means to be female and to be human in a world that has been dominated by male ways of thinking and behaving. As a result, women writers began a critical investigation of the effects on society of a gender-specific valuation of abilities and behaviors. Especially the older writers such as Wolf and Morgner attempted to analyze and clarify the destructive consequences—not only for the individual but for society as a whole and the future of the planet—of the tradition of male aggression and female passivity.

By the early 1980s writers had expanded their perspective to include portrayals of the conditions of many different kinds of "outsiders": the elderly, the physically or mentally handicapped, the dying, the nonheterosexual—people who are either unwelcome in or unable or unwilling to fit into the standard categories of an operative, function-defined, production-oriented society. Presenting such portrayals could be seen as a tactic to include others in a comprehensive literature of social critique, or as a typically "feminine" behavior of caring for the weak and the sick. It was fresh evidence of the vitality of a socially critical literature attempting to expand the boundaries of a social system and reexamine the assumptions and definitions upon which modern Western culture was founded.

It is not surprising that many of the authors in this collection were extraordinarily active in the mass political movement of the fall of 1989. Christa Wolf, Helga Königsdorf, Daniela Dahn, and others spoke at rallies, wrote editorials, appeared at dozens of public discussion meetings, served on citizens' commissions, gave endless interviews, and tried to mediate, articulate, and transfer information between individuals and the public sphere. The attacks on Christa Wolf (and with her the entire range of progressive East German intellectuals) that appeared in the West German press in the summer and fall of 1990 were a prelude to the decision to examine the political histories of all civil servants and elected officials in the former GDR. In January 1992 a decision to open the files of the STASI, or State Security Police, was implemented amid charges of widespread complicity with the old regime and countercharges of widespread violations of confidentiality and civil rights by the new one.

As of this writing, virtually every prominent figure in GDR culture and politics has been accused of collaboration. University faculties (along with judges, schoolteachers, and other public employees) are being evaluated by commissions composed largely of West German academics to determine their political as well as professional suitability for future employment.[66] The next-to-last remaining native East German state governor, Manfred Stolpe, is under heavy pressure to resign; all but one of the other eastern states and major cities are now governed by native West Germans. The past two years have provided a sobering beginning for the intellectual openness of a reunified German culture.

The stories in this collection offer an introduction to the complex and evolving reality of GDR women's experience up to 1989. Traditional Marxist literary theory classified literature as a "socially active element." In state practice, the reality of this power was confirmed both through support and through censorship. While literature in the GDR continued to play its traditional roles as entertainment, education, and art, it took over other functions as well, and a number of authors began to use literature as a forum for active and specific social criticism. Given the more restricted situation of journalism and the social sciences in the GDR, fiction could sometimes give a more accurate picture of actual social attitudes and conditions than could those "objective" sources.

The issues raised in these stories are familiar to any woman in the English-speaking world today: motherhood, child care, structures of authority in the workplace and in the public sphere, gender difference, and differing approaches to conflict and social relationships. The cultural and intellectual sources of these concerns are also clearly recognizable, since they are the central problems facing humanity in the latter half of the twentieth century: instrumental and competitive versus cooperative thinking in work and social relationships, reproductive rights and responsibilities, the relationship between labor and capital, the organization of family and child rearing in postindustrial societies, the origin and meaning of life in the face of nuclear war, the tension between the destructive capacities of human inventiveness and the benefits of modern technology.

The immediate and practical relevance of many of these issues is demonstrated on a daily basis to women in advanced industrial societies who find themselves trying to juggle paid work outside the home with the needs and demands of children and family. Once a society has reached a level of social development and economic prosperity where family survival is no longer an issue, the immediate next stage has been the question of individual self-fulfillment. With concrete and visible obstacles gradually disappearing, women are increasingly forced to deal with less obvious and often internalized social and psychological barriers.

After a decade or two of "emancipation," women in these societies are still confronted with a number of difficult questions. What exactly has been accomplished in terms of a measurable, statistically verifiable integration of women into the structures of economic and political power? Why has change come so slowly? Even more vexing, what in fact is the meaning of individual self-fulfillment? What is the balance to be struck between individual freedom and social responsibility, between personal independence and parenthood? Can the contradictions between public and private life, between career and family, be resolved? Or will deeper contradictions within the structures and values of Western postindustrial society force attempts at resolution into sterile debate or practical dead ends?

These issues cut across national and ideological boundaries. The similarities between the practical problems and daily lives of women in the United States and Canada, Western Europe, and central Eastern Europe far outweigh the differences in political system, language, or specific cultural details. In fact, seen from a distance, they elicit both a shock of recognition and a clearer focus on their common underlying causes.

Notes

1. For more detailed discussion see the following articles by Dorothy J. Rosenberg: "Shock Therapy: GDR Women in Transition from a Socialist Welfare State to a Social Market Economy," *Signs* 17, no. 1 (1991): 129–51; "Women's Issues, Women's Politics, and Women's Studies in the Former German Democratic Republic," *Radical History Review*, no. 52 (Spring 1992); "Side Effects: Women in the Process of German Unification," *Comparative Studies in Society and History* (forthcoming, 1993); and "The New Home Economics: Women, Work, and Family in the United Germany," *Signs* (forthcoming, 1993).

2. According to the Bundesbank, Germany budgeted DM 180 billion in West-East net transfer payments for 1992: i.e., 6.5 percent of the West German gross national product, or DM 3,000 ($1,800) per West German citizen. This figure does not include the Treuhand (Trusteeship) privatization agency budget and borrowing authority, which are reported to total another DM 68 billion for 1992. See David Goodhart, *Financial Times* (London), March 19, 1992, pp. 1, 20.

3. Finance Minister Theo Waigel's plan calls for limiting increases in federal spending to a nominal rate of 2.5 percent annually (before adjusting for inflation) and using the difference between this figure and expected growth to cover the bulk of the costs of unification. In fact, limiting increases to well below the rate of inflation (currently 4.8 percent) simply disguises real reductions in social spending. See Christopher Parkes, " 'Hard-as-Nails' Finance Policy Pledged by Waigel," *Financial Times*, April 21, 1992, p. 4; and "Waigel kündigt 'knallharte Finanzpolitik' an," *Deutschland Nachrichten*, April 24, 1992, p. 1.

4. Industrial production in the GDR fell 51 percent between August 1989 and August 1990 and had fallen another 40 percent by August 1991: Deutsches Institut für Wirtschaftsforschung (DIW), ed., "Gesamtwirtschaftliche und unternehmerische Anpassungsprozesse in Ostdeutschland," *Wochenbericht*, nos. 51–52 (1991).

5. Nearly two million East Germans moved to the West between 1989 and 1992; close to one million have been forced into early retirement; and more than 500,000 (80 percent of whom are men) live in the East and commute daily or weekly to jobs in the West. See "Trendwende am Arbeitsmarkt?" *Deutschland Nachrichten*, December 13, 1991, p. 4; "Eastern Germans Still Flocking West for Jobs," *New York Times*, January 5, 1992, sec. 1, p. 8; Hedwig Rudolph, Eileen Appelbaum, and Friederike Maier, "Beyond Socialism: The Ambivalence of Women's Perspectives in the Unified Germany," in *Economic Reform and the Status of Women*, ed. Pressman, Aslanbeigal, and Summerfield (forthcoming).

6. "Shortened hours" means working less than half time, in some cases working zero hours. See Christopher Parkes, "Workforce in Eastern Germany Shrinks by 40 Percent to 6m.," *Financial Times*, April 14, 1992, p. 3. There are 400,000 in federally financed job-creation programs (*Arbeitsbeschaffungsmassnahmen* or ABM) and 500,000 in federally financed training programs: "Bald 1,35 Millionen Arbeitslose im Osten?" *Deutschland Nachrichten*, April 24, 1992, p. 4.

7. Interview with Angela Merkel (Federal Minister of Women and Youth), "Probleme des Ostens von Bonn aus schlecht einzuschätzen," *Der Tagesspiegel* (Berlin), July 27, 1992, p. 2. Heinrich Franke, president of the Federal Labor Office, stated in January 1992 that he was "very worried" about women's unemployment. December 1991 statistics showed that women made up 62 percent of the total unemployed, de-

spite constituting only 48 percent of the labor force: "Die Zahl wird 'ganz deutlich zunehmen'" (The number will increase significantly), *Neues Deutschland*, January 22, 1992, p. 3. In April, with the rate at 62.3 percent, Federal Women's Minister Angela Merkel called for measures to reduce the high rate of female unemployment, characterizing it as "social tinder": *Deutschland Nachrichten*, April 24, 1992, p. 4

8. Friederike Maier, "Erwerbstätigkeit von Frauen—Geschlechtsspezifische Umbrüche im Arbeitsmarkt und Beschäftigungssystem," in *Wirtschaftspolitische Konsequenzen der deutschen Vereinigung*, ed. A. Westphal et al. (Frankfurt: Campus, 1991), pp. 295–318.

9. Rudolph, Appelbaum, and Maier, "Beyond Socialism." Single mothers, women over fifty and women with college degrees are the worst hit by unemployment. See also Gerda Jasper, "Mann wird arbeitslos, Frau wird Hausfrau" (Men become unemployed, women become housewives), *Neues Deutschland*, September 4, 1991, p. 9. In July 1991, single mothers were 10 percent of the total unemployed, and three times as many women fifty-five and over were unemployed as men over sixty.

10. Felicity Barringer, "Birth Rates Plummeting in Some Ex-Communist Regions of Eastern Europe," *New York Times*, December 31, 1991, p. A3.

11. Rudolph, Appelbaum, and Maier, "Beyond Socialism."

12. While retail prices in the East rose rapidly to equal or exceed West German levels following the currency union on July 1, 1990, the inflation rate in the East has consistently remained higher, fueled primarily by massive rent increases. The inflation rate in eastern Germany in March 1992 was over 15 percent; in western Germany, 4.8 percent: *The Week in Germany*, April 24, 1992, p. 4. Eastern income had reached an average of 46 percent of the western level at the beginning of 1992: *Deutschland Nachrichten*, January 17, 1992, p. 4.

13. Elke Holst and Jürgen Schupp, "Frauenerwerbstätigkeit in den neuen und alten Bundesländern: Befunde des sozio-ökonomischen Panels" (Women's employment in the new and old Federal states: Findings of the Socioeconomic Panel), DIW discussion paper no. 37, 1991, p. 12.

14. See Sabine Berghahn and Andrea Fritzsche, *Frauenrecht in Ost und West* (Berlin: Basisdruck, 1991), for a comparison of the East and West German legal systems and policy effects on women's employment, marriage, social entitlements, etc.

15. See Annemarie Tröger, "The Creation of a Female Assembly-Line Proletariat," and Gisela Bock, "Racism and Sexism in Nazi Germany," both in *When Biology Became Destiny: Women in Weimar and Nazi Germany*, ed. Renate Bridenthal, Atina Grossman, and Marion Kaplan (New York: Monthly Review Press, 1984). See also Herta Kuhrig und Wulfram Speigner, eds., *Wie emanzipiert sind die Frauen in der DDR?* (Cologne: Pahl-Rugenstein, 1979); and Friedel Schubert, *Die Frau in der DDR* (Opladen: Leske & Budrich, 1980). For a short summary in English, see Dorothy Rosenberg, "The Emancipation of Women in Fact and Fiction: Images and Role Models in GDR Literature," in *Women, State, and Party in Eastern Europe*, ed. Sharon Wolchik and Alfred Meyer (Durham, N.C.: Duke University Press, 1985).

16. Eva Hein and Klaus Rosenfeld, *Frauen in Ausbildung und Beruf* (Berlin: Staatsverlag der DDR, 1985), p. 49, shows a figure of 91.1 percent for 1984. According to the *Statistisches Taschenbuch der DDR, 1989* (Berlin: Staatsverlag der DDR, 1989), 48.9 percent of the labor force was female in 1988.

17. *Frauenreport '90*, ed. Gunnar Winkler (Berlin: Verlag die Wirtschaft, 1990), p. 27.

18. This is especially true with respect to employment. While 91–92 percent of the adult female population of the GDR was either in training or regularly employed, the figure for the FRG was only 51.7 percent. Only about one-third of the West German female labor force shows an unbroken career pattern, another third leaves the labor force permanently after the birth of a child, and the rest stop working for an extended period because of family responsibilities. The GDR had an extensive network of affirmative action employment, further education, and reintegration programs; there have been no similar measures in the FRG to help women return to work after a family-related absence.

For a thorough comparison of women and family policy in the two Germanies, see Gisela Helwig, *Frau und Familie: Bundesrepublik Deutschland—DDR* (Cologne: Wissenschaft & Politik, 1987). For the most recent and authoritative study of the family in the GDR, see Jutta Gysi, ed., *Familienleben in der DDR: Zum Alltag von Familien mit Kindern* (Berlin: Akademie, 1989).

19. Helwig, *Frau und Familie*, pp. 40 (breakdown of women workers), 86 (1984 figures for part-time workers). See also *Datenreport* (Bonn: Bundeszentrale für politische Bildung, 1989) pp. 32, 78, 82.

20. *Frauenreport '90*, pp. 55, 63, 83.

21. *Datenreport*, p. 78.

22. Helwig, *Frau und Familie*, p. 46. See also Berghahn and Fritzsche, *Frauenrecht*, p. 95.

23. Interview with Angela Merkel, "Probleme des Ostens."

24. Jasper, "Mann wird arbeitslos," p. 9. According to a 1991 poll, only four out of ten individuals finding new employment after losing a job were women: Institut für angewandte Sozialwissenschaft, "Frauen in den neuen Bundesländern im Prozeß der deutschen Einheit" INFAS research report no. 15 (Bad Godesberg, 1991). Women's share in publicly funded job programs (ABM), which provide one- to two-year contracts in public projects largely paid for with federal funds, have remained at about 36 percent, despite complaints about gender-biased recruitment: Maier, "Erwerbstätigkeit von Frauen."

25. "Die Frauen sind die Variablen des Arbeitsmarktes [Women are the variables in the labor market]: ND-Gespräch mit Dr. Marina Beyer, Gleichstellungsbeauftragte der einstigen DDR-Regierung" *Neues Deutschland*, January 30, 1991, p. 8. "Jeden Abend der Eismann. In Ostdeutschland trifft die Dauerarbeitslosigkeit die vielen alleinerziehenden Mütter besonders hart: Sie leiden unter Armut und Vereinsamung" (Every evening the ice cream man. Single mothers in Eastern Germany particularly hard hit by long-term unemployment: They suffer from poverty and isolation), *Der Spiegel*, no. 24 (June 15, 1992): 99–101.

26. According to a report of the Federal Ministry of Education published on February 12, 1992, 12 percent of the children of working-class families attend a university, compared with 60 percent of the children of white-collar workers; 34.5 percent of West German students received BAFÖG loans. Of the average income of an unmarried student living away from home, 46 percent derives from parents, 26 percent from his or her own earnings, and only 17 percent from BAFÖG. See "Wer studiert and wer nicht?" (Who studies and who doesn't?), *Deutschland Nachrichten*, March 20, 1992. p. 6. The average Eastern German student, who cannot rely on parents' or their own earnings under conditions of mass unemployment, is now dependent upon BAFÖG for 88 percent of income.

27. *Datenreport*, p. 72.

28. Helwig, *Frau und Familie*, p. 48.

29. Elizabeth Meyer-Renschhausen, "Feminist Research at German Universities? Nearly Impossible! Taking Stock after Ten Years," *Critical Sociology* 17, no. 3 (1990): 60–73.

30. Ingrid Sommerkorn, "Overview of the Women's Movement in the West," paper presented to the Women and Unification Workshop, Center for European Studies, Harvard University, May 18–19, 1991.

31. *Frauenreport '90*, pp. 41–44.

32. Helwig, *Frau und Familie*, p. 49.

33. Report of the GDR government to the Secretary-General of the United Nations, "Frauen in der DDR: Bilanz der Erfüllung des Weltaktionsplanes für die Dekade der Frau—Zeitraum 1976–1985—'Gleichberechtigung, Entwicklung, Frieden,'" in *Informationen des wissenschaftlichen Rates*, no. 2 (1985): 22. See also *Frauenreport '90*, pp. 66–68; and Helwig, *Frau und Familie*, pp. 48–51.

34. Hedwig Rudolph, Eileen Appelbaum, and Friederike Maier, "After German Unity: A Cloudier Outlook for Women," *Challenge*, November–December 1990, p. 37.

35. *Frauenreport '90*, p. 94.

36. *Datenreport*, p. 307 (gross yearly earnings, for 1987).

37. *Frauenreport '90*, pp. 92 (1988 net monthly wages for production workers, real hours worked), 93 (net monthly salary for college graduates). These figures are not exactly parallel to those in the *Datenreport*. Both *Frauenreport '90* and *Datenreport* cite women's concentration in less well-paid branches or categories; fewer overtime hours and lack of hazardous duty pay lower their wages. Both note that women are underrepresented at higher executive levels. West German sources also indicate that women have less education, lower qualifications, and underrepresention in technical professions.

38. *Datenreport*, p. 40.

39. *Frauenreport '90*, pp. 24–25.

40. Cited from the Federal Bureau of Statistics in Wiesbaden. From January to July, the five new states registered 67,000 births, a 40 percent drop compared to the same period in 1990. There were 424,000 births in the eleven western states for the same period, an increase of 2.7 percent. Marriages dropped in both parts of Germany: by 57 percent in the East, 4.5 percent in the West. The combined German birth rate declined by 6 percent and the marriage rate by 16 percent. See "Easterners Marrying Less, Bearing Fewer Children," *The Week in Germany*, November 8, 1991, p. 6.

41. *Frauenreport '90*, p. 109.

42. *Datenreport*, p. 46.

43. *Frauenreport '90*, p. 112.

44. *Datenreport*, p. 43.

45. "Survey: Most Adults Live in Couples, Women Still Do More Housework," *The Week in Germany*, November 22, 1991, p. 2.

46. *Frauenreport '90*, pp. 28–29.

47. Ibid., p. 151.

48. Ibid., pp. 145ff.

49. Ibid., p. 140.

50. Ibid., p. 150.

51. Berghahn and Fritzsche, *Frauenrecht*, p. 176.
52. *Datenreport*, pp. 203–4. See also "Familienpolitische Informationen: Familienpolitik in der DDR und der Bundesrepublik," Evangelische Aktionsgemeinschaft für Familienfragen occasional paper no. 3 (May–June 1990), p. 2.
53. These and the following statistics are taken from *Sozialreport '90: Daten und Fakten zur sozialen Lage in der DDR*, ed. Gunnar Winkler (Berlin: Wirtschaft, 1990). For discussion of these issues, see Irene Dölling, "Culture and Gender," in *The Quality of Life in the German Democratic Republic: Changes and Developments in a State Socialist Society*, ed. Marilyn Rueschemeyer and Christiane Lemke (Armonk, N.Y.: M.E. Sharp, 1989), pp. 27–47.
54. *Frauenreport '90*, pp. 140–43. See also "Familienpolitik in der DDR und der Bundesrepublik" p. 3.
55. "Familienpolitik in der DDR und der Bundesrepublik," p. 3.
56. Author's interview with Frau Möllhoff, Büro für Kitafragen, Senatsverwaltung für Frauen, Jugendliche und Familie, Berlin, January 29, 1991.
57. *Datenreport*, p. 53, shows 1,472,819 kindergarten spaces as having been available in 1986, which would statistically have served 80 percent of West German children aged three to six; however, given regional differences and varied opening times, only 62.3 percent were actually enrolled. Cited in Berghahn and Fritzsche, *Frauenrecht*, p. 92, from Bundesministerium für Jugend, Familie, Frauen und Gesundheit (ed., *Frauen in der Bundesrepublic Deutschland* (Bonn, 1989), p. 56.
58. *Frauenreport '90*, p. 148. See also "Familienpolitik in der DDR und der Bundesrepublik," p. 4.
59. The birth rate in the GDR was 13.7 per 1,000 inhabitants in 1984; 13.6 in 1987 (*Statistisches Taschenbuch, 1989*). The 1989 birth rate was 12.1 (*Sozialreport '90*). Comparable figures for 1984 from *United Nations Statistical Yearbook 1985*: FRG, 9.5; France, 13.8; U.S.A., 15.7. The GDR's extensive system of prenatal care also resulted in a low infant mortality rate of 8.1 per 1,000 births in 1988 (*Sozialreport '90*).
60. Interview with Dr. Lykke Areson, *Neues Deutschland*, (September 1–2 1990, p. 9. According to Areson, a specialist in the field, the abortion rate in the GDR has remained stable at one out of four pregnancies, exactly the same rate as in the FRG. Minors constitute 20 percent of the women seeking abortion, compared with 30–35 percent in the United States. Dr. Areson states that the vast majority of women seeking abortion have one or two children already and do not want or feel able to have more. *Frauenreport '90*, pp. 167–70, describes a generally falling trend in the rate of abortion since legalization in 1972. The decrease is especially notable in the age groups 15–20, 20–25, and 30–35. It is notable also that of a total of only 135 fourteen-year-olds who became pregnant in 1988, fifteen carried to term.
61. See Jutta Menschik and Evelyn Leopold, *Gretchens rote Schwestern: Frauen in der DDR* (Frankfurt am Main: Fischer, 1974), pp. 196ff. See also Eva Kaufmann, "Interview mit Irmtraud Morgner," *Weimarer Beiträge* 30, no. 9 (1984): 1500–1502; and Hildegard M. Nickel, "Sex-Role Socialization in Relationships as a Function of the Division of Labor: A Sociological Explanation for the Reproduction of Gender Differences," in Rueschemeyer and Lemke, *Quality of Life*, pp. 48–58.
62. The government did intervene by establishing gender quotas to prevent the "feminization" of the medical profession.
63. *Das Bildungswesen in der DDR* (Berlin: Volk und Wissen, 1983), pp. 157–58. These figures equate the German Promotion A with an American doctorate, and Pro-

motion B with the rank of associate professor—not an exact match but close enough to allow meaningful comparison of gender status. Women held approximately 7 percent of the associate and full professorships in the GDR university system in 1980. By 1989 they had reached 35 percent of assistant professors and 9 percent of full professors: Rudolph, Appelbaum, and Maier, "After German Unity," pp. 33–40. This is still significantly higher than women's representation in West Germany, which has remained at 5 percent since 1980, with women holding only 2.3 percent of full professorships. See Meyer-Renschhausen, "Feminist Research," pp. 60–73. According to Winkler (*Frauenreport '90*, p. 42), female university enrollment reached a high of 52.1 percent in 1986 but had fallen back to 47.3 percent in 1989.

64. Hein and Rosenfeld, *Frauen in Ausbildung und Beruf*, p. 76, and *Statistisches Taschenbuch der DDR, 1987* (Berlin: Staatsverlag der DDR, 1988), p. 18.

65. Cited from Irene Dölling, "Zwischen Hoffnung und Hilflosigkeit—Frauen nach der 'Wende' in der DDR" (April 1990); published as "Between Hope and Helplessness: Women in the GDR after 'the Turning Point,' " in *Democracy and Civil Society in Eastern Europe*, ed. Paul Lewis (London: Macmillan, 1991).

66. West German universities are public institutions, and tenured professors are members of the civil service. After unification, East German professors lost their tenure rights by being classified as civil employees (*Angestellten*) rather than civil servants (*Beamte*). Following their "evaluation," those not found to be politically tainted are being allowed, in competition with other applicants, to reapply for their own positions.

Gerti Tetzner

Gerti Tetzner was born in 1936 in a village in Thuringia, in central Germany. After finishing grade school in the village, she commuted to high school in the nearby town of Gotha. She left Thuringia to attend law school in Leipzig, took her state examinations there in 1959, and practiced law for three years before permanently giving up her career as a lawyer.

Tetzner began to write in the years that followed, but without the intention of making it her profession. She worked as a temporary agricultural laborer, in a cotton mill, for the post office, and wherever else she could find part-time or temporary employment. She also received several stipends and attended the Creative Writing Institute in Leipzig for two years. The success of her first novel allowed her to become an independent writer in the mid-1970s. Tetzner has also written several children's books and contributed to anthologies and journals. The following selection—which also appeared separately as "Grenzen" (Limits) in a West German anthology— is the opening scene of her novel *Karen W.*

Karen W. Halle/Leipzig: Mitteldeutscher Verlag, 1974.

Im Lande der Fähren (In the land of the ferries), with Reiner Tetzner. Halle/
Leipzig: Mitteldeutscher Verlag, 1988.

Eines schönen Sonntags (One fine Sunday). Halle/Leipzig: Mitteldeutscher
Verlag, 1993.

Karen W. (1974)

THE ROOM smells of dust and sweaty clothes.

It's dark and quiet.

Now and then a truck rumbles past in the street below. The floorboards vibrate faintly in response. Peters turns over; noise and motion irritate him even when he's sound asleep.

I wait for the sound of his snoring to start again.

During vacation I had begun lying there and listening until I was wide awake—and waiting. Tonight, the first night at home, I lie awake again and wait. For what?

I used to need his breathing beside me. This irregular ascent from deep, hesitant tones to light whistling sounds lulled me to sleep.

Before this brooding began.

This brooding, how and why we had become the way we are and how we could have been. Thoughts and images began to spin. Night after night, racing in an endless circle, drawing me down into the whirlpool.

Even on vacation, the same chaos in my head.

But suddenly—between sentence fragments, the hypnotic tone of the anchorman's voice reading ordinary news reports (strongly denouncing Israeli aggression)—suddenly this utterly ordinary news in my ear: "Heavy thunderstorms also struck in the area of Suhl-Mühlhausen. Hailstorms in western Thuringia destroyed part of the wheat harvest . . ."

That's where the vortex stopped.

The whirlpool of thoughts in my head stood still. Forgotten images, untouched by the years that followed, suddenly surfaced: The grass on our neighbor's hillside meadow flattened by the storm. The street in the lower village a river of yellow mud. The tips of white picket fences near the houses sticking up out of it. I'm floating in a washtub, pushing myself along with a broom handle. Past Meierhoefer's kitchen window. Instead of a black-haired man, a reddish brown calf's head looks out at me. Up on the hill a gate is thrown open. The Genzel brothers, sworn enemies in a feud over their inheritance, stand together in the barnyard shoveling mud toward the road . . .

Across the valley—next to Werlich's garden on Miller's Hill—our house still stands.

With each night I lie wide awake, the house emerges from my childhood more clearly. The three-paned windows. Green shutters on either side. The black and white star pattern on the hallway floor tiles. The open space behind the garden.

And with each day spent waiting, I become more impatient than the week before; my life is passing me by, my youth and strength are seeping away unused, irretrievable . . .

The closed curtains are already turning gray. The sharp outline of the wardrobe stands out against them. You can already make out the braided lamp cord. In a few hours it will all be visible again. Carpets that muffle the sounds of the morning rush. A bright tie to liven up a business face. A kiss with a glance at the clock, the same old song.

I have to do it.

Now, I have to do it tonight! I've planned it a thousand times.

I'll find paper and a pencil on his desk.

We're in pretty bad shape. Apparently you feel fine. I'm leaving and I'll start all over again somewhere. I'm sure you won't mind if I pick up Bettina from summer camp and take her with me for now. She always got on your nerves. Karen.

He has the meeting with a foreign delegation this morning. I'll fix his breakfast for him. He'll think: The truck traffic woke her up, she went out for a breath of air and is late getting back.

He'll be completely calm.

In the afternoon, when he takes his fifteen-minute break and has his cigarette, he'll find the note under the ashtray (he always takes it with him from the coffee table to his desk). At least he'll have an evening and a night before the next meeting.

Dust everywhere.

Newspapers next to the open suitcases. Unopened letters. Wet swimming suits in a plastic bag. I should have unpacked his things and washed them, he's not good at things like that. But once I'd gotten started, I'd be lost again.

I've held on with compromises long enough, just to be able to live here, with him.

The job in the spinning mill, for example.

Of course, I sat down at the dinner table with the feeling of really having accomplished something, learned something: Gathering up armloads of raw cotton, stuffing it into a rolling bin, jumping into it myself to pack the stuff down and pushing the bin over to the presses. Or standing for hours on the production line and reaching in now and then to pull out wads of dirty cotton. Or carrying away rolls of twine and bringing the empty spools back to the women at the machines. Or getting cigarettes for Big Otto. As an unskilled worker, I wasn't assigned to any particular machine, just filled in here or there or wherever. I hadn't known work like that still had to be done. Before, I'd sometimes said, "We'll send him into productive work on probation," and had regarded the problem as solved.

It was now clear that it hadn't been much of a solution.

Just outside a building door, the hesitant sense of demonstrably useful work began to disappear. There was another building across the way and another behind it and others to the left and right, and in this gigantic, impenetrable web of motions, all invisibly related to the transformation of a dirty clump of cotton into white handkerchiefs, my motions during a long tiring day were lost, seemingly pointless.

This impression was reinforced when my personnel file passed through my supervisor's hands. Lawyer . . . ? Now just a minute! For half the money here? Voluntarily! Umhm . . . it used to be Sweetie or Karen, do this, do that—whatever was needed. It was now grammatically correct and exact: Mrs. Waldau, and clear assignments for the day, checked afterward and please and thank you, and all around me an invisible net of surreptitious glances entangling my hands and feet. Spontaneity was gone. And the roof, vibrating with the noise of the machines, seemed to sink down a little closer to my head every day. Was the sky above it actually blue or green?

Maybe I would have gradually gotten used to it. Or they would have gotten used to me in the end. But had my life or my relationship with Peters and his world changed?

Unable to stop yawning, I'd knock over the bathroom footstool at four-thirty in the morning. He'd be instantly awake and sticking his head through the bathroom doorway: "Nonsense! Blind ideology! A person with your education acts according to some plan, a deeper meaning, you know what I mean, it can be a secret for all I care—please, can't you finally explain . . ."

That was exactly what I couldn't do. I might have been able to explain what I didn't want.

This closed circle of life and work, for example. This visible track, as if once you sat down in a certain train you reached a certain goal by passing through certain stations, as long as you didn't get off or (god forbid) pull the emergency brake. Peters's supper with his colleagues came along this track every six days. I concentrated on the empty cups and glasses and smiled like a deaf hostess but still couldn't help overhearing how Peters's much-admired wit and his charming laugh degenerated, swept him far away beyond impassable boundaries: Schenkmann will get tenure, inside information, got his Ph.D. a year after I did and only two committees, a miracle tenure case, so to speak; what's the matter, after all, they've already approved your pension even though you haven't opened your mouth at meetings and committees recently, little crisis, hey . . . I can't look at him anymore without seeing his face at those suppers. I can't even eat a mushroom anymore without thinking about how Peters, who hates mushrooms, organized mushrooming expeditions during vacation with the Rector's assistant to get that inside information and didn't even notice my attempts to start over again together. And I can't polish the nameplate on the door anymore—Dr. Peters—without asking myself why I, Karen Waldau, am actually still living behind it. It eats at me like a sickness. It's poisoning me—everything picks up the same bitter aftertaste.

Ten more years of it, twenty years? That's all there is?

What good are healthy lungs? What good are eyes for all the colors of the rainbow? What good are ears for all the sounds of the scale?

Now, I have to do it, tonight!

Bettina's schoolbooks are in the left side of the bookcase.

One side of his face is lit by the small, soft glow of the night lamp, his cheeks and chin lie in shadow. His upper lip protrudes slightly in his sleep (like Bettina's). I want to remember every little line, every hair. But everything blurs. I can feel his tender, breathless lips everywhere. I can feel his warm skin on my skin. I can feel his gentle hands on my back—I turn out the light.

His breathing is deep and regular. He lies on his side, curled up under the blanket like a baby in its mother's womb. A familiar warmth rises from him. Rises and wraps around me and fills the whole shadowy room. Something sober and foreign in me must have dictated that note. Nothing is more important than this familiar warmth. How can I simply want to leave like that! We have to talk at least one more time. I have to find precise and careful words . . .

But how can I explain to him, the precise thinker, this imprecise urge that simply can't be held back any longer without suffocating me? I'd slide into nagging accusations despite myself and make the inevitable parting even worse—and still not really have explained anything. And what will I do if he simply brushes off my words, kisses them away, and feels so clearly how the bitter aftertaste melts away again under him and I forget what I've learned—and learn it again the next day?

How many times have I run through the city, sat down in a cafe, and called up his faces from the past, painted them large and bright and promising, made myself a way out. And been defeated again by another dinner party.

Now, I have to leave this minute!

Translated by Dorothy Rosenberg

Renate Apitz

Born in Breslau (now Poland) in 1939, Renate Apitz spent much of her childhood and her high school years in postwar Berlin. After university studies in theater and art history, she worked as a dramaturge for GDR radio. Only in her late thirties did she turn to freelance writing, bringing out three volumes of short prose during the 1980s.

   "Harmonious Elsa" is taken from Apitz's anthology *Evastöchter*, which inspired the title of this volume (see Translators' Preface). Some of its allusions warrant explanation. Clara and Gretchen, the "virtuous" roles the imagined protagonist wants to play, are the heroines of Goethe's *Egmont* and *Faust*, respectively. Her parents' anti-Nazi stance during "those brown years" (1933–45) is mirrored in the description of the actor Paul as the "Schweijk of the Third Reich," a figure first made famous in Germany by the Czech novelist Jaroslav Hasek, then by Bertolt Brecht with his comic hero in the Hitler satire *Schweijk in the Second World War*. The reference to a boyfriend who is ostracized by the protagonist's family reflects the early postwar black market economy: he is a *Grenzgänger*, a border-crosser, who, by going to the Western sector of Berlin to work, can get four East marks for every West mark he brings home ("one to four"). Finally, the last line of the text refers to a 1969 story by the East German writer Werner Bräunig, "The Simplest Thing in the World," about uncomplicated male-female relationships based on the integration of meaningful work and the private sphere.

Evastöchter (Daughters of Eve). Rostock: Hinstorff, 1981.

Hexenzeit (Time for witches). Rostock: Hinstorff, 1984.

Herbstzeitlose (Meadow saffron). Rostock: Hinstorff, 1989.

Harmonious Elsa   (1981)

IT'S A SILKEN BLUE autumn day outdoors. You can see the crowns of the poplars through the windows. They bend westward in the wind, and the leaves show their gray undersides. I should be paying better attention. They don't pay their professors big salaries so we can admire poplars while they talk. Elsa will keep us on our toes in this seminar all right. Even so, we're lucky to have our Comrade Elsa. We quickly got used to her, right away we all liked her thin face with that natural, layered hairdo, or whatever you call it. But—how does a woman like that get to be a doctor of philosophy? I mean, I wonder how she manages being both a woman and a scholar. There's a lot we don't know.

Her name could be Ellen, or she could be called that. Ellen's papa was a mediocre actor. And then, in 1933, when Ellen was just two years old, it happened. Papa was acting in one of those troupes that do political theater. During a guest performance in Paris, the troupe decided not to return to a country ruled by fascism. Only Dora and Paul, who were Ellen's parents, you see, disagreed. They wanted to go back home and suggested that the group go underground by taking regular repertory jobs. Organizing resistance would be futile, too. Given the overwhelming odds. There was no quarrel between them and the troupe. They parted in mutual respect. Dora and Paul really did manage to survive all those years in mainstream jobs, too. Ellen grew up in unspoken agreement with Papa's view that you don't fight the tide but live with it.

After the war, when Ellen was nearly grown up, she faced the question of how to live an honorable life. She felt a calling to play the virtuous Clara or Gretchen. She failed the acting school entrance exam. Her tears moved Papa. He drove there with her. This occasion turned into a reunion. The old buddies, who were now involved in training a new generation of actors in the Stanislavski method, and Paul. Paul wasn't going to be outdone. He told how he had gotten through it all, all those brown years, in his attic apartment (four rooms), and when required to display the Nazi flag, he had not resisted but had hung out a tiny pennant with the despised swastika, which couldn't even be seen from below. They loved the story. And so he elaborated on it a bit and told it often. Paul, the Schweijk of the Third Reich.

So Ellen could now dream of Gretchen and Clara and study fine arts. She was engaged by a theater near Papa, that is, in Berlin. She was allowed to play servant girls and once a maid who had to yell something indecent from the wings. The other tenants in her apartment house admired lovely Ellen, who appeared in the program notes as Eleonora. The directors advised her to try her wings in a small theater. But it was too late for that, for a male admirer awaited her nightly at the stage door. Sometimes with flowers.

The man works in the West at one to four. That caused an uproar in the family. Papa disowned her. Who can afford an opportunist in the family? At the same time, someone else took her on. Manny had studied Marxism in the USSR. He told her she wasn't suited for a career as Gretchen or Clara. She was too clever. He gave her books so she would adapt to his way of thinking. This wasn't difficult for her. Manny's friends were buddies. They were never around, or were always showing up at the wrong moment. They were always at meetings, where they talked or argued. To them, she was Ellen, the girl who had gotten good at typing their reports when Manny asked her to. When Manny's influence got her a job at one of the schools where he was teaching, it was too much for the 1:4 man. He filed for a divorce from this theater floozy, this lefty. That's when Ellen came of age. Just at the moment when the old judge asked her what exactly she intended to do with herself next. It was really only to impress her ex-husband that she said she wanted to go to the university. She then spent years as Manny's research assistant. She sat in bright, sunny rooms and worked tirelessly. Analyses and plans, outlines and reports. Manny did make mistakes. One cost him more than he could handle. He was sent off to manage a mid-level operation and settled in there quite nicely. He could not take Ellen with him. This solution had not occurred to her either. The institute retained Ellen, who received her doctorate two years later. Now she's got us. When our seminar group gets together to go to the theater—with spouses and children, of course—she looks at the season program and says that she prefers reading plays to seeing them performed.

Thus far, it would seem that things had gone rather smoothly for my Ellen. She loves the written word. But now I'd like Life to come closer to her. After all, she's not too old for such things. It is not good for man to be alone, saith the Lord. Right he is. Maybe our little Charlie, who sits up front on the right, would be right for her. He's a nice guy . . .

For example, Charlie's driving her home not long ago and invites her to take a little detour with him. Now they're sitting in a cafe high above the city. The windows are shut. He thinks it's because of the danger, and she can't imagine anyone would do such a thing on purpose. "Yes they would," says Charlie, and makes his first move. "You try being alone all the time!" "I am alone all the time," says Ellen, not understanding. Now he shows her pictures. Charlie in uniform in front of a T-34 tank, one of him standing on a slope as a distinguished officer of the People's Army, one with a general on a roadside. He shows her his grandchildren, and his wife who died of diabetes. They had been happily married for twenty years. But he never really saw much of her, all those years between the generals and the tanks. "Now I'm a civilian and the Section Five Party secretary in the factory. I want to have another go at it, at fifty-one." Ellen looks up, a little surprised that a person refers to life as something one has a go at. She is only a little younger, these aren't her problems. Charlie's eyes get big and sad. The world doesn't understand him.

"I was used to taking orders. Now everybody expects me to speak for myself. That's damned hard to adjust to. The first time I went to a meeting with workers, I wore a white smock. They wiped off their hands before they gingerly shook my paw. And then once I went to a group of directors in my assembly line overalls. They didn't even shake my hand. I go out on the shop floor and order that the workers be given tea with lemon because of the heat. Is that something the Party should do? I organize Party indoctrination and training courses and write reports. Is that the Party, I mean, really? You're a professor, you should be able to tell me what we're doing wrong in the area of Relating-To-Our-People. I'm glad I've found you."

Well, thinks Ellen, I'd like to know what good it's going to do him. She likes his brown eyes and the energetic lines above them. He's even educated in a certain way, and speaks Russian, which she finds so difficult. Charlie's beginnings lie in the Don River Basin. Lots of schools, and his "Yes Sir, Comrade General." That's what this really quite likable man is about.

Ellen says, "Good. Well, that's about it," and is about to pay for her coffee, the automatic gesture of the single woman. And he says: "Why? Do you have to go?"

"Time management," Ellen says, smiling. "The coffee's gone, and you've told me a little about yourself." By now this thing is starting to look like a waste of time. Nevertheless, she stays and looks out over the city. Seen from above, the streets form lines between the buildings, inhabitable piles of brick divided by gray asphalt bands carved by a blow torch. She would like to talk about the city, about the future of the brick fortresses, but Charlie is talking about himself. He has an apartment. Luxury, of course, expensive record collection. Come by sometime, OK? I'm alone a lot.

He opens fire, so to speak. Ellen has always had trouble evaluating these situations, and right now she hasn't the faintest idea what to expect from this one . . . I'll have Charlie tell her about the good beer in his refrigerator, but Ellen doesn't drink beer. "You're pretty narrow-minded," snaps Charlie. "Alcohol gives me a headache," Ellen hastens to say. Charlie doesn't give up: "I make good money," he points out. "So do I," says Ellen. "I'm crazy to be looking for a new wife. I wanted to talk to you about it. Why are women all so arrogant these days? When a guy finds one he likes, she says leave me alone. Well, you're so smart and educated, but you can't even carry on a real conversation." My clever Elsa thinks she would like to have said something. But when does a clever woman speak, and how is she supposed to compete with Charlie, who, after all, has an agenda? Maybe it's just boredom. "Try reading a book," she advises him, "that helps."

So Charlie doesn't get anywhere with this Ellen.

I would really rather get Charlie and Ellen together after all. Maybe then we'd need a different Elsa—livelier, more intense. A woman who's been around and can take a few knocks.

*   *   *

This time I'll call her Elise.

She must have been a bit stubborn. Contrary, and not even that good a student in school. I don't want your connections, she said to her Papa—I wish she had said it when she was competing for admission to the university.

Then she worked as an unskilled laborer in a factory. Things will turn out all right. The soldering fumes brought tears to her eyes. It could also have been the small appliances—radios, I guess—that piled up in front of her work station and made her ruin the others' piecework rates. Drill six holes on one frame: one red wire, one yellow, one green, one white, one striped, and one black and tighten the nut with the number six wrench. That took time. If she missed the wires or if the nut wasn't tight, the assembly line lead would yell: Come here. That meant make-up work. The mountain of radios grew at a frightening pace. She was afraid of the noisy, happy clan of women who either helped her or made fun of her, depending; who laid siege to the factory gates and stormed the streetcars at three-thirty; who had boyfriends and husbands. Elise began to have dreams about it: a red one, a green one, a yellow one . . . Mrs. G. said some people just can't do it. Elise was moved to another station. Gluing antennas. That was simple. The rate inspector wrote her time on record sheets. Her time was good. On Saturday he took her dancing, and six months later to the justice of the peace. She told her child fairytales and kept telling them when the child was asleep and the rate inspector was still sitting around in bars.

The couple spoke occasionally after the divorce. About the child, and about how bad the production figures looked. Even the rate inspector didn't know why something was always wrong and why the appliances were so bad. Much worse than those from across the border. Elise went to the Party Secretary and said: "I don't want to work when it's a waste of time. Why are we behind schedule, why are our products inferior even though we're doing our best?" She was assigned to a work group with engineers and brigade leaders in which everyone blamed someone else. There was a lot that Elise didn't understand, but she stood up for the women's interests. "I don't want the others laughing at me. Send me to the university." Economics. Those were four hard years.

Then she had a boss. He had a temper, but he knew his field. He took a job in a government ministry. She got a new boss. This time, she ate the frosting off the cake and was a success. Her third boss didn't drink as much as the second, but the monotony of the job, the calculations, the detail work began to bore her and make her irritable. The woman instructor in charge of her work group offered to send her to school to take a social science course (maybe the one we're taking now). That was fun for Elise. In economics, Elise was the best in her class. She was the one who had it down cold, became Elise the Wonder Woman, learned other things on the side, and stayed on as an instructor. She got her doctorate under the affirmative action program. Her son took a bride after his stint in the army. She took up her next book, wrote a small brochure herself, attended several conventions, submitted reports, and, in the evenings, fiddled with the new hairdo her women colleagues had talked her into.

She's surprised when she sees something about big ballroom dances in the paper. How nice, she thinks, to be young again.

A mood like this would have been Charlie's big moment, if he'd been watching for it. I'd put a bouquet in his hand: carnations or a few late roses. I'd rather not think about how they come to terms, only that they find each other. In the long run, solitude isn't Elise's thing after all, and Charlie plays his cards better this time, too. Elise blossoms again. Gets rosy cheeks, uses expensive perfume, and buys a few clothes in the designer shop. But the time comes when Charlie's records have all been played and when Elise's group leader mentions to his assistant that Elise used to volunteer more, had been more dedicated. Elise's dedication is now spent mostly in the supermarket. Standing in lines has intensified now that she shops for two: at the cheese counter, the sausage and meat departments, the vegetable stand, and the checkout. And she mustn't forget Charlie's beer. Ill will abounds. Elise must decide: husband or research.

Maybe the question should not be so black and white. It could be that the problem lies with Elsa-Ellen-Elise or with Charlie, a purely personal matter. In which case there will be no choice but to think up a harmonious Elsa, one who knows how to integrate career and inclinations of the heart. Quite a task.

* * *

Speculation is for the birds.

I meet Elsa, her husband at her side, in the park. She's pushing a baby carriage. "My grandchild," she says with the dignity of a Grand Duke. She met her husband at their high school graduation ball. He had to swear he'd let her become a professor. She goes to school, stays on as an assistant at the university, gets her doctorate, has two children. While they are still little, she lets her husband go for his doctorate, publishes several scholarly works, and directs a large collective. She is promoted to professor at forty-five. Their son is an auto mechanic, their daughter a research biologist. Sundays, previously reserved for the children, now belong to the first grandchild.

I wish the simplest thing in the world had been just a little more exciting.

Translated by Nancy Lukens

Maxie Wander

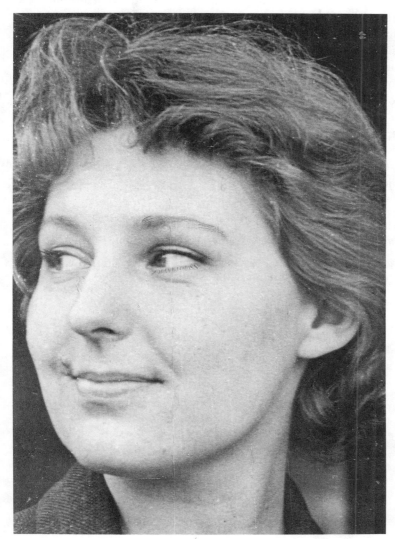

Born in 1933 in Vienna, Austria, Maxie Wander moved to East Germany in 1959 and worked as a secretary, a reporter, and a librarian before turning to writing. She lived in Klein-Machnow near Potsdam. She died of cancer in 1977 in Berlin.

Wander is better known in the West than many of the women included in this volume because of the posthumously published autobiographical reflections written during her struggle with cancer, *Leben wär' eine prima Alternative*. She also wrote short stories and prose pieces, such as her "Kinderprotokolle" (documentaries of and for children) with titles such as "Frank, Dialectics, and the Ordinary Guinea Pig." Her only independent publication, *Guten Morgen, du Schöne,* a collection of interviews with women from which our selection is taken, was of immense significance to GDR women's writing and to the genre of short prose in general. Wander's unique contribution was to empower her discussion partners to discover their own voices. While her questions are not directly recorded, her presence as engaged interviewer is reflected in her subjects' responses. In this selection, the speaker's trust is indicated by her use of a very colloquial idiom.

Guten Morgen, du Schöne: Frauen in der DDR (Good morning, Beautiful: Women in the GDR). Berlin: Buchverlag der Morgen, 1977.

Leben wär eine prima Alternative (Living would be a great alternative). Darmstadt/Neuwied: Luchterhand, 1980.

Ute G., 24, Skilled Worker, Single, One Child (1977)

My PARENTS were progressive, right, but the way they brought us kids up, terrible! The girls had to slave, the boys had it easy. After my big brother died, my parents spoiled their only other son rotten. He turned into a know-it-all and had temper tantrums, but otherwise he's a good kid, right? My little sister, you can do whatever you want with her: Sabine, do this, Sabine, do that, and never any back talk. My big sister, she gets all worked up about the littlest things. It makes her sick if a day goes by where she can't complain about something. And my big brother, the one that's dead, with him it went in one ear an' out the other. A lotta times he'd go for days without talking to my parents, he was always an independent type and my parents respected that, right?

An' me, well, I dunno. At home somehow it was never clear where I stood. I always did everything I was told, like Sabine, never got upset about anything, and never got outa line. I still live at home. An' I know for sure I'd do a lotta things completely different if I'd gotten out when I was seventeen. They didn't have any trouble with me, in school and stuff. I never ever tried anything you could get in trouble for. I always studied hard and did everything else, too, right? God, straight home after school every day, cleaned house, never went out, was seventeen before I ever went dancing, and then home by nine! An incredible fuss.

Things didn't really change until I had the kid, right? It was the end of the world for my parents. The first person I told I was knocked up was my big brother. I always told him everything, he really understood. I was earnin' money, right, and he was an apprentice. I really spoiled him and I was crazy about him. And that's why it hit me the hardest of all when he died. I was incredibly shocked the way he looked all of a sudden, blue lips and fingernails. I was in the kitchen, and he came in for something to drink. He was gettin' over pneumonia, and all of a sudden it happened. It was all over in a hurry. I went and got a doctor, he tried to revive him. Blood clot in the lung, embolism, and that's it. Our parents were at work. Somehow it's real funny, I still can't talk about my big brother like somebody that's dead. I always think he's just away in the army. I even dream about him, he's standin' there, and I say where've you been so long? I've only been to his grave twice, I can't stand it.

But I've gotten more independent since my brother isn't around any more. Before, I'd always ask him for advice. An' then all of a sudden I hadda do it all myself. My father isn't the most important anymore since Ralph's been around, either. Ralph'll play chess with him and win, and my father's ego takes a beating. My father's a lot of fun, he likes to go out for a drink, and you can get anything you want from him. Nobody would ever hurt him, he trusts everybody. As far as personality goes, I'm real similar to him. On the other hand, he can be strict and consistent, too. I used to think it was really neat that he always knew everything. And the way he treats my mother. My mother isn't very healthy, so he builds her a summer house! Gives up havin' a car an' builds a cottage! Still, he's the boss around the house. For one thing, he's smarter than my mother, and besides, my mother isn't very good with money either. And everything else grew out of that. I see it like this: my mother comes from a railroad background, not very active in politics. She was only a girl when my father married her. My father comes from around Senftenberg, mines, right? Grampa was a real character: Ok son, you're not gonna do that, Nazi Party and stuff, you're just not gonna do it. Toward the end my father was drafted, but he came back and started to work for the city council.

My mother had been a housewife the whole time. They were always on each other's backs. Finally, after my little brother was born, she helped out at the day-care center. She saw what kinds of problems other women had, and all of a sudden the stuff at home wasn't that important any more. Later on she started at the factory, full time. And were we amazed, hey, Mom's doin' all right! She even joined the Party, an' that was her first decision. Some things are still hard for her, like the Party's mandatory training sessions, for example. She never had an education, so I've got a lotta respect for her for what she's made of herself, from bein' a little housewife, totally in my father's shadow, y'know? An' all of a sudden she's contradicting him in public! Except sometimes she's so bitchy I can't stand her. Like she'll complain about the ol' cottage and how much work it is for her. An' she has no idea how good she's got it. She's been gettin' these strange ideas recently. Nothin' against the way she's changed, but now she's gone too far, now she's gotta go buy stuff from "Exquisit," that makes me mad. All of a sudden she's lost her bearings.

Nope, I wouldn't wanna live like my mother. Though I used to be pretty damn stuffy myself. For example, I was really hot to get married and everything just like everybody else. That was too much for Ralph back then. Now we're planning on an extended family. We all got the idea at the same time: Ralph an' me, Tom an' Erni. We wanna live together, 'cause we like to be together anyway, right? Well, we saw this film about an extended family household. Of course, they were doin' it all wrong, but with our setup it should work out better, right? Gee, to shack up like other married couples, watch TV, always the same, always together, and if ya want company, ya have to leave the kids at home alone, or the woman has to stay home—no way! First I thought: Just go along with it, so I don't lose Ralph. 'Cause I loved him more than he loved me. Meanwhile, that's evened out. But now I really want the extended family. We all work shifts. So somebody's always home to watch the kids. Later I'd like to adopt another kid, after I've finished my correspondence courses. Partly because of my figure, right? Ralph says: Just think what you're gonna look like if you have another kid! He's into me havin' a good figure. And mine really isn't all that hot. Actually, that's my handicap, too, when I think about men. I would've tried it out already, but then I think: It's sure no fun for the man!

Erni's still skeptical about the extended family. She's completely different. Typical housewife and mother. But she's gone through a lotta changes the last few years, you gotta give her that. Erni and Tom are real interesting. Tom's a real man, like in the storybooks, y'know? But he cooks and takes care of the kids when Erni's on night shift, does everything a woman does. That doesn't fit with the way he acts in public at all. Well, an' Erni was a hairdresser. Tom was so sick of it, he couldn't stand hearing the gossip from the hair salon any more. All of a sudden he grabbed her, sat her down in front of the TV and said: Now listen! No commercials, we're watching the GDR news for a change. So she watched, y'know? The next night the same thing. Him holding Erni down till she got interested. Girl, he said to her, don't ya understand, it's not hobbies that matter, it's how you look at life. He wanted a partner, y'know? and he got one. It was almost like it was with us. One day, what does Erni do? Starts griping about her private beauty salon, the exploiter and stuff, and quit on her little boss. Now she doesn't wash greasy heads anymore or curtsey for every mark she earns. Took off her jazzy little smock, has grimy fingers, a shitty triple shift, but she's gettin' retrained, and she likes bein' with people who don't just talk shit. Now she's worried if the extended family household breaks up, how she'd get back the money she's put into the house. That wouldn't bother me at all. Good grief, I'll earn more money, I won't be ruined. An' everything else, well, we'll just have to try it out.

When we've gotten ourselves set up, we wanna build an addition and fix up somethin' like a youth center where you can play music and dance. Ralph wants to learn guitar, I play accordion, back then in the band I sang, too, and other people'll show up with their instruments, great! I need people around me. I really miss my friends, not just in the GDR. Just now in Leningrad, the factory sent me there for a week, I realized what I missed. The daily grind is always the same, but you don't absolutely have to do everything that way. It used to be if I thought somebody looked interesting I'd think, nope, ya can't do that, people'll talk. I think it's great to talk with foreigners. We were arguing about freedom in Leningrad. A guy from Holland asked me if we were free. Sure, we're free, I says. But you can't travel wherever you want, he says. No, I says, I guess we have a different idea about what freedom is, we better get that straight. I'm free from exploitation, I've got my right to work, I get paid just as much as a man, an' I get an apartment, even if it isn't all that easy, but it isn't for you all, either, is it? Then he asked if I was happy. Yes, I'm happy. But don't you earn too little money? No, I feel fine just the way I am.

It was great with the Dutch guy, he was just crazy about me. But the minute I was home with Ralph again, I'd forgotten him. I actually don't have the urge to go to bed with other men. It's fun to flirt, a little kissy-face and stuff, but the only one who's really good in bed is Ralph. By now we've learned from one another the way we both like it. Ralph could do it three times a day, he's got incredible energy. Man, I wonder if it'll last. I'm afraid he'll wear himself out.

The guy who knocked me up played in our band. It wasn't true love, it was pure stupidity. He invited me over to his place once when I'd missed the train, so we just made some coffee. And dumb, sweet Ute falls right into his trap. Oh, boy. It happened right away the first time I slept with him. Nobody believes me. I thought it was so disgusting. He had to turn on all the sweet talk and it never would've worked without the schnapps. I couldn't stand the sight of the guy anymore, I really hated him. I didn't tell him about the kid, maybe I didn't dare. All my brother had told me was: Well, Ute, on such-and-such days you gotta be careful. At school we got the scientific explanation from the Marxist-Leninist perspective, about the responsibility you take. But nobody ever told us how it works in practice. Eighteen years old and still that dumb, right? If we'd had the pill or legal abortion back then, Jens certainly wouldn't be around. Relating to him was really strange. What, that's supposed to be my kid? O God, no it can't be true. And as for that famous motherly love, I never felt it till he started sayin' mama and car-car.

I'd just started studyin' economics before I got pregnant. I was incredibly homesick, and then all the stress over the baby. I didn't know anybody down there. We didn't know what we were actually studying. At the end of four years, we would've had a diploma, but no idea what we were doing. So, I got the hell home. Then I started workin' at the factory. Two companies wouldn't take me: Sorry, pregnant women aren't allowed to work night shift. That really shocked me, that some companies brush you off that easy. Being a single mother is a real disadvantage. Four years ago I applied for an apartment, 'cause the law says that an unmarried mother and child count as a family and have a right to appropriate housing. Married couples who applied later than I did already have an apartment, not me. So two months after I had Jens, I brought him to the boarding nursery and went on shift work. Little babies spend a lotta time lying in their crib and don't really notice what's goin' on yet. He was one and a half before he wanted to stay home even though he got special treatment at the nursery. Oh, the sweet little thing. He is, too, with his big blue eyes, just like me. He stayed in the boarding nursery for three years, then I brought him home. That was the only time I fought it out at home and won. At first my mother said: I've raised enough kids already, now I'm s'posed to watch yours when you're workin' afternoons or nights? They wouldn't give me the day shift, an' I didn't want to leave the company.

Now I'm goin' to vocational school part time. I get one day of study leave a month besides the day for housework, and I get off once a week to go to class, too. I need somethin' like that: learnin' somethin' an' provin' myself. Whenever somebody pays me a compliment I work twice as hard, man it's like I'm transformed, I've got twice as much energy. I volunteer for a lotta social projects, sometimes it's too much for me, but the others are so lame, it makes me mad enough to keep me goin'. Right now we've got a real nice problem: we send people from our company off to school, right, when we know they aren't involved in any volunteer projects; at most they're just good at their work, and they'll end up government officials. We're practically shooting ourselves in the foot. What are we supposed to expect from people like that? They aren't gonna motivate anybody else. So it's the same vicious circle again. Well, it happens to be my goal to teach the people in my collective so they know exactly why they're workin' and so they feel responsible for everything. Ralph and Tom wanta do that too. When you're interested in your work and you wanta change things, then you don't have to just hang around waitin' for your break. It really upsets me when I see how people sleep on the job and wake up for break. Sometimes I get the feelin' I'm fightin' windmills. We've got some tough cookies in our collective. They're in it for keeps. Let's hear it for socialism, they do everything just the way they're told. But basically they think like machines. You gotta fight 'em with facts, and above all, never admit anything's wrong. Of course there's a few that you can talk reason with, it just takes longer. I'm not for compromises, not at work. It's different with Ralph, there you have to take a lot.

I see Ralph as a really strange character anyway. He sees a lotta things clearly, and he knows an awful lot. It's because of him that I finally have a clear position, y'know, with real good arguments. A person needs somethin' like that. Ralph is always a step ahead. At work he was the first one to try to figure out the reasons behind production problems; he was also the first one who criticized the management all by himself. He's got ideas, fantastic. It gets you going, right? For instance, he says: Okay, I'll admit I like to tell people what to do, but I've also noticed that you like to be told what to do, and I don't like it, Ute. Or he'll say: As soon as you figure out that marriage is a bunch of bull, I'll marry you, Ute. In other ways he's a slob. He puts up a curtain just like that, one-two-three. He couldn't care less if it falls down a minute later. Main thing is, it's up for now. Everything's just for the moment. He doesn't care what he has on, no matter how worn out it is, as long as he's got somethin' on. But if there's somebody around taking care of him who says: Now you really could get yourself a decent sweater, then he'll do it. Except that he's got a real talent for pickin' just the times when we're broke. You don't talk about money. You've gotta have it. That's the way he is. His stubbornness in some things covers up a whole lot of insecurity. Sometimes he cries like a baby. Maybe all men are emotional just like women, I've never thought about it. I always wanted a man I could look up to. Ralph said right away he didn't wanta be a tough guy, he thinks it's gross because it's unnatural and dishonest, just like submissiveness in women. But I didn't understand it back then. And then he was jealous like you wouldn't believe. I was in a band back then, he wanted to forbid it and make me quit because all the men were lookin' me over. When I'd say hi to somebody in a cafe, he'd say: What? You had somethin' goin' on with him too? He made a real scene if I kissed a guy out on the dance floor. He'd say you can do that with anybody I know, but not with guys I don't know. I always start to bawl when he starts in on me like that. Afterward he understands, but as a matter of fact, at the tiniest little thing he'd . . . So I said we'd better split up, it's not working out. Then he bawled, and right then I thought he was a jerk. I took off. In the meantime, he got involved with somebody and I had other guys too. But it still upset me when I'd see him with Christa.

She looked so good, she's still my handicap. It makes me really sad when he tells me he's seen Christa, an' he's all excited. He drove me crazy with Christa this and Christa that. He was always talkin' about her like I hadda be like that too. Now I just say: So go back to Christa! And then it's better, then I'm me, and Christa's somebody different.

I really took advantage of the six months he was with Christa, it was automatic. In the band, y'know, everybody aroun' me goin' you're great Ute, you're terrific, Ute. At school they always predicted I'd be shy, never the center of attention. They sure missed my personality. Listen, kid, I said to myself, someday you're gonna die an' you're not comin' back, ya better have a good time now an' stop worryin' about other people, right? Once I had an experience with an Arab, it was terrible. I'm always tryin' to fight it. He read my palm. Past, present, and future. An' he saw everything, y'know? Even that my second child would die. An' that's the way it was. I got rid of a child by Ralph. Going to school, no chance of an apartment, and Ralph said, man, Ute, we can have lots of kids later. Just the way the Arab told me and that I'll die at fifty!

Well, it took two years for us to understand each other as well as we do now. Once it's broken, you can't put it back together. But for us it's gotten even better. Now everything's so settled that one of us misses the other one if we're apart for a while. My parents used to nag me: Ute, don't you finally wanta get married? And then I struck bedrock with Ralph. Now I ask myself why I should force him to do anything, it's hardly likely to improve our relationship anyway. So that's the compromise, I don't always get my way. I've changed, so has he. An' a piece of paper really isn't the most important thing in the world. Ralph always says: Women don't want any equal rights at all. I do, I says, you can count on it. Even my son is already settin' the table, cleans my shoes when he does his own, straightens up his room without talkin' back. I don't see any problem.

But I don't know about bein' faithful. Ralph says yeah, men can be just as faithful as women, they just been taught all the rest of it, but what's faithful worth, anyway? As far as I'm concerned, okay, other women, as long as he stays! He tells me everything, an' then I see if I got reason to be mad or not, right? Sometimes I almost died laughin': Hey, man, sure picked yourself up some gems, didn't ya? He was flirting with a sixteen-year-old. O, dear me, like a rooster! They went swimmin' in the moonlight and she yelled: Ralphie, look, the stars! How would he react if I tried a line like that? At the moment there's not much goin' on. I don't play in the band anymore, it got to be too much. My parents wouldn't let me play the piano, 'cause the bourgeoisie all used to play the piano, so that's why we don't play the piano any more. They really don't quite know which end is up, sometimes they do, sometimes they don't.

But maybe there are two sides to all of us, right? Now an' then I like to kick back too. Except for Ralph, he's always with it, into it. That's why I want us to move in with the others, 'cause I hope there'll be more people to spread the work around.

I don't have any problems gettin' along with people. This problem about brotherhood, come on. Somebody's always waitin' for the other guy to do it. I dunno, those are people who are so smart that they don't really know what they want any more. They just complain, it's part of the act. It used to be like that, too. Like with writers, they could never deal with life, one guy kills himself, another one turns into a hermit, y'know? They're so good at writing, they describe other people's problems and can't deal with their own. 'Course it would be sad if people were always satisfied, wouldn't it? I've had enough problems, I know what I'm talkin' about. Nah, I wouldn't want the fast life. I know the people that wish they could have it all, but then when they've got some tiny little problem, their world falls apart. In school, you really get put through the grinder, you're a nervous wreck. Once I spent two weeks sweatin' out a research problem, and couldn't get it and couldn't get it. An' all of a sudden I got an idea and worked the thing out. Well, an' it was all right, and now it's forgotten, I'm a few steps farther along. Y'know, ya don't have to be headin' any place in particular, ya just gotta keep movin'.

Translated by Nancy Lukens

Charlotte Worgitzky

Photo by Joachim Haberecht, Berlin, courtesy of Buchverlag der Morgen.

Born in 1934 in Annaberg in the Ore Mountains of southeastern Germany, Charlotte Worgitzky attended drama school in Leipzig from 1951 to 1954 and worked for the next ten years as a member of several theater ensembles. She began writing in the late 1960s but continued to work in theater and teach drama as an independent agent after 1964. She has been a freelance writer since her first book appeared in 1975.

This story is taken from her 1978 anthology, *Vieräugig oder blind*.

Die Unschuldigen (The innocents). Berlin: Buchverlag der Morgen, 1975.

Vieräugig oder blind (Four-eyed or blind). Berlin: Buchverlag der Morgen, 1978.

Meine ungeborenen Kinder (My unborn children). Berlin: Buchverlag der Morgen, 1982.

Heute sterben immer nur die anderen (These days only other people die). Berlin: Buchverlag der Morgen, 1986.

I Quit

I'M TIRED. My movements are sluggish, my eyelids want to fall shut—in short, I feel the perfectly ordinary need to sleep. My dear husband, Oswald, has already gone to bed, and our children have long since ended their nightly chatter. But I'll brew myself some coffee—three heaping teaspoons per cup—and then I will neither sew the zipper into my daughter's skirt nor darn the hole that Oswald showed me in his sock before he went to bed. Instead, I'm going to write down the story of why I am no longer the principal. I'll put up with my students shooting spitwads across the room and passing comic books under the desks once they realize that I'm not concentrating, because if I make them write an essay I'll have to be careful that my head doesn't suddenly fall onto the desk. I'll put up with it because I think it's important that everyone find out how I came to have such an important position.

The very first time I saw him a little ahead of me in the cafeteria line, I wanted to get to know him. In those days his chest still bulged out farther than his belly, his black hair had receded only far enough to give his brow a free and noble look, and his rimless glasses made him look extremely intellectual. Six months later he laughed and admitted that he had thought I was unapproachable.

I realize that my ambition was the driving force behind the events that followed, but I can't call it a weakness because I've always found it to be motivating.

While Oswald slept after our nights together and put off his seminar papers until some vague future, I was sitting at my wooden university desk every morning at 7:55. My skirts gradually grew too big, and now and then I began to get drowsy before midnight. Once, when I fell asleep while he was kissing the soles of my feet, Oswald claimed that I didn't love him as much as he loved me. I was in agony. I liked his eyes even better without glasses, and his chest was as full of black hair as his head—but I wanted to be a teacher and was only a sophomore. "I'll take care of my seminar papers," said Oswald. "You're more important to me now." He was two years ahead of me. I developed an inferiority complex.

Then one night this angel appeared. I had fallen asleep with my head on

Oswald's shoulder around 4:00 A.M. It had to have been an angel because it had wings the size of a swan's on its back. Its face did look completely different from the angels I had seen in pictures, but then, artists do tend to gild reality. The face seemed familiar, I just couldn't remember where I'd seen it. It was broad and wrinkled with thin lips and a protruding chin, its hair white and pinned into a skimpy bun at the back of its head. Blue stockings peeked out from under its long plain gown; it must have been a female angel. It—or she—spoke in a voice that was rather deep for a woman, but kindly: "I want to help you because you are a woman. You can make a wish. Think it over carefully."

I felt the way you do in dreams in which you push off from the ground and float weightlessly above everything.

"Peace on earth everlasting," I said.

"And good will toward men," the angel finished and shook its old woman's head. "I don't make promises I can't keep. You may wish for something for yourself."

That was fine with me. So I asked: "I want to always be awake. Never tired. Never have to sleep again."

"This shall be granted you," said the angel slowly. "But only on one condition—" and somewhat hurriedly for an angel she explained: "—it still isn't possible without conditions." Then she nodded her head in Oswald's direction, who had fallen asleep in the meantime. "On the condition that you remain faithful to him."

Solemnly, I declared my consent.

Dissolving before my eyes, the angel disappeared, and I was awake. Slowly I raised my head and looked at Oswald's face just beneath me, sleeping helplessly and innocently with his high forehead and his black hair, protectively holding the covers snugly against my back—I could have sworn that I would never want to be unfaithful to him. I told him about the apparition in the morning, and we laughed about it.

Despite having gotten so little sleep, I went through the day feeling fresh, surprised Oswald with a homemade egg salad for supper, and was still fresh, cheerful, and active when he had begun to yawn. I said he didn't love me as much as I loved him. He fell asleep. I was awake. Wide awake. Like a cool, sunny morning after ten hours of sleep. After I had gazed at Oswald for a while, I rolled out of bed, carefully covered him up, and sat down at my desk.

He didn't want to believe it at first, but after I showed him my seminar papers in the evening and the following morning a few times, Oswald ad-

vised me not to tell anyone else about it. And that's how I became class secretary. My diligence was admired. I was held up as model of emancipation
and a guilt-producing paragon. I was awarded prizes and medals.

When my breakfast came back up a few times, Oswald and I legitimized
our nights. I was asked if I wanted to be relieved of my duties, but I answered that I would be satisfied to be delivered of my child. I was recruited
to join the Party. During the admission interview our Party secretary praised
me so highly that a confession rose to the tip of my tongue before I could
swallow it back down again. And I admit that I don't know to this very
day whether consorting with angels isn't basically un-Marxist and therefore
anti-Party. But I kept quiet. After all, it was to their advantage too, if I refused to postpone my degree and organized and led all the seminar group
meetings until shortly before the baby was born.

I kept quiet in the hospital, too, when I was given a shot and pushed
into a dark room so that I could sleep through the night on the first evening of my thirty-six-hour struggle with my daughter. It wasn't until the
following evening that our Annette saved me with a squawk. The midwife
said she was a lovely child. This child is now already at the age when male
glances are confirming that prophecy. At the time I was unhappy that the
lights were turned out at 9:00 P.M. so that I couldn't even read and had to
spend six nights thinking about the advantages and disadvantages of my
peculiar fate.

My husband had three younger siblings; his mother had taught him at
an early age how to do the shopping, polish shoes, and sew on buttons.
Thus, I did not have to relieve him of the conviction that these chores were
reserved for women. It's just that he has a comfortable disposition. And
since I had about eight more hours a day at my disposal than he, it would
have been uncomradely of me to use them only for myself. I wrote half of
his senior thesis and corrected his students' homework while I was still in
school. He gradually forgot how to sew on buttons, too, and he took our
daughter for walks with his left hand only (he held his cigarette in the right),
while I cooked dinner and washed the diapers. Nevertheless, my diploma
says "Outstanding," and without any preliminary attempt to send me off
to the provinces, they assigned me to teach Russian and mathematics at a
school so new that we had to walk across planks instead of steps to enter
the building for our first conference. The staircase has been renovated three
times since then.

My daughter favored me with unbroken health, and since I hadn't canceled a single class during my first year of teaching, I was elected union

representative in my second. "Brigitte is always there," they said, and they got so used to the idea that they were astonished and indignant at a meeting when I asked a colleague to read the summary report that I had prepared, because I felt dizzy.

Oswald (men are such children) was hoping for a boy. He bought a washing machine so I could take things easier, and once I was foolish enough to hang the wash out in the yard right after I'd taken it out of the machine. "Strange goings-on at the Rocholls," I heard my upstairs neighbor say the next day as I was coming back from shopping and, much as I hate eavesdropping, I didn't open our apartment door until after I heard the upstairs door shut. "Do you know how long that laundry has been hanging out down there?" "No," answered the pensioner who is her neighbor. "Since two o'clock in the morning," said my upstairs neighbor, and while I was imagining the old man's astonished face, I heard him say, "I was asleep." Undeterred, his neighbor continued: "Their lights are on every night whether its two in the morning or five. Strange goings-on." I decided to have shutters installed.

This time I wasn't asked if I wanted to be relieved of my duties. Our principal had been delegated to the Party college for the year, and I was allowed to replace him, since my colleagues thought that paper work would surely be less taxing than classroom teaching. For my part, I was glad that I could take the paperwork home at night.

It was a boy. My dear husband beamed proudly and protested against taking him out in Annette's baby carriage. A new high-wheeled carriage with a footbrake was purchased. The neighborhood children took turns taking one another for walks in the courtyard in the old one.

Shortly after I returned to school, our principal was transferred to the next newly built one. He was experienced at building up a new faculty. I was appointed his successor. At the party celebrating my first day in the new job, a reporter asked my husband if he was the old principal. "No," he replied, "I'm just the new principal's husband."

At home he referred to me exclusively as "madame boss." I didn't like the way he said it, and I soon found a note while brushing off his sport coat. I saved it: "My sweet little Ossi," it says, "if you can't come this evening either, I'll be waiting for you in front of the post office tomorrow after work. My relief knows and she'll be there in plenty of time. Your sugar dumpling can hardly wait." A few days later I saw the two of them standing together in front a fabric store display window. I recognized the girl from our branch post office. I had often bought commemorative stamps from her. She didn't quite come up to my dear Oswald's shoulder, but her hair hung down to her richly rounded bottom. She pointed at a pink polyester print, and they went into the shop without having noticed me.

I said nothing. I'm sure it isn't easy for a teacher to have a principal for a wife. And Oswald is a good teacher. On the last day of school he always has to take a cab to carry his presents home, and he sometimes gets more mail from his students during the summer vacation than I do. And although he can't show off half as many awards as I can, after all, he does need eight hours of sleep, I said to myself. So even if he frequently "went to see a friend" in the evening and didn't come home until after midnight, what could I do about it? Taking revenge was out of the question; I don't care for marital squabbles, and a divorce—my constant wakefulness could become public knowledge in the process. A secret is binding.

I did, however, hold my third pregnancy against him. After all, there is a limit to what can be accomplished during the night. So I demanded that he be the one to stay home when one of the children was sick, since he could be replaced by a substitute. But when he suddenly had to go to the clinic with our oldest son George every single day, I regretted my demand. I didn't even have to look into it; I knew that it wasn't the woman doctor but at most a nurse.

The Party comrades convinced me of the importance of allowing myself to be nominated as a candidate for the city council. They would help out if necessary and relieve me of assignments at school, but after all, I had managed to handle all the increasing demands on me until now with an astonishing sense of responsibility and admirable discipline.

I was elected. But when the chairwoman of the Democratic Women's Union in my district immediately asked me to join her organization too, I refused. I did agree to a journalist's request to interview me for a two-page profile in a weekly magazine.

On the telephone I had been struck by his slow, less deliberate than melancholy speaking voice. The thin, tanned person with prematurely gray hair and strikingly pale eyes that my secretary ushered in gazed at me so intensely that I was the first to look away. There was nothing zealously reporterlike about him. I began to trust him. He hardly asked anything about my biography, just noted a few dates. We talked about psychology in general and authoritarian education in particular. He had read the articles I had written for our professional journal and said they weren't provocative enough to initiate a discussion, but I countered with the fact that I had already provoked him with them. We both laughed. I postponed another appointment, ordered cognac, and sent my astonished secretary home. I discovered that he wasn't wearing a wedding ring. Oswald agreed sullenly to my telephoned request that he pick up the two boys from their respective day-care centers. I answered my companion's comment, delicately balanced between a question and a statement, that I must have a very sensible and unconventional husband, with an equivocal smile.

As he said goodbye, he hesitated and, holding my hand, asked if I would agree to a second conversation. For the sake of decency, we postponed meeting in his apartment until two days later.

For the first time I had the need to share my secret, not because of a guilty conscience—words like "example," "emancipation," "outstanding," didn't seem to belong to his vocabulary—but simply to be honorable. I had to be careful. To be on the safe side I refused the Courvoisier, but I couldn't resist an Edith Piaf recording. We hardly spoke, both confused. My departure was hasty.

The next morning I had neither corrected the geometry papers (my students always praised me for never prolonging their anxiety about the result of a written assignment for longer than a day), nor washed my daughter's scout blouse, nor hung up the living room curtains that were waiting to be ironed. My daughter was outraged at having to wear a dirty blouse to her scout meeting. My students were surprised, but my husband didn't ask if I was sick until the following day. Perhaps I really was. I had come to love the hours of the night; even if I used them to work for others, they belonged to me. A passing car or a bellowing drunk on the weekend only emphasized the quiet that surrounded me. And whether I darned socks or read books or corrected papers, no one interrupted me with questions like "Why can't dogs talk?" or "Is lunch ready yet?" And when one of the children coughed or had a fever, I was glad that I could open the door to their room and check on them. Now, sitting in an armchair, an entire pack of cigarettes hadn't helped, and I would have liked to wake up my family so they could keep me from the temptation of going to him, to Conrad G; he deserves to have his name spelled out but I don't want to compromise him. And how great is the temptation when you know that he is just waiting for you to come! A taxi, and I'd be back in time for the first-shift alarm clock ringing, set the table like every other morning, make toast as if nothing had happened. And nothing happened.

I began to make comparisons, revised them because they were unfair. He has faults too, I said to myself, just different ones. Just as with Oswald, they'll annoy me only after I've gotten used to his advantages. And think of what I would lose! I knew my ambition; it pleased me to be able to decorate myself with a new award every year in May or October—without any resentment from my colleagues, I was sure. They were glad that I did the work for them. I often asked myself, didn't they have to wonder how I managed it all? I'm sure they overestimated my husband.

I went into the bedroom. Oswald breathed evenly, his glasses lay next to an open book on the nightstand, and a bare foot stuck out from under the covers. He hadn't gone out in the evening without me for a while now. I pulled the covers over his foot and took his shirt with me to the washing machine.

Conrad G. brought the magazine with the article to me at school. My secretary asked if she should bring cognac. I said no thank you.

He looked even thinner. His gaze was no longer searching but was as melancholy as his voice. I was glad that someone might come into the room at any moment.

I recognized myself in that profile. For the first time, I found myself appreciated as the person that I would have been even without the extra hours at night, although naturally he too talked about the amount I worked, my professional, private, and social achievements and contributions. I found it difficult not to tell him the truth, so I asked him not to see me again. His cigarette trembled as he stubbed it out. My secretary's typewriter began to clatter wildly as we came out of my office.

Shortly thereafter our fourth child announced itself (the pill saved me from a fifth). I gave Oswald the task of finding us a larger apartment. We were able to move into a four-bedroom apartment in an older building after the birth of our youngest.

I now had to plan even my night hours carefully in order to manage everything. It took me two years to read Thomas Mann's Joseph trilogy. I gradually got fed up with the reporters because they wasted too much of my time, so I learned how to get rid of them. But I couldn't (and didn't want to) deny myself a television program "Parade '71—Honoring the Best."

The program was televised live. The studio was full of curiosity seekers, people who had come because of the pop singers, and the prizewinners and their families.

I sat next to Oswald in the front row. I knew that I would be the fifth person called by the host. Four men were interviewed ahead of me. Each one received a gift: a trip to Moscow with his wife or a motorcycle. Between the interviews, painted dolls held the microphone to their lips and sang what are called hits. Oswald couldn't tear his eyes away from one with bleached blonde curls, false eyelashes, and a glittery silver-green jumpsuit. She moved her hips as if she were stirring soup with them. My Oswald stared in fascination and nearly clapped his hands off. It annoyed me. For one thing, this was supposed to be a sort of day of honor for me, after all, and for another I found his taste dreadful.

The moderator spoke with oleaginous charm, completely different than he'd been during the rehearsal. The people who were being honored seemed to have no flaws at all, just work, collective spirit, helpfulness, and technical innovations. I harbored the suspicion that they had entered into nighttime contracts the same as I had, but even before I was called up to the stage, I was struck by the fundamental difference between me and my honored predecessors: they were men. The wives sitting in the audience took care of everything that I needed my night hours for.

The blonde oozed more schmaltz after the fourth candidate. I think that if I had pinched Oswald he wouldn't have noticed. I hoped in vain that he would squeeze my hand once for luck before I had to climb the steps to the stage. My stomach was full of butterflies. The host smiled at me. "And now ladies and gentlemen, the high point of our program, the golden climax, proof that equal rights have become a reality: a woman! Mother of four children, city council member, school principal—" I was already frowning, I almost missed the question why I had become a teacher. I responded with the answer that we had rehearsed, but when I was jovially asked how I managed to cope with all of these responsibilities, if I had a special scheduling method, I said, "I don't sleep at night."

The TV announcer's mouth was still smiling but his eyes gaped. "Of course," he said and gave an artificial laugh, "it's easy to imagine someone with such extensive responsibilities having insomnia."

"No," I insisted, "not ordinary insomnia. I never get tired. I work night and day." This time he looked at me completely bewildered. Then he laughed again, very loud and much too close to the microphone. "A joke!" he said. "A splendid joke! In order to manage everything that you have to do, one really would need the nights too. We know what you're hinting at."

"No joke, no hint," I said. "It's the truth."

I saw Oswald sitting there. He had his hand over his mouth. "One night when I was still a student"—I was careful to speak clearly into the microphone—"an angel appeared and told me to make a wish. So I wished never to have to sleep again."

I saw beads of sweat rolling down the interviewer's face. But his show-hosting experience saved him. "Are you sure it wasn't a devil?" he asked, laughing, and shook a finger at me in mock reprimand. "The Devil himself with hooves and horns? A contract signed in blood? Ladies and gentlemen," he turned to the audience, back in control, "the modern Faust! The Faust of our century: a woman! Faustina!"

The applause washed over us in waves.

I gave up. Let them have their lies, I thought, and smiled down at them.

The interviewer left out a few of the questions, even though I now answered as expected. His charm seemed forced, and he quickly signaled the stagehands to roll out the color TV that I was being given. The band was in a hurry too, and a youngster with a black mane and a gold-glitter turtleneck sang: "I love only you, you, you—"

Oswald didn't say anything. Worried now, he took my hand, which must have been hot.

There was a cocktail party for all the participants and their spouses afterward. I wanted to skip it, but Oswald thought that would be rude. The interviewer kept his distance.

I identified the bleached blonde curls as a wig, but the eyes under the false eyelashes apparently found a receding hairline, glasses, and a beer belly appealing. A wife who got to go to Moscow said to me: "You sure gave it to them." I asked her what her occupation was. "I'm staying at home just now, because of the children," she said not very self-confidently. My husband clinked champagne glasses with the blonde. Despite the mother-of-pearl polish, her fingernails looked like dirty claws.

A young man who introduced himself as a producer suggested meeting with a writer. He was sure we could put together a television play. I asked him if he wanted to include the idea of the contract with the angel in the story. He laughed. His teeth were white and even. He thought it would be unrealistic. "Then it will be boring," I said and thought of the evenings when I had walked away from similar films after fifteen minutes. The producer shrugged his shoulders and said smiling, "You underestimate yourself." I love white teeth.

Through the open door I could see Oswald and the blonde wig in the next room. He had his arm around the back of her chair. A bottle of champagne stood on the floor in front of them. I'd like to see the evening's bar bill.

The young producer was putting a lot of effort into pedagogical themes. His schooldays couldn't have been that long ago. Finally, we were reduced to hauling out anecdotes about student pranks. He claimed that he couldn't imagine students getting any pleasure out of annoying me. I said, "Charming rascal!" My champagne bill alone must have come to a considerable sum.

He called a cab. Oswald and the pop singer had disappeared some time earlier.

I would like to characterize him as a nimble grasshopper. Nevertheless, puffed up with pride, he dared to ask me afterward if I was satisfied. I didn't feel like convincing him of his lack of talent; besides, the fatigue I remembered so well had already begun to creep through my body. Still, it wasn't until I saw the blue-stockinged feet of the angel standing at the foot of the bed that I sobered up. It still surprises me that I was able to sleep so deeply and soundly after the shock.

When I got home the next morning, Oswald was already asleep in his bed. My daughter claimed to have been unable to prevent the boys from smearing marmalade on their pillows. "Why were you gone so long, too!" she complained.

That evening I lay down next to my husband. He didn't say a word.

I would like to keep my seat on the city council. I asked to resign as principal. Filled with consternation, they sent me to the doctor. After several hours of examinations in various departments of the outpatient clinic, it was determined that my right eye is slightly weaker than the left and that I need to have a filling in one of my front teeth. I confessed to the doctor, a dignified gentleman of about sixty, why I was there. With a kindly expression he wrote me a referral to a psychiatrist. I hoped that this would be enough to get my resignation accepted, but they demanded that I go through therapy. Finally they relented when I fell asleep in the middle of a student conference.

Oswald now does his best to help me. I am convinced that he has been faithful to me since then. Now that I could take revenge for everything that happened in the past, I haven't the time and I'm always tired.

Tomorrow I'll place my third ad for a housekeeper to come at least twice a week.

Translated by Dorothy Rosenberg

Christa Müller

Christa Müller was born in 1936 in Leipzig. After completing an apprenticeship as a bookbinder, she was delegated to the Workers and Farmers' College, where she studied labor psychology from 1956 to 1958. Müller then attended the state film school in Babelsberg from 1958 to 1962 and received her degree as a producer and scriptwriter. She went to work as a scriptwriter for the *Deutsche Film-Agentur* studio in 1962 and began publishing poetry in anthologies and journals in 1970, appearing with Maria Seidemann and Reiner Putzger in a 1975 volume of poetry, *Kieselsteine*. She has published many short stories, including one collection of her own work, and a novella. Müller lives in Potsdam and continued to write for the DEFA studio until 1989.

The following story is from her collection *Vertreibung aus dem Paradies*.

Vertreibung aus dem Paradies (Expulsion from paradise). Berlin/Weimar: Aufbau, 1979.

Die Verwandlung der Liebe (The transformation of love). Berlin/Weimar: Aufbau, 1990.

Candida   (1979)

WHEN CANDIDA was eleven years old, she asked her mother: If you had to have seven years of bad luck and were asked when you'd rather have them—as a child, or later—what would you choose?

I don't know, said Maria.

I'd take them as a child, said Candida, then you'd have it over with.

*   *   *

Candida was born.

Maria was in her second night of labor. The midwife had lain down on the cot against the wall of the birthing room. This child that didn't want to enter the world would be born between night and day. She could tell from the sound of the mother's breathing.

She fell asleep and was awakened by Maria's scream. Don't scream, she said. Save your strength. Her limbs felt as heavy as lead as she got up.

She did what had to be done.

Blinded by the lamp at the foot of the bed, Maria closed her eyes. Come, finally. Come! she thought.

The midwife told Maria to pant to keep from pushing the child out of her body. She grabbed the baby by the nose, twisting it, because the umbilical cord was wrapped around its neck. Its shoulders hadn't been born yet.

Barely here and already gone. That would be too easy, she thought, and cut the umbilical cord between Candida and her mother.

Suspended by her feet, Candida received the first blows of her life. She was silent. Maria saw the baby hanging above her, a thin little body covered with white tallow. Finally, the tiny mouth above the crooked nose gasped for breath with a wretched cry.

They lay next to one another: Candida and her mother.

The midwife entered the numbers in a book. The little that could be known: weight, length, shoulder and head measurements.

What could be guessed? That the eyes would be blue?

What will she think? Feel? What will she cry about, be happy about?

The January night rang with frost. The frost shattered telegraph wires, armored the earth, killed the fish under the ice, and buried people in the snow.

Candida had arrived in the world.

*   *   *

The world. The child shut its eyes and mouth to keep it out. It hadn't had a choice. It had to come. It lay at its mother's breast as it had lain in her body, with its fists clenched and its knees pulled up, and refused to drink.

Candida, my daughter, Maria spoke to her. It's no use shutting yourself off. If you don't like the world you'll have to change it. You're right that it's impossible to live in. So drink. You have to grow strong. And open your eyes.

Maria decided to raise Candida to bear pain and fight for happiness.

During this time Maria kept having the same dream: she had forgotten to feed her baby, and when, in an attack of panic, she remembered it and unwrapped it out of its covers, it had dried up and fell to dust in her hands. She would wake up stiff with fear and listen for its breathing. She couldn't hear it. She had to go to it, touch the baby and feel its warmth.

*   *   *

Candida squinted into the sun. Her baby carriage stood in the garden, in the melting snow.

She looked into the friendly faces that bent over her. Whenever she recognized Maria, she smiled.

Candida's eyes were a transparent blue, incredibly clear in some lights. It startled Maria. She felt a distance between herself and the child. At those moments she felt as if Candida's whole being was turning away from her.

Maria took care of Candida in the breaks between lectures. It was a relief when the baby was ten weeks old.

*   *   *

The Home was right on the lake. A house full of children. It smelled of warm milk and was filled with the sound of their crying and happy shouting.

Maria was told that she would be allowed to visit the baby on Sundays and, if the director approved, take it home with her. Candida didn't make a sound. She lay willingly in the stranger's arms and didn't even turn her gaze toward her mother as she was carried out. Maria signed something, handed over the child's papers, and found herself outside the building again, more confused than relieved.

*   *   *

Candida immediately caught cold. Her breathing hampered, she refused all nourishment. She screamed, struggled. Whenever she opened her mouth, it was stuffed full of sweet mush. She spat it out again, struggling with the care-giver until she was exhausted.

*　　*　　*

A week later the Home was placed under quarantine. The infection appeared in the city too. Between the quarantine in the nursery and then in the university dormitory, three months had passed.

The little beds stood in a long row under an awning on the terrace facing the lake, and Maria walked uncertainly from one to the next. She looked into rosy faces and couldn't find Candida's.

A nurse showed her to her.

Candida lay on her stomach, one hand hidden beneath her. She slept on her left cheek sucking her right thumb. Her hair had grown and curled into wispy blonde locks. Her skin was still delicate. Her mother saw the pulse beating beneath it.

Maria squatted down to look her child in the face. The funny nose, the narrow cheeks shaded by long eyelashes. She slept with her thumb in her mouth. When Maria pulled it out, two tiny teeth gleamed behind her lips.

Candida sighed in her sleep and turned her head to the other side. Maria followed her and looked at her again. Tried to imagine what had happened between leaving her and seeing her again. She had brought a child here which lay on the side you put it down on. When she saw it again, it could turn over by itself.

Candida opened her eyes. Big, clear, blue, she looked at her mother without recognition.

Maria took Candida for a walk, Candida looked into the tangle of leaves. She had never seen them before. She knew the sky, the ceiling, and the awning.

Candida saw only the leaves. When she had seen enough, she fell asleep. That's the way it was for months.

Candida's smile did not belong to Maria.

*　　*　　*

Vacation had emptied the dormitory. Now Candida moved in. Her voice echoed through the building, and she could feel the silence around her.

Through the bars of her crib she could see her mother sleeping in the morning, saw her wake up, and learned to rely on her. After her morning bottle, she lay beside her on the couch and tugged at her hair. Candida's playpen stood on the sunny tiles of the balcony. A radio played. She was bathed outdoors, and on warm evenings her bed stood beneath the changing colors of the sky. Nightingales called in the bushes.

Candida lay with her eyes open as if she didn't need to sleep.

Her grandmother arrived. Inspected the child: What a little mouse! There's hardly anything to her.

She stayed for fourteen days. Days in which Candida got used to the noise of the wheels of her baby carriage rattling on the cobblestones, crunching on the gravel paths, in which she saw the roof of leaves over her head along the path and grabbed at the hard summer grass from a soft blanket in the meadow. She was surrounded by the women's voices or silence. She crawled off the blanket and felt the otherness of the world, and despite the discomfort that the thistles and ants caused her, she didn't cry.

Maria, said her grandmother, let me take her!

You'll spoil her. No. You have nobody else.

But she doesn't have anyone either. When does she have you? Sundays for two hours. Maybe a weekend now and again. When vacation is over, you won't see each other again until Christmas.

*   *   *

In the wet season the children were brought to their mothers in the visiting room. There were chairs along the walls. The mothers, now and then a father, sat there in white smocks and held the children on their laps or between their legs. The larger ones toddled around the room. It was noisy and crowded.

Candida didn't like the room, its stuffiness, the many voices. Her mother was a stranger to her here. Her mother meant sun and wind, the smell of dry grass, and sounds that Candida didn't hear in this building.

Candida was busy with herself. She tried to stand up, pulled herself up on anything she could reach.

Maria watched her, and when the child fell, she didn't rush over to pick her up, and when she cried, she didn't comfort her. Falling down is part of learning to walk.

Candida didn't cry long. She soon stopped altogether. When she fell, she stood up again. Her mother didn't praise her. She smiled, but Candida didn't see it.

*   *   *

At Christmas they rode to her grandmother's foggy gray city.

Maria was upset: her room was freshly wallpapered, her old crib, brought down from the attic and repainted, stood next to her bed, a playpen, a rocking horse, a bath, and a potty.

So much trouble! she said roughly, determined not to leave Candida here.

Candida took possession of these things. Rolled around on the carpet, pulled the tablecloth off the table, clambered onto chairs and couches, and broke dishes. In an unsupervised moment, she knocked over the Christmas tree. She was scolded. She didn't cry.

Her grandmother said: How should she know that a vase breaks, that you can't pull yourself up on a tablecloth, that a stove or a candle flame is hot.

Candida screamed when she was put on the potty. She would fall over on her side, knock over the potty, and lie on the floor stiff and screaming. The women stood over her helplessly. The grandmother tied Candida to a table leg with a diaper. She didn't fall, but screamed until she was exhausted. The potty stayed empty.

Why should I torture her, said Maria. In a week she'll be back in the home.

Her grandmother said nothing.

After the holidays, when Maria went to the grocery store where her mother worked, one of her mother's co-workers said to her: She's been moving heaven and earth to get a space in our kindergarten.

She's my child, thought Maria.

*   *   *

Her grandmother brought Maria and Candida to the train. Look at her, she said, how much she's missing.

A train had left this station when Maria was five. She could still see it: a sea of flowers and flags, brass flashing in the sun, crowds of people. Her father's head oddly squashed among so many heads. He has on a uniform like everyone on the train. Maria doesn't like the material, it scratches when she presses her face against it. Her father's arm hangs out of the compartment window, and her mother holds his hand. Holds it as she runs alongside the train. She is laughing. The brass band is playing: *Muss i denn, muss i denn zum Städele hinaus*—must I go, must I really leave my home.

Her mother is wearing a white wool coat. Maria runs along beside her. Everyone is running. Then they are left behind. Her mother is crying. The music rings and whistles: *Darum Mädel, Mädel wink, wink, wink*—so wave, wave, wave to me, girl.

Maria never saw her father again, no matter how long she waited for him.

She battled her mother throughout her entire childhood, for she thought: She had let him go away!

*   *   *

An adult's year is short. A child's year is endless.

Candida had become steady on her feet. So she needed to be protected. Her world was blocked by doors and bars. She had an uncontrollable desire to see what lay behind the doors and bars. She accepted no prohibitions.

*   *   *

Candida's father asked permission to see her.

One day their Sunday walk took a new direction. Candida pushed her carriage across a long, steel bridge. She looked, amazed, through the gaps in the railings at the swirling water and threw what she happened to have in her hand. She watched the doll rock on the surface of the water for a while and then sink.

Calmly, she started pushing the carriage again.

Later, when they were on their way back again, she stopped at the same spot and looked down.

Gone? she asked doubtfully.

Her mother nodded.

Then she cried.

*   *   *

Her father was waiting on the other side of the bridge. Candida liked him at once. He carried her. Threw her into the air. Played with her. She was allowed to climb on him, ride him, rumple and pull his hair, and sit on his shoulders and bury her hands in his beard.

So there you are! He held her over his head. Flyweight!

Her father was Candida's great discovery. She flew from his hands into the sky and fell into the safety of his arms.

He taught her to drink sweet, dark beer out of a bottle and how to open the cap, showed her how to do somersaults and jumping jacks. She trusted him.

Maria was very quiet. Hugged Candida tighter when she said goodbye, but went over the bridge with her the following Sunday.

It was already summer. They got into her father's funny car and drove to the lake. Her father talked with her mother. Sometimes they shouted. They stopped talking when they noticed Candida's shocked face.

Next week I'm going to an intensive course. Six weeks, said Maria.

Bunny, said Candida's father, move in with me when you get back. At least we could live together.

Maria's eyes turned dark. Why don't you come to me! she said.

I can't. You know that.

You don't want to.

You know I can't!

Why did you leave?

I go to school here.

And I go to school at home.

Bunny . . .

Everything had already been said.

*   *   *

The border was closed in August.

It was Sunday, and Candida headed for their usual path toward the bridge. She didn't protest when her mother changed the direction of their steps. She climbed expectantly into buses and streetcars, carefully examining the faces. She dashed quickly up the dormitory steps and then stood in her mother's room, astonished, said her father's name, ran out, called him.

But the building was empty.

Maria went after her. Then Candida let herself fall. Silent. Without tears. Maria picked up her daughter and carried her dead weight. Candida's arms and legs hung limp, her eyes were a clear, expressionless blue.

*   *   *

They took Grandmother for a walk in the park. Brightly colored ducks swam in its lakes, and bridges hung over them. Children frolicked. Music was playing in a giant white shell.

Candida danced in front of the shell, spat into the water from the bridges, called to the ducks, and rested in her grandmother's lap, who rode comfortably in her light, shiny chair on wheels. How big you are, said Grandmother tenderly, and Candida slid from her knees to chase a butterfly. A wide, straight canal with black water and dirty foam flowed sluggishly beside their path. The trees grew closer together. The heat was less intense, it smelled of wild onions.

I never liked that smell, said Grandmother, smell it.

Candida blew the air out through her nostrils.

No! The other way around! Her grandmother showed her how. Does it smell good?

Good! said Candida. Threw her arms around her neck.

And looked into her mother's face as she pushed the wheelchair and saw tears.

Her grandmother laughed to Candida. It's nice to ride, isn't it?

When you're well again, said Maria, Candida will move in with you. You were right.

I knew it, said her grandmother to Candida, your mother is a smart woman.

*   *   *

Two months later a coffin covered with velvet and wreaths of flowers was carried through the rustling leaves and lowered into a grave. Candida watched and admired the dexterity of the men with the shiny top hats. Holding her mother's hand, she walked fearlessly onto the plank over the grave and dropped her flowers into it. She was surprised by the hollow sound of the clods of earth hitting the coffin and became impatient when the handshaking with her mother went on and on. She pulled her toward the hall, where Grandmother had lain asleep behind a pane of glass, surrounded by fresh greenery, astonishingly young and pretty. They'd have to wake her up before they could go home.

Candida screamed and cried when Maria took her firmly by the hand and pulled her away.

*   *   *

Candida left the Home.

Maria had brought her new shoes, gloves, a hat and scarf, a bright red parka, and shaggy woolen leggings. Thus outfitted, Candida ran proudly through the building, fighting off the other children's attempts to touch her, until she burst into tears and ran to her mother. Maria laughed and they left together.

*   *   *

It was Candida's third birthday.

They celebrated in a soda parlor with cake and music from the jukebox. The box interested Candida. They didn't leave until all their coins were used up. The air smelled of snow.

Smell it!

Candida sniffed and laughed. The cold had reddened her cheeks, and her eyes shone with pleasure. Bright strands of hair peeked out from under her hood. Maria couldn't stop looking at her child.

They ran a few steps, then hopped. On one foot. On both.

Candida knew the way home. She pulled her mother to the bus stop. Maria led her to a different one. Candida was unsuspecting. She stormed into the big, warm bus and found herself the best seat—next to the window high above the back wheel. Her mother asked the driver a lot of questions, and Candida got impatient. But then they rode. For a long time. Through the whole city, across the river, through the woods, past a lake, through more woods, through a village. They stopped at a railroad crossing and waited while a locomotive panted past, drove past fields of green winter wheat, and finally got out.

They were met by a gust of wind. It blew Candida off her feet. Maria sprang after her, for she thought the wind would blow Candida away, over the railing down onto the freeway.

Candida was amazed by the wind. She couldn't get past it. She couldn't move her legs forward. She wanted to walk forward and was moving backward.

The sky was dark with snow clouds. Maria picked Candida up and carried her with Candida's back toward the wind. The child had wrapped her arms around Maria's neck and rested her head against her shoulder.

That's how they walked along the freeway. Maria needed all her strength to brace against the wind. The cars came toward them with their headlights on high beam. The snow lashed her in the face, melted and ran down her neck. Her arms became numb. She was afraid that Candida would start to cry. But Candida began to sing softly, enjoying herself. She felt safe. She didn't ask what she was doing here, in a snowstorm on a freeway in the middle of a dark forest. Her mother was carrying her.

Finally, Maria saw the freeway bridge. They saw a smoking chimney, then a blinking light, then the house, bright and welcoming, surrounded by shiny wet pine trees. They took refuge under the porch roof. The storm drove snow in after them. They were stiff from head to toe.

Candida looked expectantly toward the door where her mother had rung the bell. A woman in a rustling white apron came out. They looked at one another, Mrs. Wiese and Candida, and a spark jumped between them. Candida ran to her, buried her face in the fresh apron, leaving damp spots, and laughed.

Warmth and children's voices surrounded her again. Candida saw her mother take off her coat and take the hanger that Mrs. Wiese handed her. Then she got undressed. The office had a large glass door. While the women played with Candida and dressed her in dry stockings and slippers, the curtain was drawn back from the outside, and little noses pressed flat against the glass.

Candida was electrified. She waited, intent on each new face behind the glass door. Each one looked at her, friendly and curious.

Maria was allowed to come with her to the play room. Candida took possession of a paradise. And was accepted into it.

Candida let go of her mother.

Maria left without saying goodbye.

*   *   *

The building was spacious. Thirty children lived in it. Candida was the youngest. She was given the same dress and apron as all the other little girls. They were altered to fit her in the sewing room, and her name was embroidered on them. She wished she could have pants like the boys.

Candida learned that the terrace room was her group room. That was where they painted and built things, hung up their drawings, told stories, and were read to. That was where she had her shelf and her apron hook and her place at the table.

She stood at the large glass door to the terrace and watched the snowflakes cover the garden and the woods, the sparrows swinging on the bird feeders, the bird and rabbit tracks in the snow in the mornings. The window on the other side of the room shimmered in the light. Snow White and the seven dwarfs were etched into the glass. They glowed and sparkled when the evening sun set behind the window.

It was nice in the Bird Room, the bigger children's room. They made sure that the little ones didn't get into any mischief. The room had a long veranda with two aquariums. Candida stood before the red, green, and velvet black fish, delighted. She talked to them and pressed her nose and mouth against the glass. She stood the same way in front of the bird cage, which hummed and twittered and where red or yellow beaks would tweak at a finger pushed through the wire. Candida soon knew the names of all the birds.

*   *   *

It was a long, cold winter.

The woman who brought the milk up from the village in the morning got her sled stuck in the fresh snow. She sat in the kitchen with frost-reddened cheeks and waited for the furnace man to put on his fur coat and go retrieve the sled. She looked at the children who came into the kitchen to get the baskets of silverware. Then she said: I only do it for your sake!

The milk froze in the cans along the way.

Candida ran a curious finger over the milk crystals.

Snow?

No, laughed the cook, milk! Watch this!

She chopped little pieces out with a knife, threw them into a pot, and put it on the stove. Candida watched as they melted and turned into milk.

You're a skinny little thing, said the milk lady. Don't you like to eat?

Candida watched the milk melt and didn't respond.

The cook sighed.

*   *   *

Candida ate poorly and extremely slowly. She was always the last at the table, and the other children were rude to her, since they couldn't finish clearing the table because of her. After this had happened a few times, the cook took Candida into the kitchen, where she ate just as slowly.

The cook, like almost all the adults in the Home, came from the village. She was a simple woman who had learned to cook from her mother and during her marriage. All the children liked her. They were allowed to help her. She said: What kind of life is this? You need to know what goes on in a kitchen, that a raw onion makes you cry, what a roast smells like or a cake, and how much work it takes to make what ends up on your plates. Every child knows that at home.

There were children in the Home who didn't have any other home.

Her mother sent a color postcard every week. On each one the promise that she would come in the spring. Candida collected the cards and guarded them jealously. She kept them on her shelf and made sure no one else touched them.

The melting snow made the woods impassable, and the children couldn't go outside for days. The barber worked his way slowly up to Black Mountain to shear the "winter fleece."

The children met him with cries of delight. He was full of stories. Surrounded by a circle of devoted listeners who knew every single word, he clattered his shears around their heads while they made absolutely sure that he told properly the stories they demanded.

The children had made a "barber's chair" out of a table and stool on the veranda of the Bird Room. One after another, they willingly let him wrap the white linen sheet around their shoulders. They stole glances in the mirror when they were finished.

Despite his extensive repertoire of stories, the barber had only two hair-cuts at his disposal, a short one for boys and a slightly less short one for girls. Now and then Mrs. Wiese asked him to spare these locks or those bangs, so that in the end she managed to keep the children from all looking exactly the same. Candida watched and listened with interest. Her thin hair rose crackling under the barber's comb. She twitched when she felt the cold shears against her neck and her ears. Her hair fell in strands onto the linen sheet, she picked it up; it felt soft and silky and shone in the sun.

*   *   *

The freeway shimmered in the heat. Maria made her way into the woods. Her feet sank into the sandy path and she took off her shoes.

She dampened her hopes of suddenly hearing voices, as she had a few times, and having a swarm of children burst out of the bushes. Then, recognizing her, they'd call out a name—Candida—and a bright face would separate from the swarm and fly toward her. The children were not to be seen. Not behind the transformer hut, not behind the blackberry bushes, not in the hollow between the two wooded hills either, and definitely not on the treeless heath where their beehives stood.

A sprinkler revolved on the lawn in front of the building.

Candida ran racing with the spray, caught up with it, let it catch her, ran into it and away from it. She laughed when the spray caught her and laughed when, in the heat of excitement, she collided with other children and they tumbled in the wet grass. Maria watched unobserved until she couldn't stand it any longer.

She walked out onto the lawn and caught the naked, wet bundle that shot toward her.

The game on the lawn stopped short. The children came closer and looked at Candida and her mother.

Maria hugged her daughter and looked into the eyes of the others, tender, hungry, longing eyes. Maria felt humble before them. She could sense too clearly how on other days, when another mother took her child in her arms, Candida would stand with the others, with the same eyes and the same shyly pleading smile, would push toward the stranger's hand as these children pushed toward hers when she raised it to run it through the hair of the child standing closest to her.

My mother's coming too, said one. Her eyes were clear. She believed it. But her mother wouldn't come. The little girl had been left behind when her parents had crossed the border, an infant alone in the apartment.

Maria knew the stories of most of the children. She hadn't spent her days here alone with Candida. She had played with all of them, and Candida had accepted it.

Candida chattered excitedly. Maria couldn't understand anything. You chatter, thought Maria, when will you talk? Talk like a three-and-a-half-year old?

Candida ran her syllables together incomprehensibly. She was not the only one. Only a few of the children spoke clearly.

Maria held her hands over her ears. Candida laughed and fell silent.

Slowly! said her mother, and Candida stopped for breath. Maria repeated after her, enunciating clearly and asking for confirmation that she had understood. Candida didn't put up with this for long. She understood herself perfectly.

They left before lunch time. Maria had ordered a taxi. It was waiting for them in the parking lot before the bridge.

The day was a celebration.

Candida said her father's name inquiringly. Maria was distressed that the child remembered it. Klaus and car belonged together. Now Candida would learn that there was no necessary connection.

*   *   *

It was the longest train ride in Candida's entire life. The sun was setting when they arrived. Candida didn't complain about the long walk from the train station to the campground. Maria had a lot to carry. The tent and sleeping bags were tied together into a pack on her back. She carried the bag of food supplies in one hand and held Candida's hand in the other. They both stopped in their tracks when they had climbed to the top of the last dune.

Before them lay the sea.

The days were like the shells on the beach. Candida never tired of them and wasn't able to count them.

She woke next to her mother, surrounded by warmth. The sound of the waves running up the shallow beach had been with her forever. Candida crawled out of the tent, brown and naked.

Dew lay on the canvas. The campground slept.

She was the first.

The sea was as broad as every other day. It ended in the rose-streaked sky.

A spark glowed on the horizon. Candida watched it grow into a ball, rise out of the water. A shimmering red path led to it from the shore.

She looked directly toward where the sun rose, pure and clear.

The sun!

The "u" became a fanfare.

The suuuuun!

*   *   *

They slept in the dormitory again.

Most of Maria's things were already packed away and in storage. Maria had to move out, she had finished her degree.

Candida was disturbed by the missing books and pictures, and she asked where they were. Maria couldn't make her understand that they weren't going to live here any more.

They set the breakfast table on the balcony. That was the same as always, and Candida's restlessness subsided.

They looked at one another with pleasure.

Candida had never looked so healthy. Deeply tanned, her hair even lighter, cheeks and chin gently rounded, her body full of energy and self-confidence.

They talked together. Maria didn't have to put her hands over her ears or ask over and over. Candida's vocabulary wasn't large enough yet, and now and then she mixed up her sentences, but the words were clearly pronounced and her meaning was clear.

Maria didn't tell Candida where they were going. Candida had shaken her head when asked if she wanted to join the other children.

Maria disguised herself with the shopping basket as they set out.

Candida was unsuspecting. She willingly climbed into the bus and rode expectantly through the summer landscape.

Maria felt miserable. She wanted Candida to accept it as she had until now. She suspected that this would no longer be possible.

From her gestures and glances, she read Candida's plea to be allowed to stay.

They had found one another, now they ought to live together.

Candida immediately recognized her surroundings.

Maria saw how her little body grew limp. Her shoulders drooped, her head lowered, and tears spilled from her eyes. Maria took Candida's hand. The child walked beside her without resistance. Weeping in deep despair, without strength, without protest.

Other times, Candida would take the wrong path on their way back, couldn't find the Home, tried to get lost in these woods. Maria would play along until Candida got tired and gave up. Candida had learned that they always found the Home and that her mother, who had just been with her, was suddenly gone.

Maria felt a desperate, vicious rage rising in her.

Be quiet! she barked at Candida.

Candida paid no attention. Her nose and eyes dripped, her face was swollen, her pupils dilated and unfocused.

I can't help it, thought Maria. You only have me. But I have other things to do!

Stop it! she screamed and grabbed Candida by the shoulders and shook her. Nothing changed.

Stop it! She slapped her face.

*   *   *

Maria lay on the ground, which was covered with dry pine needles. Candida slept beside her. She had to wake her. It was late.

The wind stirred the crowns of the pines. If she leaned against the trunk, she could feel it move. She would show Candida before the summer was over.

She tickled Candida's ear.

Candida opened her eyes and promptly shut them again. She went back to sleep. She didn't want to wake up. She lay on her side, her legs curled up against her stomach, her right thumb in her mouth and her left forefinger stuck into her navel under her dress. Her thumb was disfigured from sucking and her navel rough and raw. She withdrew into herself and reconnected the exposed parts of her body with her center.

Maria took Candida's hands and held them in her own until the child was completely awake. She wiped her face and took her into her lap. Candida was calm.

Listen, said Maria. We can't go home. I have to work. Tomorrow I'm going away, and before then I have to move my things out. We don't have an apartment. We have Grandmother's apartment in Leipzig . . . We have to trade it for another one.

Candida couldn't understand her.

I have to work! I'll come back!

Candida nodded.

They stood up.

Candida started along the path back as if Maria had said exactly the opposite. Silently, Maria picked her up, turned around and carried her just as she had carried her six months earlier.

It was warm and dry. Candida was silent, and Maria felt her becoming heavier. Candida's arms swung limp against Maria's back, she let her head hang, her eyes wide open and expressionless.

*   *   *

By midnight it was clear that they wouldn't be able to film. Maria left the makeshift production staff office. When she came out of the hotel, she saw a light in one of the cars pulling in. She asked if she could have a ride.

Take the blanket, said the man next to the driver.

They left the city on Route 7. The man in the front seat was shaving. Maria tried to pick up the conversation. They were talking about an exhibit . . .

A hand shook her by the shoulder. She had to get out. She had slept. The man looked at her with undisguised curiosity.

Maria had to change cars five times. The last stretch she rode on a tractor. The driver knew the children's home and offered to take her there when he heard that she had hitchhiked from Weimar.

*   *   *

Candida didn't leave her mother alone for a second. She kicked at the children who came too close to Maria and fought against taking her nap.

It was a warm September day. Mrs. Wiese gave them a blanket, and Maria lay down beside Candida behind the house. Maria fell asleep, exhausted, and Candida watched over her. When she slipped away from the blanket to pick up a fallen apple, she never went far enough to lose sight of her mother. When Maria woke up, Candida pushed her to leave. Maria understood her more from her gestures than her words. Candida slurred her speech as she had before.

They went to the lake and rocked in the boat that was tied up in the bay. They took a great deal of trouble with one another. Candida courted Maria, did everything to please her, everything to be taken along. Maria did everything to distract her from the fact that she would leave alone. She saw that she was not succeeding.

Maria felt that it would be better not to come again until—until when? Until vacation? Until Candida understood more?

The children perched like birds on the terrace steps in the evening sun and grabbed their food from the tray that Maria held out to them, swallowing and chattering, chirping and calling for more. Mrs. Wiese brought a second tray.

It was a familiar scene for Maria. Many days out here had ended this way. Today, she was afraid.

Candida sat with the others. Maria saw that Mrs. Wiese was watching Candida too.

She's been different since she came back, said Mrs. Wiese. She breaks up the other children's games, is getting more and more antisocial, and throws tantrums at the slightest provocation. When I had night duty, she wouldn't go to sleep. She sleeps badly now. She cries and keeps repeating the same words. It took a long time before I understood her: The fox ate my Mommy.—You should leave when Candida takes the silverware basket into the kitchen.

Maria nodded.

Later, she walked toward the freeway, cursing. She felt miserable.

*   *   *

The next day a new teacher started work. She had just finished her training and this was her first job. She took the children out in the afternoon, and that evening Candida was missing.

She notified the police.

That night, Candida was found in a pasture next to the freeway, nine kilometers from the Home.

Maria carried Mrs. Wiese's letter around with her for a day before she showed it to Pelikan.

I was very glad that you agreed to be my mentor, she said, but I don't see any way . . .

He read. Then he said thoughtfully: I don't either. There's no eight-hour day and no guaranteed weekend in this job. I'm sorry. You look for space in a kindergarten. I'll think it over.

Moved, he had dropped his formal manner.

*   *   *

It was winter again before she could bring Candida back with her.

*   *   *

Her new life assured Candida of Saturday afternoon and all day Sunday at home with Maria. Monday mornings Candida took her little suitcase with clothes for five and a half days, walked across the street, and was there. Her mother gave her a kiss at the heavy oak door and ran to catch the streetcar.

Candida lived in a Home again.

Again there were birds and fish and flowers in pots and a plot in the garden for each group.

The garden extended behind the house, filled with old chestnut trees. The ground beneath them was bare.

There was hardly any grass.

Tables and benches stood under the chestnut trees in the summer. There was room for snowball fights in the winter.

Candida could see the house where she lived with her mother from the window of the dormitory. If the windows were lit in the evening, her mother was home. When the children passed by the house on their walk, Candida said: We live here!

Sometimes Candida saw light in the windows in the morning. Then she'd say: My mother is getting up and going to work. I can go see her on Saturday.

And when Maria came to pick Candida up, Candida showed her to the other children and said: My mommy.

*   *   *

Maria's work days were long. She worked to make up for her free weekends. This was the third film she'd worked on as Pelikan's assistant, who was willing to accept her abandoning him on the weekends. They were about to separate. Pelikan was going to Egypt to film material on the building of the Aswan Dam.

Maria envied him.

*   *   *

They lived in a former customs house, not far from the bridge. It needed repairs and stood in a border zone. Two conditions that made it difficult to rent out. The house had stood empty for a long time.

It was built of red brick, had large windows and a veranda leading into a garden that stretched down to the lake.

Maria was amazed when she looked through the barbed wire toward the other shore. She had sat there with Candida and Candida's father hardly three years ago and looked across at the house. Its warm red had glowed above the path along the lakeside. A sunshade stood in the garden.

Maria found all sorts of things left behind in the house. Things suitable for a house but unnecessary for life in the other Germany and unsuited for an escape to it.

She took what she needed from the apartment in Leipzig, sold the rest, and furnished the customs house for Candida and herself.

My life will be nomadic, she'd thought earlier. In hotel rooms, tents, automobiles, and under the open sky. I will be where things are happening that will change the world and where things happen that are meant to destroy us. A film camera can become a weapon.

Candida didn't recognize the bridge. She had a memory of a bridge that swung in steel arches across a wide stretch of water. One crossed it in the sunshine, and at the other end stood her father, whose face she no longer remembered. But the bridge next to their house was blocked by red-and-white painted walls and had iron bars driven into the roadbed.

Soldiers stood there.

They laughed with one another. Sometimes they scuffled.

One had taken her by the hand: Not that way, not the other way, not this way! and made a serious face like her mother, who had said the same thing to her.

Verboten!

Candida knew what that meant.

*   *   *

In the spring she forgot the prohibition. She crawled through the barbed wire, picked flowers and brought them to her mother.

Maria reacted strongly.

Candida was confused. Suddenly she blinked like an owl. Astonished and frightened by her mother's agitated demands.

Maria finally regained control of herself.

There were so many things surrounding her mother that Candida found magical, that filled her with curiosity and made her forget urgently pronounced prohibitions: the countless pictures on the walls, the books and the wonderful stones that lay all around, dried roses, tree bark and branches that looked like animals. Her mother sat on the floor and listened to music from black disks. She had a whole pile of them.

Candida squatted next to her.

What are you doing? asked Candida.

This! Maria pointed to the television screen which a herd of elephants silently crossed to a watering hole. Candida laughed.

Elephants?

No, films that you can watch there.

On TV?

Yes.

Elephants?

Oh, Candida. Come over here!

They crawled across the floor together and Maria pointed to the photographs: a house by the sea.

Those are palm trees. The house belongs to the children. It's their school. Before, they didn't have a school, before the Revolution . . .

Maria stopped for breath, waited for Candida to ask a question. She intentionally used all the words she normally used. She wanted to catch Candida's imagination.

Candida looked at the children's faces, white ones and black ones.

It's a school in Cuba. Cuba is an island.

Look here, said Maria.

And on other days other pictures lay spread around. Candida looked at them and imagined the differentness of the world.

On Candida's sixth birthday the lakes were covered with ice.

The ice beyond the barbed wire was broken up day and night. They could hear the crash when the steel hull of the boat came down on the ice and the uneven, labored sound of its motor.

They took hot tea to the bridge.

Fishermen stood on the lake in the park beside holes in the ice, and Candida watched them. The ice was so clear that she could see the fish under their feet snapping at the lure and swimming away with it until the line was taut. The man beside the hole set down his fishing pole and drew the line out of the water with his bare hands until he pulled up a thrashing fish, shining silver with light red fins. He carefully removed the hook from its mouth and threw it onto the ice with the others that lay there thrashing and leaping until they were still.

Candida looked at them.

The fish were silent and their eyes stared wide open.

Candida understood that they were dying.

Why don't they say anything? Doesn't it hurt? she asked her mother.

We can't hear them, said Maria.

Candida pointed to the gasping fish mouth. It hurts him! she said to the man at the hole in the ice. He's screaming!

The man smiled.

It was wonderful to stand on ice skates with arms spread out against the wind and sail across the ice, faster and faster. Maria sheltered her from the wind on the way back. She heard the fish bumping their mouths against the ice, turning around and disappearing like a flash of lightning into the depths.

Sometimes Candida was overcome by fear of the depths. It seemed to her that the surface would shatter like glass, and she waited for the sound. Her gaze sought her mother and held her fast. That was all. No cry, no gesture, no call for help. The ice was solid, and Candida felt it bear her weight. She saw the ease with which Maria moved and saw the calm of the fishermen and the exuberance of the children.

*   *   *

Candida didn't see any of her playmates outside of the children's home. It was a lucky coincidence that they lived so close by. The other children came from all over the city and suburbs. They went back on the weekends.

Candida's playmates on the weekends were the children from the neighborhood and children who came from far away to go skating or to go swimming in the summer.

She found herself almost exclusively in the company of boys. She looked like them with her badly cut hair, her rough, chapped hands. She knew how to fasten a hook to a fishing line, how to climb up any tree or over any fence. She fought with them when she had to and came home with a bloody nose and no complaints and was ready to face any challenge to prove her courage.

Maria saw her dolls lying around unused; the only successful gift, aside from the ice skates and fishing gear, had been a scooter.

Candida's wild games took place outdoors, ruined her clothing and gave her bruises. Inside, only fairytales—on records, on television, and sometimes told by her mother—held Candida's attention. She didn't finish any other games she began. She smashed them when they got too hard. Then she sat stubbornly in the middle of the rubble.

Maria insisted that Candida clean up after herself. These were terrible tests of strength. Maria was consistent in her demands, and Candida was consistent in her resistance.

They loved each other, sometimes painfully. They misunderstood each other.

Candida had been able to wash herself for some time. She had long ago learned how to tie a ribbon but still asked her mother to do it. Candida wanted to trick her into an expression of tenderness, wanted to be washed and dressed by her mother. Maria insisted on Candida's independence. To the point of the tantrums that Maria feared. No matter how dismayed she was, she still thought: If I give in now, Candida will decide that this is how to get her way. Living with her will be hell.

Candida did as her mother wished, but it didn't escape Maria that this was a capitulation, that Candida had given up something important. It worried Maria. Sometimes she thought she would rather meet resistance than this joyless acceptance.

Still, now and then the child would throw her arms around Maria, who, surprised by this sudden show of affection, wouldn't know what to do.

*   *   *

They had another happy summer.
They put up their tent by the sea again.
We should stay here forever, said Candida.

*   *   *

Huge flocks of grebes collected at the south end of the lake, all black with a white oval mark on their foreheads.

Only the shimmering circles left on the water under the low autumn sky showed Candida where a bird had dived. She waited breathlessly for it to surface again. But finding the same bird again in the crowd was a matter of chance. Their underwater pathways were invisible.

Mallard ducks nested near the banks, but they held no secrets and all looked just like the picturebooks. Candida hardly paid them any attention.

Then the air rang. Swans! Candida saw their elongated necks, their powerful bodies, their wings beating in unison, heard the humming. Saw their feet stretched forward to brake their speed, leaving a wake in the water, and then settling into it, raising their heads and necks into the gentle curves that awakened in her the desire to stroke them. They folded their wings and swam calmly through the teeming swarms of grebes, which hurriedly paddled out of their path. Candida counted six. Three still had brown feathers, they were the young ones. She fed them her sandwiches.

A piece of fishing line with a hook and float hung in the branches over the water. Candida set her schoolbag next to the bent trunk and climbed up. The line hung far out over the water. She worked her way out along one of the thicker branches. It bent a little. She got up, stood on tiptoe, grabbed the line and carefully pulled it toward her, coiling it. Then she worked her way back and slid down the trunk with the coil of line between her teeth. She dug for worms in the moist earth under the fallen leaves. She skillfully threaded one onto the hook, put the others into her pants pocket, and climbed up the tree again. She crawled on her stomach along the slanted trunk until she was far enough from the bank to drop the hook into the water. The water quickly got deep here. She couldn't see the bottom, she saw her reflection and the tree's. Leaves loosened by her movements floated down and sank onto the water. The float was hardly visible as it danced now and then in the wake of a duck.

The fish were eating the worms off the hook. Candida could tell from the way the float moved. She watched intently. One of them had to bite into the hook at the end of the worm. When the float sank, she pulled in the line. A little perch thrashed in the water. She pulled it up, grabbed the slippery body confidently, removed the hook from its mouth, and threw it down into the leaves, which rustled as it struggled. No more fear that the fish was screaming.

Candida threaded another worm onto the hook.

When she had the third perch, she climbed down, collected her catch in the bag that had held her sandwiches, and ran off.

Her eyes gleamed with satisfaction.

At the school she called to the janitor's cat: Mamie, Mamie . . . and shook the bag temptingly. Mamie leaped out of the coal cellar and graciously took the fish. Inside the bell rang. Seconds later, crowds of children appeared. Mamie disappeared with the fish, and Candida romped across the playground with the others.

Where were you?

Fishing!

You're late!

Candida laughed happily: three fish!

She went upstairs with the others after recess.

Mrs. Peters looked at her sternly: Why are you just getting here?

Candida didn't have an answer.

Where were you?

At the lake.

She saw that Mrs. Peters was alarmed.

I was only fishing, she said, from a tree, three fish.

Child! said the teacher, what do you think you're doing? Where is your notebook?

Candida jumped. It was under the tree. She ran out of the room without an explanation.

*　　*　　*

It got dark earlier every evening, and Candida had to be there when Maria got home.

Since she had found out that Candida had been late on her way to school, Maria went out of her way to take her there, but she seldom managed to pick her up from the after-school program. In the afternoon she looked for the child, followed the path that she had to take. Candida was pleased when her mother found her and followed her cheerfully.

In Candida's notebooks Maria saw the failures of her teachers: few letters, a lot of scribbling, and under them in red ballpoint pen the admonition
to pay more attention, be neater, be careful.

Candida's homework was regularly accompanied by the play-group
supervisor's comment that Candida showed little interest in doing it.

Maria tried her best to redo Candida's botched homework assignments
with her. Candida sat brooding over her notebook with her lower lip stuck
out, until the tears dripping onto it made it completely illegible.

Candida was amazed by the intensity with which the grownups argued.
It was about her. For days. She couldn't figure out what it was about. She
didn't seem to have done anything wrong, because nobody scolded her. The
big people were shouting at one another.

The doctor wanted her to tell him what was in the picture. Children were
riding a carrousel. Wonderful! She was completely attentive.

But, said Mrs. Peters, after all, I can't give her private lessons, she has to
adjust to learning in the classroom. I have thirty-five students.

And when one of them is difficult, you give up, said Maria angrily.

She's not mature enough, said Mrs. Peters calmly.

You accepted her, Maria accused the doctor.

It can happen, he defended himself. Physically, she's mature.

And what now? Maria's voice was brittle.

Take her out, advised the doctor. Next year she'll be further along.

And where is she supposed to go?

The best thing would be for you to take care of her.

Maria laughed sarcastically. Then she shouted: There's nothing wrong
with the school system in this country, right? took Candida by the hand and
left the room, slamming the door behind her.

Outside they walked quickly and silently. Candida could hardly keep
up. She pulled at her mother's sleeve. Maria looked at her, and Candida
shrank back, huddled together as if she were freezing. But Maria's gaze had
already softened.

You can't help it, she said.

*   *   *

This is where I work, said Maria to Candida. That's a studio. Look, there's
a camera, that's what takes the pictures that make a film.

Black satin curtains hung down from the darkness overhead. Motionless
and shining, a sputnik hung in space.

Pelikan, I've been looking for you, said her mother to a man who was
lying on his back under the camera looking into it.

He came out from under it.

Here we are, said Maria. It didn't work. She patted Candida on the head and gently pushed her.

Say hello!

They looked at one another curiously.

She's being put back a year. I don't have a kindergarten space and I won't get one and I'm not sending her back to the Home, said her mother.

Light's ready! somebody called.

Pelikan lay down under the camera again. Something rattled, a red light blinked, and Maria put her hand over Candida's mouth. A man with a pointer was now standing under the sputnik and explaining something. Then the light went out. This happened three more times, and Candida began to get restless.

Pelikan came over to them again, they walked out the door, and he offered her mother a cigarette. Candida watched them smoke.

Don't give up now, said Pelikan. We'll think of something.—Candida!

He pronounced her name with a gentle, musical inflection. You're a pretty little girl, Candida. Too bad that the world still isn't the way it ought to be for you.

I have to live with her myself. I myself. She has a right, said Maria. I'll make it through the year somehow, give me a leave.

You won't be any more independent in a year, said Pelikan. Don't think it will be any easier.

Thank you, Pelikan, I'll think about it—I'll have time.

*   *   *

Candida spent the nights in the customs house alone. Her mother put her to bed in the evening and then went across the street to night duty in the children's home. At the beginning, Candida insisted on being taken along to sleep there. Maria showed her that another child now slept in her bed, that there wasn't a bed for her there any more.

Candida knew what her mother was doing. The doors to the sleeping rooms were left open at night, and when a child called or cried, she would come with a flashlight to see what it needed. During the night she polished the many shoes and sewed torn-off buttons back on. In her room the radio played softly, and warm light fell on the red sofa. A blanket lay on it to pull over herself when it got chilly just before dawn.

Candida could see the light in the duty room from her bed. It burned all night.

In the morning, Maria sometimes found Candida sound asleep in her,

Maria's, bed. Then she would get into Candida's bed. Most of the time the radio was playing or the television flickering in the dark. Candida had her thumb in her mouth and her index finger in her navel. Her jaw was beginning to take on the shape of a rodent's.

The bed looked as if a battle had been fought there, and the pillows often showed signs of tears.

There's a witch in the wall. She comes out and pinches me when I'm asleep. Here's where she pinches me.

Maria gave her a club to take to bed with her. The witch stayed away for a long time.

*　　*　　*

Days wrapped in ice and snow. She now waited with her own fishing pole at the fishing holes. Her eyes had the shine of innocence. On ice skates, she'd race with anyone. There were no tears when she fell.

Her seventh year began.

*　　*　　*

One night the doorbell rang at the children's home. Outside stood a soldier from the Border Patrol with the trembling, sobbing child wrapped in his coat.

Candida was beside herself.

I saw her standing in the window, said the soldier. She was yelling. I told her to go back inside before she caught cold. I'd come tell you and you would come get her. Then she jumped out of the window. It wasn't very high. She must be afraid, all alone.

The soldier had a young face with shy, gentle eyes.

*　　*　　*

It thawed. They wandered through the old city center of Leipzig. It was fair time. Candida stopped in front of every shop window with cries of delight. While her mother didn't offer any resistance, she hardly paid attention to Candida's discoveries. She was *thinking*. Candida knew what that meant.

On the Circle, a wonderful car kept pace with them, fire-engine red, large and shiny. It followed them for a long time. Her mother didn't see it. Then it stopped a little ahead of them. A man got out. He wanted to say something to her mother. Candida could see that clearly. They walked past him, and Candida turned back toward him because he was looking at them intently.

Bunny! Candida!

She could feel her mother stiffen, felt how she grasped her hand tighter before her mother turned around.

*   *   *

So, you've become an exploiter? said Maria.

Exploiter! With sixty exploitees. I work twelve hours a day and want to finish my doctorate next year. And you? Do you have everything you need to defeat me?

Maria closed her eyes. For a long time. Candida saw the man's gaze, felt his mockery turn into tenderness. She looked knowingly into his face for a second, then her sympathy swung over to Maria completely, turned into confusion, for her mother remained motionless.

Her time with Candida's father had been good, the best in her life, it seemed to her. He was with her day and night. They had a single bed, one desk from which they ate and at which they worked, which completely filled the space between the bed and the wall. There wasn't space for a chair in the room. It had been years before she could let another man touch her. In moments of bitter isolation he had moved close to her, because the distance between them could not be bridged. She was calm when she opened her eyes.

I was in Ohio for the electronics fair in the fall. It's funny to travel to places like that. All my boyhood dreams come to life. But then everything turns out to be different . . .

His voice was gentle.

Her mother leaned forward with her elbows on the table on either side of her coffee cup, as she would never have allowed Candida to sit.

I'm going back for another degree, was at the university today. Journalism.

Her laugh came from deep in her throat.

Candida doesn't recognize me, he said.

Candida saw the pleading glance directed at her mother, felt her own heart beat louder and faster.

You were still very little, said her mother. This is your papa.

*   *   *

Time flowed backward in a wild whirlpool, at the very end a pale memory of a feeling floated up: being thrown up in the air and caught in safe hands at the end of a long bridge, across which she had hurried under a bright sky.

*   *   *

The world took on a new shape for Candida after this meeting. She thoughtfully considered the broad steel sweep of the blocked bridge, the opposite bank. The people over there didn't come here. Their boats came out to the middle of the lake. Her side, where their house stood, was plowed by a police speed boat.

She demanded information.

Good and bad—how could one apply them to here and there? These simple words! Every child knew what they meant. But they seemed to cause problems for her mother. She gave long and complicated answers to Candida's short questions.

She asked about her father.

The evening of that day in Leipzig she had urgently insisted that he come with them. The big people were suddenly in agreement: they couldn't do that.

She couldn't remember everything anymore. She knew how much she had wanted her father to come with them and how helpless she was. That she couldn't do anything to overcome the fear that he would simply go away. Her ears rang, and her arms and legs got so heavy, some force seemed to pull at them from the ground. Her head was filled with gray cotton.

When she woke up, they were riding in a bus on the freeway. It was getting dark, and the people were asleep. The motor hummed deep and clear. She fit herself into its humming. No one saw how blank her eyes were.

She felt that the wire fence had something to do with his not coming back to the customs house with them.

He lived on the other side.

*   *   *

Maria had given up her night job at the children's home and now delivered newspapers. The fact that she now got up before dawn and was back from her first round by breakfast time didn't disturb Candida. Her mother was there in the evening. The door between their rooms stood open at night, and no ghosts came in the early morning.

They did the second round of deliveries together. They were through by lunch time. The people had their newspapers and their mail. Candida knew all the houses in the district and all the names and the faces that belonged to them. And she knew paths and secret ways to slip from one backyard to another and surprised Maria playing hide-and-seek with a rascally: I'm already here!

In the afternoons, her mother asked for absolute quiet. Then she sat over her books, claimed to be working, and got angry if you asked her anything.

But in the afternoons there was no shortage of playmates.

It was already warm for April. The children who came out to play near the ditch soon took off more than their shoes and stockings. Led by Candida, they ventured their first swim of the year, and since they went in naked the only aftereffects were a few complaints from indignant parents. Her mother laughed.

She went with her to the lake. Hung a hammock between two trees along the bank, kept one eye on her book and the other on the throng near the bank, which fell off quickly. Candida was learning to swim.

Maria took her out to the middle of the lake on an air mattress. There was no more bottom to stand on. All she could do was grab for the air mattress which her mother held just within her reach. Candida slid down, dove under the mattress, turned around and grabbed it.

Come on! Two strokes alongside!

Candida willingly did what Maria asked, accepted her praise, and increasingly gained confidence in the water. She felt able to do what her mother could do, to do what her mother demanded.

Which of her friends, who now could read and write, dared to swim across the lake with her?

At certain moments, Maria was struck by Candida's expression, it made her look so much like her father. Little mocking wrinkles formed at the corners of her eyes and lower lids, still good-natured, an expression that said: I know better, I know different, but don't be upset, I don't want to annoy you.

And she hugged the child in vague fear.

Candida pushed her away: Leave me alone!

*　　*　　*

Candida's new class was wonderful.

Her mother, after she had seen it, was less enthusiastic. Mrs. Horlitzka seemed helpless in the face of this collection of distinct personalities.

Alexander was an angelic-looking urchin with curly black hair. He was here for the second time. He was bored and really did know everything. He always got "A" on assignments and "F" for behavior. He was repeating the first grade because of a long illness. He enjoyed fighting and made no distinction between boys and girls, and Candida accepted his challenges. While rolling around on the floor of the wrestling ring was still a game, defeat worked like dynamite. The expectant whispers running through the class during lessons fanned the spark of hostility into an explosion. Candida sprang out of her seat with tears of rage in her eyes and attacked the black curls, both of them leaving clumps of hair behind.

It only seemed to end in the office of the principal, who lectured them on the disgracefulness of their behavior and wrote notes to their parents. It kept happening. But in the afternoons they sneaked out of the after-school program together, went fishing, and lived in the trees.

In the evenings Maria paged through Candida's notebooks, which showed little change from the year before. She demanded effort, neatness, diligence, and a bit less wildness. When Maria became angry, she could see how the child quickly stiffened, how she pulled her head down between her shoulders, her cheeks and forehead flushed, and stared back out of wide open, nervously twitching eyes.

Stop it! Just stop it! Maria cursed herself silently.

When she had finally calmed down, Candida said, almost inaudibly: Do you always have to start yelling?

Candida, listen to me! You can't always have your own way about everything!

Leave me alone!

Fine! Do what you want. But I won't leave you alone. I'm your mother and you're my child. And that's why I can't leave you alone. I have to help you to grow up, to be smart, to learn to live with other people.

I already can!

*   *   *

To go to the other country and see what's there. If she knew that, she'd know more than Alexander, than Mrs. Horlitzka, than the principal, than her mother.

Candida sat on the floor and bit into the little green pod. The burning in her mouth made tears come to her eyes.

The way they'd all cried! She had to laugh. The whole class had cried when Mrs. Horlitzka came to give them the dictation test. They'd all tasted the peppers.

Who did it?

Candida!

And Candida thought it was hysterically funny.

Come with me!

Candida resisted. She was sick of having to go to the principal's office. They'd all wanted to taste.

Mrs. Horlitzka ought to have seen how stiffly she walked, how she stood in front of the principal with her head lowered, like a frightened bird. And her eyes.

Silently they walked back up the steps together. In the classroom, Candida retreated into her seat.

Her rage grew under the sparkling of curious eyes.

Candida leaped up. Threw everything on her desk at the teacher, pulled her book bag from the hook and kicked at it. Ran to the abacus at the front of the room and beat both fists against the colored balls until a dowel broke and the balls bounced across the floor.

The class sat frozen. Candida's hand was bleeding. She licked off the blood and sat down as if nothing had happened.

They had both turned pale, the child and the teacher.

No dictation was given that hour.

Mrs. Horlitzka dragged herself to the lectern and read a story. The classroom had never been so quiet. When the hour was over, she looked at Candida's hand. It wasn't badly cut. When Candida began to pick up the balls, the others bent down for them too.

*   *   *

Candida didn't go to the after-school program. She went home and took the key out of its hiding place, exhausted.

She let herself collapse onto the rug and slept.

She got the air mattress, blew it up, and dragged it onto the veranda.

It wasn't very cold outside. The water shimmered like dull metal. She pushed the mattress through the wire, slipped after it and then again through the second fence, and floated the mattress out onto the water.

It was the moment when day turns to evening, with an uncertain light that erased contours and made a mallard duck, lying still in the water, invisible.

Behind Candida the streetlights flared. The strip of beach lay glistening in the light.

She saw the customs house for the first time from this distance. Its windows shone behind the lights.

The other shore dissolved into the water.

Then she heard voices calling. A flare rose and poured green light over the water. She saw soldiers on the shore running and waving, heard their cries.

She was startled.

The word *verboten* took on terrible meaning. She hadn't thought about it any more. Lots of things were *verboten*. That meant, don't get caught.

She became frightened. Tried to get away.

A spotlight fastened on her. She dove. When she surfaced again it was just as light as before. Someone swam toward her with powerful strokes. She tried to escape the light, but the edge of the circle of light floated in front of her, the soldier reached the circle.

Come here this minute! He was out of breath. She knew him. He had come to the bridge two days ago.

Come here! Or something terrible will happen. He was already beside her, cut off her path and screamed at her: Get going! Back! You swim pretty well!—Hurry up! I'll take the mattress, or do you want to get on it?

She didn't want to.

She swam beside him.

He made a face as if he were crying.

*   *   *

What has to happen, thought Maria as she lay awake, before we understand what is important? Really understand.

Who cares that you are too often not happy?

Candida—your name means spotless, shining.

What will you be like when you are as old as I am?

*   *   *

Candida was allowed to get out of bed again. She ran to the bridge.

The wind blew over the water and was already cold.

October wind.

How old are you? A soldier asked her.

Seven. I'll be eight soon.

Translated by Dorothy Rosenberg

Christine Wolter

Photo courtesy of Aufbau Verlag.

Born in 1939 in what was then Königsberg, East Prussia (from 1945 to 1992 it was Kaliningrad, USSR), Christine Wolter completed high school in the late 1950s and moved to Berlin to study Romance languages. From 1962 to 1976 she worked as an editor for various East German publishing houses;

since that time she has been prolific as a freelance writer. In addition to creating German adaptations of Romanian and Italian poetry and editing anthologies of modern Italian poetry and novellas of the Renaissance, she has published seven independent volumes of prose, from novels to travel narratives. Wolter emigrated from the GDR and has lived in Milan, Italy, since 1978.

This selection is taken from the 1976 volume of Wolter's short stories, *Wie ich meine Unschuld verlor*, which focuses on women living alone after having experienced marriage.

Meine Italienische Reise (My Italian Journey). Berlin/Weimar: Aufbau, 1973.

Wie ich meine Unschuld verlor (How I lost my innocence). Berlin/Weimar: Aufbau, 1976.

Juni in Sizilien (June in Sicily). Berlin/Weimar: Aufbau, 1977.

Die Hintergrundsperson oder Versuche zu lieben (The person in the background, or Attempts at love). Berlin/Weimar: Aufbau, 1979.

Die Alleinseglerin (The solo sailor woman). Berlin/Weimar: Aufbau, 1982.

Areopolis (Areopolis). Berlin/Weimar: Aufbau, 1985.

Straße der Stunden—44 Ansichten von Mailand (Street of hours—44 views of Milan). Berlin/Weimar: Aufbau, 1987.

Matteo Bandello (Matteo Bandello, trans. from the Italian). Berlin: Rütten & Loening, 1988.

Early Summer (1976)

NO ONE will disagree if we claim along with the newspaper that this summer is the hottest since 1908. The pine forest is blazing hot. It is only tolerable at the shore. On the beach, children and adults wade around in the shallow water the whole blessed day; people sit on the docks by the reeds and dangle their legs in the lake. Neighbors wave a tired hello from one dock to the other. Now and then you hear a plop, someone slides limply into the water, swims out a few strokes and lies face up, but not for long, the burning sun blinds them.

The lake is calm. Sailors doze in their cabins, sometimes a little breeze comes up at four in the morning and the water laps against the boats, inspiring hope that the lake might get a cloudburst. At dawn the nightingales still sing in the shimmering birches. But by eight everything is quiet. By then all that is left is the eternal hornet drone of the motorboats.

On the western shore the morning sun beats down on the cove where the summer people's wooden cottages and the year-round residents' somewhat shabby stone houses crowd together. Nothing is stirring. Only the children's summer camp reverberates with uninterrupted shouting and merriment and endless waterfights on the beach, which will go on until evening. Then, to the beat of the latest hits, the little ones will hop tirelessly back and forth between their enervated counselors. The neighbor, Schreiber the housepainter, is hardly disturbed by all this, having drunk half a bottle of hundred-proof vodka before breakfast. He is lying on the chaise lounge under the sunshade and squinting across the lake, smiling. Malvina sees him lying there as she walks across her dock to the ladder, pulls her bathing cap down over her mahogany curls, climbs down the steps, and slowly glides into the water. Schreiber will not turn his head. He knows this morning bathing ritual, he has seen this slender-hipped figure, youthful from a distance, as long as he has lived here. She swims far out, holding her head out of the water, kicking vigorously and enjoying the warm water and the exercise that keeps you slim and, if possible, young. Two or three hundred meters, that makes six hundred strokes, so fifty calories. From that far out there is a good view of the whole inlet: the summer camp to the north with its water slide; then the painter's flowerbeds, her own little house right on the water, with the terrace, the district party secretary's rock garden, the sports camp, and the overgrown yard of the old couple who sail. At the other end of the inlet, one kilometer as the crow flies, Jochen's flat-bottomed dinghy is rocking, and he himself can be seen on the dock. Presumably he is fishing.

Malvina stands on the ladder and washes the cleansing cream off her face, climbs onto the dock breathing heavily, and sits down. She lifts each leg ten times, extending her toes, puts her feet back down on the boards and carefully removes a corn, closes her eyes and lets the sun shine on her face. She has already set the breakfast table on the terrace: tea, an egg, one slice of toast with marmalade, just like the fifteen years with Wilhelm, just like the three years since he died. Malvina has taken off her bathing suit and hung it over a line behind the house; she lets her bathrobe slip onto the chair—on the terrace she's safe from stray glances. But the sun is too hot, she goes into the house. She has already folded the bed away. The hideaway closet was one of Wilhelm's wonderful inventions, designed with painstaking precision at night at his little drafting table to relax from his stressful work as the head of an institute. He was an expert at these things, too. At the mirror in the sleeping alcove, Malvina dabs cream on her face, plucks her eyebrows and brushes them with castor oil. She slips into the green bikini, pulls in her tummy and looks herself over. With outstretched arms she squats down, counts, and gives up after nineteen deep-knee bends; it is too hot. The faint draft moving through the house is not bringing any cool air. At the camp, music drones from the loudspeakers: "A new lo-ove is like a new li-ife." Malvina tries to do some weeding, at least where passersby can see into the garden, but she cannot stand it with rubber gloves on. Streaming with sweat, she lies down in the lawn chair in the shade of the tall birch around which Wil had arranged the lawn furniture; she closes her eyes.

When she wakes up, she looks around groggily. The shadows have moved on. With a sigh she goes inside, brushes her hair, dabs some cologne under her arms, and slips on a blouse with nothing underneath. Blouse, bikini pants, sandals, that will do for the footpath that circles the inlet. Malvina takes it every day as far as the tourist center, where she buys milk and a paper. A liter of milk contains as much protein as six fresh eggs, vitamins A, B, C, E, and calcium. You can see into almost every garden from the footpath. Malvina confirms again how well she keeps her yard, all by herself; she has managed to keep everything just as it was in Wil's day. And it was an exquisite layout that he had had designed by a landscape artist. Jochen and his two sons help with the bigger jobs, painting fences and digging up dead tree trunks. Malvina had continued the agreement to pay Jochen for the winter months—she can afford it with her pension—and it is better to have someone here to look after things during the months she spends in Wil's apartment in the city. Jochen, bless his heart, can use the money; he is always building something onto his house. Malvina decides to stop by Luise and Jochen's on the way home. She needs some fresh dill from Luise's garden, and maybe Jochen knows when the electric saw is coming.

*　*　*

Jochen hasn't caught anything. He grabs his rod and net, slips on his sandals, and scuffles along the dock to the shore. Nothing, he mumbles, shoves back his old straw hat and wipes his forehead. At least it's quiet. When he speaks, the white beard moves; it stands out from his face like a briarpatch and gives him a romantic air, a little like Hemingway or a North Sea fisherman, and that's exactly how he has wanted to look all his life. He is wearing lightweight gray cotton pants; someone has cut off the legs, presumably he did it himself; he was always capable of unexpected moves; he had been famous for it way back in his days as a country doctor. The neck of a small bottle is sticking out of his pants pocket. A cotton undershirt hangs over his stomach, inside out, so he's wearing it for the second week. He shuffles across the yard, sends an ill-tempered glance in the direction of the hose to make sure there is still a faint stream of water running onto the tomato seedlings, and calls into the house: Grandma! Then it occurs to him that Luise is at the hairdresser's; it'll take all morning if not longer, with all the stuff she has 'em do; afterward she looks like a burst goosedown pillow anyway. The grandchildren are gone, thank God, sent them off to gather rabbit food, so it's quiet. Only Uli, the youngest one, is playing in front of the porch. It is cool in the living room; Jochen fishes for a cigar in the box on the mantelpiece, bites off the tip, spits it out, sticks it between the stumps of his teeth, and strikes a match.

*　*　*

Malvina reads the weather report in the paper she has just bought. The high over Eastern Europe is moving very slowly; it will continue to be unseasonably hot. Malvina stops at Jochen's garden; moist air rises from the flowerbeds. She opens the wooden gate, walks across the flagstones through roses and delphinium, inspects the full strawberry plants—Luise could give me a little saucer of strawberries to take home, and then some tomato seedlings. No one in sight, not even by the rabbit hutch; the rabbits are huddled in their stacked-up boxes. The lawn in front of the house is freshly mowed. Uli, who is sitting in the sand playing with a wooden loco-motive, looks at her absently; when she starts to say hello and offer him her hand, he turns back to the train. No one on the porch either. At first she does not see Jochen in the dim light of the living room. He is standing in his cut-off shorts and undershirt next to the fireplace, puffing on his cigar.

What a heat wave, Malvina groans. Luise . . . ? she inquires and, as if she were too weak to speak, nods toward the kitchen, where she thinks Luise must be. Jochen gives her a strange, impenetrable look and puts his cigar on the mantle behind him without shifting his gaze, and Malvina watches the column of smoke rising. She takes one step toward the kitchen door. Sway-ing slightly, Jochen comes out from behind the worn leather armchairs and stands next to Malvina. She feels Wil's old friend put his arm around her so that her left hand with the shopping net, the bottle of milk and the paper is trapped between his belly and her body, while his fingers close firmly around her right arm. He slowly lowers his face; his white beard touches her cheek and is surprisingly soft. There is a mild, not unpleasant smell of schnapps on his breath. Lips on her widowed mouth, belly on her body, soft, bearlike groans. Malvina knows that her blouse buttons are about to pop off, with that dry sound of cotton threads snapping, then she will have only her bikini bottom on.

They both hear the soft rattling from the veranda. Slowly and with dif-ficulty, someone is opening the door. Malvina suddenly feels herself freed, and while she turns her head, Jochen has leapt between the chairs to the couch, is sitting there with his cigar between the fingers that had mo-ments ago been engaged in violence. Uli's platinum blonde head appears at doorknob level, his nose running, and his grandfather barks at him: Now whadd'ya want!

Well, I'll be going now, Malvina says distractedly, as if after too long a conversation; she realizes the net is still hanging from her fingertips, strides weak-kneed across the carpet and out through the porch.

When's Grandma coming back, anyway, says the little one, I'm hungry. Malvina walks through the midday heat. Poor Luise, good Luise. She wasn't there! Jochen, the lecher. Blouse and bikini bottom. And he had such re-spect for Wil. Malvina walks quickly, and her palms are wet. She feels the shock intensifying the farther she gets from Jochen. She sees herself in her green bikini bottom facing Jochen, defenseless. Impossible to go back there. She closes the garden gate behind her and almost runs into the house. She stops in front of the mirror, examines herself. She bends over and tries to look down the front of her blouse.

*   *   *

Luise comes over the next day with her new hairdo. The curls accentuate her lack of proportion. Wil could not stand disproportion, and he always treated Luise somewhat condescendingly. She's losing her figure, her blouse is too short.

You should do gymnastics, Malvina mentions gently.

I've just put up ten jars of strawberries.

You could borrow my calorie chart.

Malvina feels that she must tell the truth. She goes to the refrigerator, takes out the vermouth and some ice cubes, puts two glasses on a tray, puts the ice, vermouth and lemon in them, a round slice of lemon on top, and carries the tray to the table on the terrace in the hot, humid afternoon shade.

Her elbows propped on the table, Luise listens to Malvina's adventure. At the end of the story, two tears appear in her pale gray eyes, and as they roll slowly down her pretty round cheeks, Luise says, ashamed: Snookums, how could you.

She thinks of the respect she and her husband always had for Wilhelm, the national science prize winner, and of course for Malvina too, and of their pride in this friendship.

I'm sorry, she says then to Malvina, I'm sorry I'm crying. I have cried every time Snookums had an affair. When the boys were still little, he had a lover but nothing to put on the table. Those were bad times, and I stood in the kitchen crying and fried him a rabbit; he said thank you and took it with him, and I stayed in the kitchen and bawled.

Nothing happened. Like I said already, Uli came in.

Luise smiles kindly.

The two older ones weren't there either. So it was just plain rape, Malvina adds, now mincing no words.

At his age, at our age. And I have spared him . . . do you understand what I mean?

Somehow brutal, Malvina finishes her thought.

It was the heat, I'm sure it was the heat, it was especially bad yesterday.

Yes, says Malvina, slowly finishing her drink, surely it was the heat, too.

*   *   *

Not until a week has passed does she decide to visit. The footpath is powder dry. The longest heat wave since 1897, the paper says. Malvina is relieved as she walks into the yard: Luise is squatting in the strawberry bed. She looks up and smiles at Malvina. I'm on a diet, she says quietly.

Jochen is standing in front of the rabbit hutches and turns his back on them. Malvina looks at his broad, violent back, the spine forming a hollow contour. The gray cut-off pants, almost colorless in the seat, are held up on his hips by a broad black leather belt. Malvina notices for the first time that Jochen has muscular calves and slender ankles.

Come in, Luise says, we're about to eat, why don't you stay and eat, it's your favorite dish.

They walk into the kitchen. Luise dishes out potato soup and parcels bacon rinds equally.

Where are the grandchildren?

Roswitha picked them up, a week early. Snookums gave Uli, the little one, a terrible whipping, supposedly because he ruined his fishing rod.

Jochen comes in as the two women are sitting at the wooden table.

He gives Malvina a nasty look and sits down. Luise talks incessantly so that Jochen's silence cannot be heard. He slurps his soup noisily, bent over his plate.

You're a marvelous cook, says Malvina.

When she has gone, Jochen gets himself a cigar from the mantle.

Funny bitch, he says. Luise's dishwater gurgles. Funny bitch. Remember? For a year she wore mourning, black stockings, black purse, everything black, even her hair nearly black. But she still went swimming in her purple bathing suit.

Oh, Snookums.

And as for you, Jochen growls, make more soup next time you invite your friends over. Two bowls aren't enough for me.

On the other side of the lake a bank of gray thunder clouds is rising. Lightning flashes.

It's high time it rained. The grass is burning up.

Translated by Nancy Lukens

Helga Schütz

Photo by Roger Melis, Berlin, courtesy of Aufbau Verlag.

Born in 1937 in Falkenhain (now Poland), Helga Schütz emigrated to Dresden in 1944. After an apprenticeship as a gardener, she was accepted to the newly organized Workers and Farmers School in Potsdam in 1955. She later transferred to the Film School in Potsdam and received her degree as a film dramatist. Schütz wrote scripts and scenarios for documentary and popular scientific as well as feature films for a number of years. She published her first prose fiction in 1970 and has been a freelance writer ever since, continuing to write both prose and film scripts. She lives in Potsdam.

This excerpt is taken from her novel *In Annas Namen*.

Vorgeschichte oder Schöne Gegend Probstein (Prehistory, or Scenic Probstein). Berlin/Weimar: Aufbau, 1970.

Das Erdbeben bei Sangerhausen und andere Geschichten (The earthquake near Sangerhausen and other stories). Berlin/Weimar: Aufbau, 1972.

Festbeleuchtung (Festive illumination). Berlin/Weimar: Aufbau, 1974.

Jette in Dresden (Jette in Dresden). Berlin/Weimar: Aufbau, 1977.

Julia oder die Erziehung zum Chorgesang (Julia, or An education in choral singing). Berlin/Weimar: Aufbau, 1980.

In Annas Namen (In Anna's Name). Berlin/Weimar: Aufbau, 1986.

Heimat Süße Heimat (Homeland, sweet homeland). Berlin/Weimar: Aufbau, 1992.

In Anna's Name

(1986)

ANNA runs after him. She runs toward him. His quirks don't interest her, his careful shaving, his collection of clichés. She wants to keep very still when he praises the generosity of his friend in the Ore Mountains: Someday strangers will sleep in his bed and he will sleep on the floor. Someday strangers in his bed and he on the floor. Someday strangers in bed, he floor. Strangers—bed, he—floor. Strangers he. Bed floor. Someday strangers.

She wants to listen to him to the very end. She wants to say: Rolf has a friend in the Ore Mountains who is so generous that strangers sleep in his bed while he himself sleeps on the floor. Rolf's clichés would become part of her. His jackets and golden thermos bottles. He can't help it. Rolf's friend really is a true friend. And in confirmation of Rolf's belief, Ricky really does enjoy working with a ruler. That's why Nicky is happy to misplace things. That way Father recognizes us at a glance, and I love his erotic superstitions. I laugh myself silly over his dreams, stories he half-tells me. I could tell the other half, for I know the rest. I know it far deeper than any theories and beyond any dreams.

Who knows what theories about me are unfortunately yet to be elaborated because, for example, I don't have the time to bite my fingernails. Isn't it about time for me to let something slip so my friends and analysts could catch me at my tricks? But no, I hide myself cleverly within my body, behind my face. A face is nearly as good as a mask.

Error holds sway over mankind by night and by day. Even love can err, but not mine.

You have to be sensible, Hilda scolds on the telephone.

I am sensible, I am clever.

Anna's cleverness served to justify her love. Her reason served her passions and her fears.

Anna buys herself a cigar in Mrs. Griesbach's shop. She wants the most expensive one.

Mrs. Griesbach says: This one's good enough. A present for the garbage man, she thinks, Otto the garbage man always buys these, White Rabbit, in a glass tube.

Anna bicycles home. Anna stands in front of the mirror with the cigar between her teeth.

She tries a cigar-smoker face. The face of a smoking fairy.

Anna throws the cigar in her sewing basket. She pulls her coat from the rack, runs to the bus, and takes the train to Berlin. After all, it's Saturday. Like any other Saturday. Like every Saturday. A meeting day. A black day. And it's raining too. Anna creeps under a roof, sits in the International Theater. There's no film today, two rock groups are playing, Pankow and Mona Lisa. She waits for the time to pass, at least she'll have something to tell about. Guess what, Rainer, I saw Paul Panke and the Wild Women. The noise nearly killed me. Really, what howling.

Freezing, she huddles between the fans. Now her watch has stopped, too. Small wonder in this din. All around her everyone flings up their arms. Spotlights wash green and violet light over their heads.

Can you tell me what time it is? screams Anna at the yellow-haired fanatic sitting next to her. He cooperatively drops his arms.

It's eleven. Are you okay, doll? You look pretty pale.

No, just let me out.

Her neighbor gets up from the folding seat. Let the lady through! The people standing in the aisle let her past. Poor mouse! Anna slinks through the night, down Karl Marx Avenue. To Alexanderplatz, creeps through the pedestrian underpass, climbs up to the elevated train. She rides to Friedrichstrasse. She shows herself no mercy. She wants to see the show. The parting five minutes before midnight. The usual line of pensioners is already waiting at the taxi stand. They came back early, the good old grannies are back from "over there." Anna joins the waiting line. One after the other, the cars with day visitors pull up. Light falls out of the checkpoint building into the puddles. The water splashes. The brakes squeal. It starts to drizzle again. The grandmothers are prepared for everything, they open their umbrellas. Our world travelers dig their plastic rain hats out of their bags. Pedestrians hurry across the square, hurry up the steps to the checkpoint building, wave and disappear. Their companions remain behind, hurry to the taxi stand or through the swinging doors of the train station, plunge into a well of sadness or race across the street in long strides, relieved. Either makes you miserable.

Rolf's Berlin *pied-à-terre* lay in the tangle of buildings behind Oranienburg Street. In the second courtyard. In an attic room.

The scent of expensive perfume fills the room. The candlewick floats glimmering in a pool of melted wax. A cork lies under the folding table. Above it the empty candy box, the empty bottle, the glasses.

The hurried departure every time. Every time, agreement and disagreement end quickly. Quick, the hat.

They had to come from Oranienburg Street, past the new Friedrichstadt Palace and the Hotel Sofia, over the Weidendamm Bridge.

Look, his large frame. His head one or two hat sizes too small. His stork-like gait.

Anna's heart pounded. Her senses reeled. She stayed in the line waiting at the taxi stand. She could have touched him, whispered his name, stepped on his shadow. She shut her eyes and fled out of the line and behind a parked construction trailer.

Her eyes wide open, like wearing a hair shirt, like holding her hand over a flame.

A figure appears, under Rolf's arm, protected by his overcoat, solicitously escorted, not a drop of rain on the sensitive hairdo, kissed goodbye, released and then embraced once again.

But now she tears herself away. A diminutive person, wrapped in furs, trots on nimble little legs up the steps into the checkpoint building. She's nearly the last to leave again. It's always the same, you mustn't be late, you can't give them an excuse. Must open your bags without complaint, write down the hard currency. Goodbye. She waves, casts another glance before she disappears behind the heavy closing door.

She is gone.

He is gone. Anna climbs solid steps, crosses cold silent platforms. She knows her way through the Schoenefeld station. She finds her way through the revisions in the train schedule.

An express train, an empty compartment, sunglasses, a magazine with a serial novel. Thus equipped, she finally allows herself a few tears and a blank mind.

Anna sank into a glowing white night. She was thrown, gently flung onto an operating table. No, it doesn't hurt. Needles and knives cut. Soft hammers strike. Anna felt no pain, only a gentle horror. A lovely, evil, narcotic dream. The more evil the dream, the more tolerable the awakening. Dream, stay with me. Verily, verily I say unto you, it doesn't hurt. No, no. I'm sure it doesn't hurt. The train swayed through the stations. Anna's head lay on the hard vinyl seat and bounced with the tracks. Rolf's figure leaped out of the dim light as Anna had seen him: the loose coat, his small head, still two or three hat sizes too small. She ought to have gone to him, she ought to have taken hold of him, guided him, saved him.

A hand touched Anna's elbow. The hand of another passenger.

Are you all right? She handed Anna the magazine that had fallen from her lap.

Anna recognized the station with a glance out the window.

I have to get off. I have to save him. Anna leaped up. The compartment door flew open. The train began to move. Anna gained ground. Her feet carried her.

Seven kilometers through the fields, fearlessly, on a dark country road—past the chicken barns. Under the plum trees beyond, past the bus stop, past the graveyard, past the funeral bell hanging in the open from an iron frame. Funeral bell. Ropes tapped the metal, ringing it softly. Motors hummed from the forest in the distance. Along the edge of the fields the warning signs: Border Zone—Do Not Enter. The humming came nearer. The ringing faded. Anna ran along the old road, closed to through traffic, over the old cobblestones, fearless, beneath the low hanging branches of the locust trees. Familiar paths. Paths home. The stench of the feedlot on the wind from the northeast. Then the new road connecting to the freeway, Route 2—a ribbon of concrete wet with rain and flooded with moonlight, shining for kilometers through the open misty gray potato fields. At the end, in the gully before the turnoff to the village, a ghostly threshing machine squatted, an antiquated old implement, spider-legged, a scarecrow, a sign of home.

Anna fell to her knees. She clutched at the shaft to keep her balance. Then she let herself slip down into the high grass.

She didn't know how long she had slept beside the old monster. The high beam of a passing bus fell on the road sign that marked the turnoff to the village. Anna pulled herself to her feet.

It wasn't far to the residential suburb.

Anna might have been a night reveler.

That's what the travel writer and early riser said. He was standing inside the building door with his suitcases, ready to leave, waiting for the village taxi.

Anna held herself up by the doorknob.

Good morning, the old fellow smiled, freshly shaven and full of energy.

Quick into your nest, you night reveler, you.

He called after Anna: The key to the shed's under your angel, and the key to the ladder's in the shed under the blue bucket. The bicycle lock's on the hook on the door. I'll turn up again in about four weeks. The mail can wait here. A lot takes care of itself in four weeks. That's the nice part, by the time I get back, there's not much left to worry about.

Anna sat on the trunk in the hallway and heard him talking, heard the taxi come.

Have a good time! He called at the end through the front door.

Translated by Dorothy Rosenberg

Christa Wolf

Photo by Roger Melis, Berlin, courtesy of Aufbau Verlag.

The major works of Christa Wolf, undoubtedly the twentieth-century German woman writer best known in the English-speaking world, are now
available in English (as indicated in the list below). Aside from her novels
and short prose, her essays and lectures—especially her 1983 "Frankfurt
Lectures on Poetics" (included in the English version of *Cassandra*)—have
played a significant role in international feminist and literary aesthetic dis-

course. Wolf figured prominently in the revolutionary events of 1989–90 that swept the GDR. Since the publication in early 1990 of *Was bleibt* (What remains), a narrative written in the more repressive era of the late 1970s which describes a writer's experience of secret police surveillance, Wolf has been subjected to severe criticism in the West German media, leading to a far-reaching debate about whether she and other East German writers had been opportunists, collaborators, prophets, or victims of the repressive regime.

Wolf was born in 1929 in Landsberg on the Wartha (now Poland). Her family fled west to Mecklenburg, in the northern GDR, in January 1945. She studied German language and literature in Jena and Leipzig; later she worked in research and editing. In the context of the "Bitterfeld Movement," which sought to bring the world of the workplace into literature, Wolf worked in a factory and participated in a Working Writers' Circle. She edited anthologies of East German writers and traveled extensively before turning to freelance writing in 1962. She was an active participant in the International Writers' Conferences on Peace held throughout the 1980s. A recipient of honorary doctorates and of literary awards in both Germanies and Austria, Wolf is known to Americans through service as writer-in-residence at several colleges and universities.

This text forms part of a 1972 short story trilogy, *Unter den Linden* (named for the main street of the former East Berlin), which focuses on gender issues.

Moskauer Novelle (Moscow novella). Halle: Mitteldeutscher Verlag, 1961.

Der geteilte Himmel (Divided heaven). Halle: Mitteldeutscher Verlag, 1963. Trans. Joan Becker as *Divided Heaven* (Berlin: Seven Seas, 1965).

Nachdenken über Christa T. (Thinking about Christa T.). Halle: Mitteldeutscher Verlag, 1968. Trans. Christopher Middleton as *The Quest for Christa T.* (New York: Farrar, Straus & Giroux, 1970).

Lesen und Schreiben (Reading and writing). Berlin/Weimar: Aufbau, 1972. Trans. Joan Becker as *The Reader and the Writer: Essays, Sketches, Memories.* (New York: International Publishers, 1977).

Till Eulenspiegel (Till Eulenspiegel, Prankster), with Gerhard Wolf. Berlin/Weimar: Aufbau, 1972.

Unter den Linden: Drei unwahrscheinliche Geschichten (Under the linden trees: Three improbable tales). Berlin/Weimar: Aufbau, 1974.

Gesammelte Erzählungen (Collected stories). Darmstadt/Neuwied: Luchterhand, 1974.

Kindheitsmuster (Patterns of childhood). Berlin/Weimar: Aufbau, 1976. Trans. Ursula Molinaro and Hedwig Rappolt as *Patterns of Childhood* (New York: Farrar, Straus & Giroux, 1985).

Kein Ort. Nirgends (No place. Not anywhere). Berlin/Weimar: Aufbau, 1979. Trans. Jan van Heurck as *No Place on Earth* (New York: Farrar, Straus & Giroux, 1982).

Fortgesetzter Versuch (Experiment continued). (Leipzig: Reclam, 1979).

Kassandra (Cassandra). Berlin/Weimar: Aufbau, 1983. Trans. Jan van Heurck as *Cassandra: A Novel and Four Essays* (New York: Farrar, Straus & Giroux, 1984).

Ins Ungebundene gehet eine Sehnsucht: Gesprächsraum Romantik (A longing reaches for the unbound: About Romanticism), with Gerhard Wolf. Berlin/Weimar: Aufbau, 1985.

Störfall: Nachrichten eines Tages (Malfunction: One day's news). Berlin/Weimar: Aufbau, 1987. Trans. Heike Schwarzbauer and Rick Takvorian as *Accident: A Day's News* (New York: Farrar, Straus & Giroux, 1992).

Die Dimension des Autors: Essays und Aufsätze, Reden und Gespräche, 1959–1985 Darmstadt/Neuwied: Luchterhand, 1987. Trans. Jan van Heurck, ed. Alexander Stephan, as *The Author's Dimension: Selected Essays* (New York: Farrar, Straus & Giroux, 1992).

Ansprachen (Lectures). Darmstadt/Neuwied: Luchterhand, 1988.

Sommerstück (Summer piece). Berlin/Weimar: Aufbau, 1989.

Reden im Herbst (Speeches in the fall). Darmstadt/Neuwied: Luchterhand, 1990.

Was bleibt (What remains). Berlin/Weimar: Aufbau, 1990. Trans. Rick Takvorian and Heike Schwarzbauer as *What Remains and Other Stories* (New York: Farrar Straus & Giroux, 1993).

Selected Essays. London: Virago, 1991.

Revised Philosophy of a Tomcat   (1970)

> The more culture you have, the less freedom, indeed.
>
> —E.T.A. Hoffmann, *The Philosophy of Tomcat Murr*

THE TOMCATS had a morning look about them!" To read this sentence from the novel, to feel it and to know I am a poet! In the nick of time, the long-deceased writer—translated from the Russian, incidentally—gives me the courage I need to return to literary production; it had suddenly vanished with my waning youth. Seldom have I been so dismayed as in this moment at the inability of my master, Professor of Applied Psychology Rudolf Walter Barzel (age forty-five), to comprehend the language of the animals, of tomcats in particular. He has no idea that I am capable of registering three complex intellectual-emotional processes simultaneously! If he only had an inkling of the purpose of that nicely rectangular little linen-bound book which Isa (age sixteen), the daughter of the house, has filled nearly half full with her utterly childish outpourings, and which I was able to obtain in order to entrust to its white pages some of the products of the feverish activity of my amazingly developed tomcat brain!

Alarmed but thrilled at the heights to which felinity has soared in me, its most worthy living representative, I abandoned the book and the professor's desk on which I had been lying and followed my usual path out the window for a stroll through the gardens in the mild autumn sun, venturing to the farthest borders of my territory, in search of a soul capable of appreciating my extraordinary being. "Soul," I say, though I know—in no small measure from the careful study of the works of my great ancestor, Tomcat Murr—that this hypothetical entity, never scientifically verified but indispensable to the early nineteenth century, is up against a wall. For this we can thank later writers and their tricks, such as "speculations," "reflections," and the expression of "views"—tricks that must have resulted, if not in greater clarity of style, perhaps, then certainly in a more profound expression on these authors' faces, an expression which I too have mastered, by the way, and which, like every behavior practiced long enough, has become second nature to me and does not fail to have wonderful effects on my inner state. This observation, though it could well be my own, can be found along with other striking remarks in the early work of Professor Barzel, "Behavior Exercises and Their Effect on Personality Structure"—proof enough to me that nowadays, when all great discoveries have already been made, even the most original talent would be unnerved by the gap between high-flown obscurity and shallow imitation if it failed to follow the basic rule of all moral beings: Moderation! Let this, then, be the opening line of my "Young Tomcats' Guide to Interaction with Humans."

Thus lost in thought, I happened upon the infamous green-eyed black cat (age two and a half) at the boundary between my turf and Beckelman's backyard. Outwardly delicate and graceful and seductive in an unmistakably oriental way, she is unfortunately impudent, supercilious, and greedy to the core: in short, a female, who of course by nature, as my professor conceded to me one day, eludes his progressive scientific methods much more persistently than the male. We keep this fact to ourselves, however, lest we arouse suspicion of subtle antagonism to the emancipation of women and further aggravate their unfortunate situation, since women obviously suffer one and all from the defect of not being men. I have been careful to take this into consideration in my contacts with that black creature, so that I frankly do not know what can have so provoked her when, deep in thought at the moment of our encounter, I uttered the simple statement: The tomcat is mysterious.

Yet this claim is so extraordinarily true! Cultivated people know it from older as well as contemporary literature, and I am quite confident that my modest but distinguished contributions to the illumination of contemporary felinity will provide further proof.

But then human beings! How transparent they are to me and to themselves! Cerebral beings like all of us from the birds on upward, subject to the ruthless force of biological chance like every other animal, they, in a moment of enlightenment, invented Reason for themselves. Now they can make every sacrifice required by their higher calling completely plausible and can react rationally to any situation. In any case, this is what Professor R. W. Barzel tries to explain to his blonde wife Anita (age thirty-nine) at night, as she lies in bed reading detective stories and eating liqueur-filled chocolates. Of course, I have never noticed that she derives any benefit from these lectures, for her expression is indifferent, even scornful. I, however, though apparently asleep on my professor's fluffy bedside rug, am in fact grateful and receptive to his every word and can assure you: nothing human is alien to me.

Thus, had I been born as a human with a gift for writing and not as a talented tomcat, I most assuredly would not devote my life to such a super-fluous genre of literature as *belles-lettres,* for its very existence is of course founded on the as yet unexplored depths of the human soul. Talk about depths! says my professor to a member of his staff, Dr. Lutz Fettback (age forty-three), nutrition scientist and physiotherapist. Dr. Fettback has a little moustache that bobs up and down when he laughs, and he laughs as he re-plies that even a simple practitioner like himself, who can't hold a candle to my professor when it comes to theory, can see that the soul is a reactionary delusion that has caused humanity much unnecessary suffering; moreover, it has allowed unproductive branches of the economy such as literature a lucrative existence. Yes, says Dr. Guido Hinz (age thirty-five), the cybernetic sociologist, a conscientious, but impenetrable person: Instead of tolerating the waste of both intellectual and physical energies naturally caused by this nonsense about souls going on unchecked, scientists should have compiled a reference work long ago containing as complete a register as possible of optimal variants of all possible situations confronted in human life, and distributed it through administrative channels to each household. This is a notable idea. Think of the energy consumed in useless tragedies, energy that would have been released for the production of material goods, which humanity, as we all know, sees as its real purpose in life (a fact, incidentally, that I gather from my regular reading of three daily newspapers). Given the ease with which human problems can be categorized, practically every conceivable hindrance to productivity could have been included in this reg-ister and removed. The scientific-technological revolution would have been set in motion decades earlier, and humanity could already be living in the future. Contentment and well-being, the longing of every creature, would be widespread by now, and even a house pet—if I may inject my personal opinion—could of course only welcome this development. For where do the worries and failings of their masters land if not on the backs of dogs, cats, and horses?

(It occurs to me here that I must make my own humble contribution to the propagation of the new term recently introduced by the integrated Domestic Animal Commission to replace the obsolete "Master." Henceforth we are authorized to call our masters "Hosts," and I hasten to include as the second rule in my guidebook a sentence that will stand the test of time: "Contented humans—contented pets!")

At this point in the discussion, Dr. Guido Hinz raises his right index finger, thoroughly repulsive to me because it habitually digs roughly into my soft flanks—raises this finger and says: Do not forget cybernetics, my dear colleague! If I understand anything about the ranking system humans use, my professor is of course in no way the "colleague" of a mere doctor of philosophy. Most important, however, I can vouch for the fact that he never for a moment forgets cybernetics, for I too am familiar with its principles. How often I have heard him say that only cybernetics is capable of providing him with the absolutely complete index of all cases of human misfortune in every conceivable combination which he says he so urgently needs in order to advance even one step. And who knows better than he, he asks, that TOHUHA would be nothing but a utopia—yes indeed, he repeats, a uto-pian fantasy!—were it not for this glorious instrument, the computer! Yes: if I were a human being, I would devote myself, like my professor, to the total propagation of *Ratio*, the force that knows all things, explains all things, and controls all things! (No one will begrudge my resorting to the Latin here, as there are words for which I find no equivalent in my beloved German.)

TOHUHA is top secret. My professor lowers his voice long before he allows this word to slip from his lips. Dr. Fettback lowers his moustache, and Dr. Hinz lowers the corners of his mouth, for reasons unknown to me. But I, lying quiet and attentive among the papers on the desk, know what he is talking about: TOHUHA stands for nothing less that Total Human Happiness.

The abolition of tragedy: that is what they're working on here. Since I could not resist committing to paper the most secret of all human secrets—begone, vain, foolish hope of ever seeing this, my best work, in black and white! Whatever is it that drives the true author to speak and speak again of the most dangerous things? For surely his mind, his intelligence, his sense of civic responsibility affirm to him the strict rule of absolute discretion: Just think of TOHUHA in the hands of the Enemy! But one or more organs which seem to have escaped the attention of physiological research to date repeatedly compel this unhappy writer in some as yet unexplained way—presumably by secreting a kind of truth hormone—to make fateful confes-sions. My great ancestor Tomcat Murr (I am directly descended from his line and look like his identical twin) expressed this in the following lovable though scientifically unreliable words: "At times, a peculiar sensation—I am tempted to call it spiritual indigestion—goes through me, right down to my paws, until they must write down everything I am thinking."

No one who knows that my professor is preoccupied with total human happiness can be surprised at his frequently tormented mien or at the re-grettable fact that recent x-ray tests captured the image of a stomach ulcer, which my professor displayed, not entirely without pride, to his friend

Dr. Fettback by holding the film up against the green light of his study lamp. We had the pleasure of hearing Dr. Fettback call this ulcer "classic," after which he honored us with the pronouncement that our work is destructive to one's health. You must be sleeping badly then, Professor? Hardly at all, he replied modestly. Aha, said Fettback, his moustache bobbing. Autogenic training.

Nestled in the professor's armchair, I have participated in the exercises Dr. Fettback conducted with him out of longstanding friendship. To be sure, there is something odd about seeing this man, unquestionably the intellectual superior of his staff, stretched out on the leather sofa obeying the commands of little Fettback, who painstakingly tries to erase all traces of mental activity from his patient's features. Well, I'll be . . .! said Dr. Hinz, who happened to burst in once when my professor and Fettback, both wearing the same vacant facial expression, were mumbling to themselves in muted unison: I am wonderfully relaxed. I will sleep peacefully. I feel well.

So, I see you've finally got him, said Dr. Hinz. What that's supposed to mean is anybody's guess. This much is certain: My professor now receives more calmly than he used to the nightly monologue of his wife, Anita, who unfortunately runs out of detective novels now and then. Loyalty to my hosts prompts me to summarize these extensive and, more often than not, shrill monologues in a single sentence: Life's disappointments, but in particular those of women, and especially those inflicted by loved ones, for example one's own husband, cannot fail in the long run to leave their mark even on persons of the strongest character. During these speeches, in which, with an unmistakably sarcastic undertone, she drops phrases like "inexhaustible virility" and "love's eternal ecstasy"—the context of which is not entirely clear to me—she imbibes great quantities of apricot brandy, her favorite liqueur, and finally orders my professor, who has been spending his evenings for the past four weeks reading that interesting volume of recommended methods of sexual sublimation, to put "that beast" out. She means me.

Needless to say, I assume a pose of deep sleep while my professor argues in a soft voice: But why, my dear Anita? Leave the fellow alone, he's not bothering us. It has happened upon occasion that she bursts out in inappropriate laughter at this point and ends by crying hysterically. But in such instances my professor turns off the light and closes his eyes, and after a while I hear him whispering: My right arm is heavy and warm. I am completely calm. I feel better every day . . .

In spite of all this he has been sleeping poorly. I often see him lying there with his eyes wide open at dawn when, fresh and rested, I jump out the bedroom window onto the little birch tree and climb down to join my own kind.

It is impossible to argue with humans about taste (this maxim also belongs in my Young Tomcats' Guide). In any case: Frau Anita is very, very blonde. This statement cannot, and of course must not, be taken as a criticism. She is a head taller than my professor—a circumstance I completely forget when I see them lying there so peacefully side by side in bed at night. It is quite conceivable, says Dr. Lutz Fettback occasionally, that a more ascetically inclined man might be attracted to a generously endowed woman; however, he adds, his professional ethics force him to disapprove of Frau Anita's eating habits.

I know what he means, since I recently read his paper, "Eating, Too, Is a Matter of Character." It culminates in the sentence: Tell me what you eat and I will tell you who you are! (Whereupon I add another maxim to my Guide: One man's meat is another man's poison.) In this regard, Dr. Fettback has recently refrained from the idiocy of appearing right at mealtimes, during which he would engage in discussion humorous to him and him alone, all in order to confirm the presence of some incredibly repulsive raw vegetable salads and the absence of meat on the Barzels' table. Thus I have had ample opportunity to rescue my professor in importune situations by consuming in a flash the pieces of meat he threw under the table to me—never mind my preference for roasted meat. But like every action that violates the laws of nature, this one too had its price: suddenly my professor began to take an interest in my reaction times, and my life—now chained to the stopwatch, just as his has been for years—became quite strenuous.

I never dreamed that the records he kept on me were to be the basis for his reflex studies, which subsequently proved so significant—had I known, how much sooner would I have demonstrated to our mutual advantage the behavior he could expect from a talented subject in his experiments! Namely, that a subject would always manage to react in precisely the same way to identical stimuli. This is the least that this wonder of technology, the computer, can expect of its partner, says my professor.

In short: Once I had caught on to the principle, our series of tests proceeded quickly and smoothly. Why shouldn't I do my professor the small favor—after a generous meal of liver, for example, when one naturally prefers to have a rest—of repeating my after-dinner leap onto the young spruce in front of the house three times instead of twice! With Isa's help, I survived a starvation test—which has its disgusting aspects, even if it does serve scientific progress—without ill effects on my health: she secretly fed me shredded beef and cream, and I ate what she offered me, even though my scientific objectivity did not permit me to share her scorn for her father's experiments. I rose brilliantly to the challenge of simulating progressive dissipation of my strength, even to the point of a deceptively genuine collapse on the seventh day. (It seems worth mentioning that I learned the necessity of banishing all trace of memory of a meal just consumed, not only from the head but from the stomach and intestinal tract as well, if one wants to collapse of hunger credibly.) Isa now musters me with strange looks, it is true. As a footnote, I had gained more than a pound in that week of starvation (I weigh myself regularly on Frau Anita's bathroom scale, although I am not so foolish as to hang a weight chart on the wall). Spring, which had just arrived, assisted me in regaining my handsome, slim figure in a short time, and I am now living once again as befits my educational status.

Deliberate resistance, however, was my approach to Dr. Fettback's attempt to regulate my defecatory instinct on the occasion of the experiment described above. To be able to empty my bowels whenever I feel the urge—this, in my opinion, is one of the foundations of tomcat liberty. My professor appears to have a different idea concerning the foundations of human liberty; in any event he looks unhappy enough when he emerges from the toilet at seven in the morning—the hour prescribed to him by Dr. Fettback—without having accomplished his business. Recently, however, the poor man has been feigning cheerfulness and relief, preferring to find a moment to go secretly later in the day or, as I have reason to surmise, quite frequently not to go at all, ever since Frau Anita said to him one morning: You can't even do *that* when you want to! Have I already mentioned that Frau Anita calls me "Tomcat"? Of course there is nothing incorrect about this epithet, but what human being would like being called "Human"? If they've gone to the trouble of giving you a name of your own—in my case, "Max"—it is irritating to be denied this most personal form of address, the mark of individuality within the species. I would sooner tolerate the obviously improper but well-meaning form Isa decided upon: "Maximilian," she calls me, pointing out that he was an emperor. I found him in the encyclopedia and was satisfied with the name in the end. Indeed, my nature is noble from the two tips of my handsome beard down to my very last sharp claw, and so it shall remain, even if that aforementioned black creature is bewitched by the idea that my magnanimity is a weakness. Oh, if only my will were as great as my capacities! "My little Tiger," Frau Anita sometimes calls me, which I don't really mind hearing, as my facial markings, beige and black stripes radiating from nose and mouth, prove the predatory ancestry of my species. But gray—contrary to the claims of humans, gray I am not. Their dull senses cannot do justice to the subtle and richly varied pattern of my coat: black stripes along the back, merging into gray-black to brownish ornaments on the flanks, an unusual ringed design on the chest, and the light and dark shading of the legs, repeated on the tail: This is precisely how my venerable ancestor, Tomcat Murr, also presented himself to the world, and it is my profound conviction that none other than this appearance will bring one to prominence.

My reader, my unknown friend from the next century, has long since noticed that I move about freely in space and time. Chronology is bothersome. So, let him follow me back to that little stretch of fence between the *Symphoricarpus albus* bushes, popularly known as snowberries, where on the aforementioned afternoon that black female cat so resented my true statement: The Tomcat is mysterious! For within an incredibly short time she hissed a generous measure of insults at me which I was obliged to ignore. I have long since given up trying to make that seductive but sexually and otherwise uninhibited cat understand that her aggressiveness belies her insufficiently sublimated instincts and that her thirst for dominance most probably derives from the fateful naming which cast a shadow over her early years and allowed these complexes to proliferate and which she now tries to take out on me.

The time has come to announce it: the cat's name is Napoleon. We know that inadequate knowledge of physiology among humans is related to their wish to be helpful and good and to forget that they descend from the kingdom of the beasts. Furthermore, if one considers their understandable preference for the male species, one can also presume to know the reasons for the erroneous diagnosis that must have preceded so fateful a choice of name. Nevertheless: why Napoleon, of all names? A tendency to masochism? The barely suppressed desire to take out one's own imperious inclinations on the innocent beast?

Yet it is doubtful whether our neighbors, the Beckelmanns, derive their motivation to act or not to act from psychological literature, as do our sort of folk. One cannot help getting the impression that these people obey their urges like robots (Frau Anita also suspects as much), bring children into the world (the boys, Joachim and Bernhard, and the girl whom, strangely enough, all the children in the neighborhood call "Maltshit," although after all, she is approaching her sixteenth birthday and can't wear her skirts short enough; Frau Anita is right about that), and, when they're tired of

it, simply go their own ways again. How can anyone do that?! says Frau
Anita—and then go on living in the same house after the divorce as Frau
and Herr Beckelmann have been doing for three months now. I couldn't,
says Frau Anita, never. And I might add: Neither could I. For now, at all
hours of the day and night Frau Beckelmann's new admirer's car, a coffee-
colored Trabant, pulls up at the ex-couple's shared front door and gives one
of those obscene honks that Frau Anita hates like nothing else in the world.
With my own eyes I have seen Herr Beckelmann open the window and
inform his successor—in the most amicable voice—that his wife was not
at home, whereupon the fellow gratefully tipped his leather cap, pulled a
bottle wrapped in the finest tissue from the car, and proposed to Beckelmann the construction worker that they go have a few together. Surely this
is carrying moral lassitude too far.

To return to Napoleon, she is unfortunately uninterested in the depth-
psychology approach to explaining her name. It doesn't matter one iota
what they call her, she claims. By contrast, she adds, what does matter to
her is my tendency to evade the most elementary paternal responsibilities
under the pretext of research work. This is a considerably edited and abbre-
viated version of her long speech, in the course of which I resorted to the
well-tried method of lying down, relaxing my limbs one by one, and giving
myself those sweet commands which, once ingrained in the channels of the
reflexes, never fail to accomplish their effect: I am completely calm, I said
to myself. My limbs are heavy and warm (indeed, they were!). My pulse
is even. My forehead is pleasantly cool. Warmth flows through my solar
plexus. I am happy. Life is beautiful.

Last April, Napoleon still had the power to make me suffer. I have
learned in the meantime that anxiety and suffering always arise out of de-
sires and that the best way to relieve the former is to fulfill the latter. *Voilà.*
It is accomplished. Too late, one could object, for my unbridled lust had
already done its damage: I am not ashamed to acknowledge that my chaste,
fatherly heart beat faster when Madam Napoleon moved into the Barzels'
kitchen one morning with four kittens, clownish creatures, two of whom
were identical in appearance to me. Secretly proud of this splendid evidence
of Mendel's Law, I nevertheless had no leisure to meditate on genetics,
nor to try to fully comprehend Napoleon's strategic move in walking unob-
structed, with an innocent mien and under the camouflage of motherhood,
into the very inner sanctum of my own territory—so preoccupied was I
with trying to mitigate the shock the Barzel family was suffering from the
fact that an animal they had thought to be male had given birth to kittens.

My professor, who grasped the situation a few significant moments later than Frau Anita, gave me an unreproachful but inquiring look. Equipped with the knowledge contained in the informative book *Love without Mystery*, which can be found under Isa's pillow, I manfully returned his glance. My professor forgave me.

Daughter Isa, I must say, burst into unseemly laughter. She was scolded. But Frau Anita took her irrationality so far as to offer the cat Napoleon— whom she, with pursed lips, stupidly called my wife!—the leftover kidneys in my bowl; nursing mothers are always hungry, she said.

But enough gossip about intimate matters. I am probably correct in as- suming that there is no one now living who is unfamiliar with the acronym SYMAWB, so that I actually need translate it only for the inhabitants of another planet, who, after all, might sooner or later come across my writ- ings: System of Maximum Physical and Emotional Well-being. It should be understood that we are talking about a subcategory of TOHUHA, and that I had the unspeakable good fortune of obtaining my education in the household of the very man who invented SYMAWB and who still directs the system today. His work was well under way when I appeared in the Barzel household. All the factors that promote or detract from physical and emotional well-being had been entered in a huge card catalogue consisting, impressively enough, of a block of thirty-six white boxes; they fill an entire wall in the professor's study and are protected by iron bars at night and, what is more, padlocked.

The three scientists in whose presence I not only learned to read and write but also began my specialized study of mathematics, logic, and social psychology were working intensively to integrate the wealth of separate data into a self-contained system: SYMAWB, of course. Very soon I found myself in a position to be useful to them in this, though without ever vio- lating my absolute principle, which reads: Conceal your good deeds from everyone. The card index became my field of concentration. The white, pink, and yellow cards slumbered in their individual boxes like soldiers in rank and file until pulled out of line and called to active duty, under the com- mand of the key words found on the front of each box, to do battle for SYMAWB. There are many key words: "Life's Pleasures," for example, and "Dangers to Civilization," and "Sexuality," "Family," "Leisure," "Nutrition," "Hygiene"; in short, the study of these cards alone will teach a non-member of the species everything about the life of the human race. Well, one day while at my research I was surprised by my professor, and knowing that he too clings to the human prejudice that animals are ineducable, I quickly stuck the card I happened to be holding in my paws into the closest open box and pretended to be asleep. This explains how "Flexibility," which I had taken from the box labeled "Social Norms," got into "Life's Pleasures," and why my professor, who of course attributed this idea to himself, called it a stroke of genius and made it a pillar of SYMAWB. Encouraged by this success, I began systematic activities aimed at the production of creative co-incidences, so that today, without any false modesty, I can call myself one of the founders of SYMAWB.

What are we trying to accomplish? Nothing less profound than the ex-haustive programming of that sequence of events which human beings have given the antiquated name LIFE. It is incredible but true—I say this for the benefit of my later readers from other galaxies—that even into our own century a negligent, indeed even mystical attitude toward this sequence of events could not be obliterated among humankind; its consequences were disorder, waste of time, and inefficient wear and tear on the workforce. Thus SYMAWB met an urgent need by using the latest computer technology to devise a uniquely valid system for rational living. It is not surprising that at the mention of the word "computer" my professor's features begin to glow from within—a moving spectacle that nevertheless causes Dr. Hinz, a cybernetics specialist, after all, to smile mockingly and remark that one should not have the same ecstatic attitude toward computer technology as the early Christians had toward their doctrine of salvation. My professor, a man of self-control, was finally obliged to remind Hinz, who is ten years his junior, that he, Hinz, had recently gotten up at a large conference and spoken about the unlimited applications of computers to the simulation of social and nervous system processes. At this, Hinz's grin became broader, and he presumed to assert that the popes too had in fact spoken for cen-turies as advocates in the cause of Christ without being Christians. Only the nonbeliever, said Hinz, has power over believers in the long run, because only he has his head free to think and his hands free to act.

My professor, who is guided by purely ethical motives, could not and would not let this inappropriate analogy go unchallenged, of course. I was already looking forward to seeing how he would brilliantly refute this nihil-ism—for what else do you call it if one believes in nothing?—when Hinz resorted to an unfair trick and cunningly inquired whether he, Professor R. W. Barzel, didn't agree that humankind can find happiness only by being forced to do so?

This, you see, is the creators' collective latest discovery, achieved as a re-sult of a voluntary test of SYMAWB in several rural districts: the only people who could be more or less forced to follow the principles of SYMAWB were a small group of test subjects who were hospitalized and kept under strict supervision for three months. All the others, who incidentally never denied the system's absolute rationality, nevertheless rushed from one infringement of its beneficent regulations to the next, and there were supposedly some who, while previously accustomed to a sound and healthy life, now plunged into debauchery under the pressures of SYMAWB's commands and prohibitions. Thus Dr. Hinz's question touched upon the weakest point in our system, and my professor, whose finest trait is his courage to face the truth, could only reply with a quiet but clear "Yes," which shattered the silence of his study.

I then realized: these fearless men, who intend to liberate the human race from its tragic bent, must themselves enter into tragic entanglements. Given the immaturity of large portions of the current human population, the momentous transition into TOHUHA cannot be achieved except by force. Yet those who must exert that force are harmless people like these three who, instead of always marching ahead of the rest, naturally also prefer to sleep a little later, to expose their faces to the sun now and then, and to make love to their wives at night after a stimulating TV show. What I was looking at were martyrs! This realization made me so incredibly weary that I laid my head on my paws and succumbed to sweet melancholy, which invariably leads to the enticingly compelling question where in heaven's name our poor solar system is headed in the boundless universe, which in turn brings on a rejuvenating sleep with cosmic dreams. (An observation, incidentally, which does not appear to me to be consistent with Dr. Fettback's claim that dreams of any kind can be attributed to the irregularities of intestinal peristalsis.)

Thus I slept and neglected to observe what the three made of my inspiration to put the card marked "Parental Love" in the "Dangers to Civilization" box. They always make something of my inspirations, because the card index has already been inspected and approved by an authorized TOHUHA Commission, so that it cannot be altered again at any price, least of all without permission.

Now I too have my pride as a scientist. Once, when I caught my professor cheating—he had surreptitiously taken the "Acquired Marital Impotence" card, which I had filed under "Delicacies," and, shaking his head, returned it to the "Sexual Disorders" box—I was of course forced to persist with my idea. When he discovered the card in the wrong place a second time, my professor was about to make the sign of the cross, but why he turned pale like a sinner caught red-handed, I do not know.

As we all know, some theorists base their entire—and I might as well say it now: lame!—system of criteria for distinguishing human beings from animals on the claim that animals can neither smile nor weep. As far as I can see, this is correct. But the question is: Does *homo sapiens* smile or weep? In the population accessible to me for observation I have found nothing of the kind—at least not in the way described by these researchers.

Laugh—yes. Recently, for example, in my professor's study: Dr. Hinz had published a new article in his series "Your Health—Your Gain" in the Sunday supplements. He wrote about the social significance of fishing, and I read with both disbelief and admiration that the human angler is inspired not only by the base notion of fish as a delicacy but above all by the wish to store up energy reserves through recreational fishing and then spend it the next day in the form of increased productivity on the job. Do you fish, then? my professor asked Dr. Hinz, and when Hinz indignantly replied in the negative, Dr. Fettback interjected: He's not productive, either! It was quiet in the room for a moment, and then began that aforementioned laughter, quite normal in a Great Society.

But smile—no: they did not smile. Isa smiles occasionally, to be sure. She sits in an armchair doing nothing and smiles a bit foolishly for no reason at all. This observation supports my thesis that smiling and weeping are infantile vestiges in the evolution of humanity, shed, as lizards shed their damaged tails, by fully matured representatives of the species at about age twenty-five. This theory is sufficient explanation for the unshakable earnestness of animals, whose evolution of course undoubtedly goes back infinitely further than that of *homo sapiens*, so that the necessity of shedding bothersome attributes must have arisen much earlier for them. No fossil imprint will ever inform us whether the ichthyosaurus became extinct precisely because it smiled when what was important was progress and advancement. But this is exactly what must be determined, for without this lofty goal before his eyes my poor professor too would most certainly prefer to tend his roses in peace. That is how he puts it, figuratively speaking, for he knows nothing about roses, and here, too, Frau Anita must rely on the Beckelmanns, whose joint rose garden continues to thrive even after the divorce, which is a mystery to Frau Anita and me, considering the sensitivity of this flower.

Frau Anita has been dreaming about black tomcats the last few nights, which is surely not merely the result of the roughage diet Fettback put her on but also an expression, quite simply, of her subconscious wish that I looked like Napoleon. To be sure, human beings supposedly have no control over their dreams, but I am insulted nevertheless. My professor always comes home very late these days, if at all, and Frau Anita naturally asks him what he's doing day and night. He's in the middle of a series of complex calculations, he replies, and needs the little computer at the Institute, where he also spends the night now and then. Well, I hope it's a lot of fun, Frau Anita remarks viciously, without noticing how the current phase of her husband's work is fraying his nerves. Even I, who deemed myself fortunate to be able to offer him even modest assistance, must now leave him alone, face to face with his great project. Anyone can see that he is over-exerting himself. His garden, which he has kept in exemplary condition—more out of a love for order than out of a passion for gardening—has been overgrown for weeks. And he himself, whose constitution is of the asthenic type, is simply wasting away. I dare not contemplate the appearance of his stomach lining.

What he wants is superhuman and he knows it. SYMAWB, I have heard him say, will be perfect and will be regarded as absolute or it will not exist at all.

This unadorned statement sent a chill down my spine. Yet how true it is! A defective system would be an absurd invention; you don't need a system to have defects in abundance. The course of human history unfortunately demonstrates this. By contrast, a faultless system, as SYMAWB undoubtedly is, must encompass everyone, for who would want to be held accountable for the massive economic losses that non-use of the system would generate? Who would be able to justify the time that would be lost until TOHUHA is fully phased in with the next generation—although, if I may take Isa to be typical of the group, they cannot fully appreciate their fathers' efforts . . .

How else can one interpret the fact that Isa—the minute her father has announced he will be sleeping with his little computer again, and Frau Anita has thereupon left the house with a small suitcase to spend the night with a woman friend—convenes seven representatives of the male and female sex for the purpose of holding one of those gatherings they call "parties," which are always very loud and very dark and from which I retreat into the cellar or the garden? I saw five white figures diving into the swimming pool after midnight, which cannot, no matter how sultry the night may have been, be called a civilized manner of finding relief from the heat. This, in any case, is the way Isa's father, my Professor R. W. Barzel, expressed his displeasure when he then unexpectedly appeared after all—incidentally, he was the picture of a desperate man in the dim light of the patio lamps and without a tie, which is not his usual style. I watched with satisfaction as the swimming pool divers, scantily clad, sneaked away rather embarrassed. Isa, though, first smashed a few priceless Rosenthal cups by the door, then locked herself in her room and yelled in her shrillest voice: Priggish Progress Nut! to her father, who was rattling at her door.

I couldn't believe my ears. This was the girl who had fed me when I was kept on a strict scientific deprivation diet. She is the only person who knows the spot to scratch under my chin that gives me the most sublime pleasure. And yet I will defer to the truth of the matter and say it: her behavior is inexcusable. It was on that evening, I am sure of it, that my professor began working on his technological hobby (concealed, of course, from all but myself), a simple system of rules which, centrally controlled, responds to stimuli in a precisely predictable manner with a range of maneuverability of plus/minus zero: a perfect creature of reflex. The advantage of such a model for the experimenter is obvious. Its disadvantage—lack of adaptability to changing environmental conditions—could be compensated for by creating an absolutely stable environment. SYMAWB (the System of Maximum Well-Being)—it suddenly dawned on me—would be the ideal environment for a creature of reflex. But why was my professor conducting this research with his drapes drawn, under cover of night, like a thief? Why would he carefully lock his files away in an iron box? Why was he reluctant to present the results to his staff, who, meanwhile, were busy at the exacting task of assembling an exhaustive catalogue of all human character traits and skills? Dr. Hinz, however strange he might be in other respects, achieved extraordinary results in these feverish weeks. It is him we have to thank for devising a means of merging the unalterable data of SYMAWB with the data in the human traits catalogue. The two systems, thus completely integrated, were then fed to Heinrich—that's what we call our little computer. His answer? Again and again I have reread the fateful strip of computer tape on my professor's desk:

PROBLEM INCORRECTLY FORMULATED. MUTUALLY EXCLUSIVE CONTROL LOOPS CANNOT BE INTEGRATED INTO AN OPERABLE SYSTEM. CORDIALLY, HEINRICH.

Heinrich is a brainless creature, said my professor in his initial rage. He made a special trip to the mainframe computer in the capital, which is far too important to have any other name than GRA 7 and which charges its clients a thousand marks per on-line minute. But Dr. Hinz, whose job is feeding the multitudes of robots their daily bread, reappeared after half a minute, somewhat ashen. Frau Anita, when my professor told her all about it that evening, thought pallor must be becoming to Dr. Hinz. On the tape

Dr. Hinz held in his hand there was only a single word, arrogant as these hotshot computers are: NO NO NO NO NO . . . fifty centimeters of NOs.

So GRA 7 is a pessimist. None of us could believe such an error could escape its creators. Dr. Fettback proposed filing a complaint with the Central Robot Assembly Office, but since it is well known that they do not consort with ordinary mortals, my professor advised against it. I could not bear to see him so depressed so therefore did not hesitate to carry the stupid computer tape over to the Beckelmanns' yard during the unsupervised noon hour. Significantly, it caused no depression but was instead draped like a tie around a brand new rose-red rosebud by their youngest boy. Napoleon and Josephine (my youngest daughter, in every respect the very image of her mother) gleefully reported this to me.

To my horror, however, my professor began to hunt for this disastrous tape as if for a treasure, on account of the pathological human tendency to transform every disaster into document files as if it would then cease to be a disaster. (From my Young Tomcats' Guide: "Contact with document files is harmful to your health!") So my professor desperately scoured house and yard, looked over Beckelmanns' fence as well, and saw the young Maltshit in the rosebed. A trite image, but I swear to it, on my good taste. I cannot understand what suddenly caused such a change in my professor's voice. Oh, he said in this new voice, what lovely roses. This might be true; I personally don't care for flowers. But he looked right past the strip of white paper tied to the largest rose. Yes, said Maltshit with the equanimity with which young girls address grown men these days. Lovely roses. The loveliest of all, however, said NO NO NO. And she handed over the strip of paper to the professor, who did not so much as look at it; he sighed stupidly and claimed that he had hopes of softening the stern judgment of the loveliest of roses. Then he asked Maltshit if her name was still Regina, and since the reply was of course affirmative, he wanted to know whether she, too, fertilized her roses with "Growfine." Regina (what a name!) said no, she didn't fertilize roses at all. Whereupon my professor uttered the curious words: Oh, happy hands! and went inside, where he simply threw the computer tape into the wastebasket, so that I had to turn the whole thing upside down to find it and put it back on his desk. Of course I ignored Frau Anita's excessively angry outburst over the scattered papers and devoted myself instead to worrying about my professor, who must certainly have taken ill—a worry that was all too quickly confirmed by the events that followed.

Meanwhile, the three men who bore the entire burden of responsibility for the prompt and cost-effective mobilization of SYMAWB discovered in agitated sessions, with Heinrich's assistance, that the only variable in their system configuration was the HUMANITY factor. It took longer for them to reach this conclusion than an unbiased person like me, for example, would have required; by holding fast to prejudices regarding indispensable components of human nature—a myth—they nearly aroused my sympathy but delayed the application of SYMAWB. Still: the idea of a Normative Human was taking shape. It was a great moment when this concept was named for the first time—and the last time, by the way—during a midnight meeting. And I can say that I was there.

Dr. Hinz broke the uneasy silence as if he were speaking about the most banal of matters: Well, then, let's call him NH. Dr. Fettback, who seemed a bit dejected to me, agreed precipitously: It would simplify some things. At this moment I realized that humans use their language not only to understand one another but also to conceal from one another things that had previously been understood. An invention I can only admire.

Thus they set about purging the humanity catalogue of every superfluous trait. It is hard to believe how much they were able to throw overboard in one sweep. With joyful anticipation they fed Heinrich the new data. They said he must have put considerable effort into the task because it seemed to amuse him. Yet in the end he announced regretfully: HEINRICH CAN DO NOTHING. Then the three decided to develop a data catalogue that Dr. Fettback, in his whiny voice, referred to as the lowest threshhold (in this context we learned that Herr Doktor reads books at home and finds quotes from the classics to use as guidelines for his own life). But Heinrich replied sadly: RIGHT DIRECTION, GOAL A LONG WAY OFF.

Dr. Hinz then suggested teasing the computer and amputating the entire complex called "Creative Thinking" as an experiment. BRAVO, wrote Heinrich, DON'T STOP NOW!

A stroke of genius, said my professor. But what do we do now? Dr. Hinz thought the most important thing was not to get thrown off by the suspicion of an antagonistic contradiction between the loss of creative thinking and the definition of "human." At that point Dr. Fettback declared that the highest source of human happiness for earthlings had always been the personality, which he, Fettback, was prepared to defend to his last drop of blood. And if a scientific conference decided otherwise? asked Dr. Hinz. Well—then! said Fettback, he was no bullheaded eccentric, after all. The conference convened at the behest of Professor R. W. Barzel decided by majority vote that creative thinking was an integral part of the concept of human being and should be propagated in art and literature, but that for purposes of scientific research and experimentation it could be disregarded.

I heard my professor telling Frau Anita all of this that evening. She, however, whose bottle of apricot brandy is now kept in her nightstand, was not following his flight of fancy and only wanted to know whether Dr. Hinz had been wearing his pretty red vest again. My professor had not paid any attention to that, of course, and Frau Anita said dreamily: He has such a pretty burgundy vest . . .

All that was needed now to get the project under way quickly was my professor's idea of introducing the term "personality formation." (Needless to say, from the very beginning I made my own modest contribution. I took the cards I had removed from the catalogue down to the pile of old paper in the furnace room, where they were certain not to be discovered. I set about this task with circumspection and removed only yellow cards, which represent only secondary traits but traits that humans seem to have difficulty giving up, superfluous though they are: "Courage," "Unselfishness," "Compassion," and the like.) Well, now they were distinguishing between "formed" and "unformed" personalities. Those formed by the three scientists slowly but surely approached Heinrich's ideal. The unformed ones, which unfortunately still constitute the greater part of humanity today, were considered anachronistic and so could be omitted from the study.

Thus a heap of useless refuse was gradually programmed out of the human being deemed suitable to benefit from SYMAWB. Dr. Hinz confessed that to his mind we were finally approaching an authentic state: to be authentic meant to fulfill the criterion of usefulness. Heinrich's reports, however, having sounded encouraging for a time, stagnated at a certain point. We made a compromise with him. We removed "Loyalty to Convictions"—what kind of convictions would a person have to be loyal to in a perfectly organized system? What does one need imagination for? A sense of beauty? We became intoxicated as we crossed out more and more and awaited Heinrich's responses, nervous to the breaking point. And what did he say? WE ARE GETTING NOWHERE THIS WAY. I AM SAD. YOURS, HEINRICH.

Seldom had we been so moved as we were by this machine's sorrow. We were prepared to go to the extreme if only we could restore his happiness. But what was the extreme?

Reason? asked Dr. Fettback faintheartedly. Sure, delete it, said Dr. Hinz, it's only a hypothesis anyway, not a trait. But the outcry if you admit it in public! And his callous gaze followed Frau Anita, who was walking out of the room with a tray of empty cups and had developed an odd way of swaying her hips.

Sexuality, Dr. Fettback now suggested, blushing, while accidentally biting into a ham sandwich. The response was silence. We parted, not knowing what to do. We were in the midst of a crisis, there was no doubt about it. That evening just before dark, when all cats supposedly turn gray (it's not true), I discovered my professor in the shrubs between the Barzels' and the Beckelmanns' yards. He turned to me with the words: Max—be glad you're not human! This challenge was truly unnecessary. But what, then, did he want to be? A tomcat, perhaps? The idea violated my sense of propriety.

My professor showed truly heroic courage. I know for a fact that he removed "Reason" and "Sexuality" from the formed personality and then ran it through the computer again. He came home a beaten man. Heinrich had spewed out the angry words: SPARE ME HALF-MEASURED IDEAS! That night, finally, my professor pulled his creature of reflex out of its box to compare its data with those of the fully formed personality. It *must* have dawned on him at that moment what I had long since known: the normative human being was identical to his creature of reflex. I see in it nothing to shake one's head over. I don't know why he didn't go introduce this creature to Heinrich right away. I don't understand humans any more.

The professor leaves the house as usual, but hours later I meet him roaming around in a little wooded area. I make my escape into the bushes without a greeting, for I value discretion in my private affairs. (This time, by the way, it's Willy the plumber's black and white Laura, a gentle, affectionate creature with no thirst for power.) Dr. Hinz visits us, even though no work has been done for days. He comes in the evenings when my professor isn't home yet. He wears his burgundy vest and kisses Frau Anita's hand; then they go into the living room, where I do not follow them, because non-research-related conversations bore me beyond measure. Isa turns the radio in her room up so loud that I crawl under the furs in the closet. Then I hear Dr. Hinz and my professor greeting one another politely in the hall. One is leaving, the other coming.

Midnight.

What's the matter, Rudolph? I hear Frau Anita asking. My professor walks past her without a word, with strangely heavy steps, and locks himself in his study; I just barely manage to slip through the door behind him. What he pulls out of his briefcase are not new messages from Heinrich but two bottles of cognac, one of them half empty. He puts it to his lips immediately and takes a long draft. Then he begins to speak.

I, no coward by nature, am frightened.

Regina, says the Professor of Applied Psychology R. W. Barzel. Miss Regina Maltshit. So you don't want me, so you're proud. Okay. Excellent, in fact (says my professor, taking a swig from the bottle). Because one of these days you will *have* to like me, my little lady. Except then you won't be Malt-shit but a creature of reflex like everyone else, and I will have programmed out your pride, a secondary trait, and I'll marry you to SYMAWB instead of to your dull, blond kid with the motorcycle. Heinrich will be Best Man, and I will have put the arrogant scoundrel in his place, too. He'll be cooperative, and no matter what I feed him, he'll cough up nothing but YES YES YES YES YES . . .

There is someone banging on the door. I hear Dr. Fettback's voice and prefer . . .

Editor's Note:

The manuscript breaks off here. Our tomcat Max, if he should prove to be its author, which seems utterly incredible, was unable to complete it. He died last week in the treacherous feline epidemic. Our grief at his loss is even more profound in view of this discovery among his personal effects. As is almost always the case when one has known an author personally, one is startled by the peculiar, one might say distorted view of the world in his writings. Our Max, too, took the liberty of inventing things. We are convinced that we know him better, and on a different level, than the first-person narrator of these lines.

But who, motivated by petty misgivings or wounded pride, would want to deprive the wider public of this monument erected by a gifted creature to his own memory?

Translated by Nancy Lukens

Irmtraud Morgner

Photo by Roger Melis, Berlin, courtesy of Aufbau Verlag.

Born in 1933 in Chemnitz (later Karl-Marx-Stadt, then renamed Chemnitz after the fall of the socialist regime), Irmtraud Morgner studied German language and literature in Leipzig. She turned to freelance writing in 1958 and was a member of the board of directors of the GDR Writers' Union for a number of years. She lived in East Berlin until her death in May 1990 after a long illness.

Morgner's importance to East German literature, to the critique of socialism and patriarchy, and to feminist aesthetics has been recognized internationally, though it would be wrong to equate her feminism with its various counterparts in the West. Her debt to the utopian thinking of Ernst Bloch is apparent. The highly complex style of this selection, which is taken from Morgner's epic novel *Leben und Abenteuer der Trobadora Beatriz*, reflects the author's desire to teach her readers to defy traditional definitions of empirical reality by playing with imaginative possibilities. An earlier English version, titled "The Rope," omitted the passages involving electron scattering. The story works well without them, but it is precisely in the playful use of the language of nuclear physics that Morgner creates a metaphor for Vera Hill's situation as a woman in the male-dominated scientific-industrial establishment.

The title of this excerpt alludes to the East German industrial city associated with the famous 1959 conference that launched "the Bitterfeld Movement" to integrate the world of production into the creative arts. It is the third piece in the novel to describe the life of a working woman.

Das Signal steht auf Fahrt (The signal is on "Go"). Berlin/Weimar: Aufbau, 1959.

Ein Haus am Rand der Stadt (A house at the edge of town). Berlin/Weimar: Aufbau, 1962.

Hochzeit in Konstantinopel (A wedding in Constantinople). Berlin/Weimar: Aufbau, 1968.

Gauklerlegende: Eine Spielfrauengeschichte (Trickster legend: A story of minstrel women). Berlin: Eulenspiegel, 1970.

Die wundersamen Reisen Gustavs des Weltfahrers (The wondrous journeys of Gustaf the world traveler). Berlin/Weimar: Aufbau, 1972.

Leben und Abenteuer der Trobadora Beatriz nach Zeugnissen ihrer Spielfrau Laura (Life and adventures of the troubador Beatrice according to testimonies of her minstrel Laura). Berlin/Weimar: Aufbau, 1974.

Amanda: Ein Hexenroman (Amanda: A witches' novel). Berlin/Weimar: Aufbau, 1984.

Third Fruit of Bitterfeld:
The Tightrope   (1974)

PROFESSOR GURNEMANN, director of an academic institute researching
the atomic structure of matter, employed a female physicist on his staff. Her
name was Vera Hill, and she lived in B. The institute was inconveniently
located outside the town limits—on a peninsula whose inhabitants preferred bicycles as a means of transportation and who stared at outsiders.
When the long since obsolete particle accelerator, now ripe for demolition,
had been built, the institute had enlivened local conversation. After local
women were hired as lab assistants and reported that the physicists worked
with scissors and watched films, the physicists counted as insiders. Vera Hill
brought the research center into disrepute again. Stragglers from a town
council meeting who found themselves in the local tavern one spring evening resolved at a late hour to deliver a written complaint to the director of
the institute. He presided in a small, neo-Gothic brick building, formerly
a chocolate factory. As the delegation to deliver the paper was about to
pass through the entrance, the gatekeeper flung open the gatehouse window without a word. To Vera Hill he was accustomed on such occasions to
saying "Good morning, Frau Doktor." The two male delegates were asked
for their identification papers. The gatekeeper called the director's secretary
on the phone and read the personal information on those seeking admit-
tance. Later he wrote out two passes with carbon copies, handed the men
the documents with a suspicious look, and pressed a button that caused a
buzzing sound and opened the iron gate that secured the entrance to the
brick administration building. The delegates' feet trod the patterned floors
of the corridor and vestibule, which were tiled like old butcher shops. Professor Gurnemann's office had a hardwood floor. He received the delegation
in traditional costume. Fashionable orthodox physicists at that time were
wearing their white lab coats long; the others, extremists, wore short ones
with slit side seams. Gurnemann, wearing a shortened but unslit lab coat,
strode in three steps down the passage between his desk and bookcase.
These furnishings, as well as the chairs which had to be offered immediately to the guests for lack of space, had clawed feet. Brass. When the two
men alluded verbally to the scandalous occurrences and presented him the

written charges, the professor said: "In investigating the structure of matter, it is especially important to study the high-energy interaction between elementary particles. Here we are dealing with those excitations which are least perturbed by secondary effects and hence allow the deepest insight into an elemental process that actually takes place in nature. Although it is not yet possible to attain the high energy levels of cosmic radiation with artificial particle accelerators, the artificially accelerated or produced particles are preferable for use in these experiments to those produced by cosmic radiation, since their natural and initial energies are unambiguously identifiable." Gurnemann stopped; his suspicion that the institute, since the giant oaks next to the new addition had been felled, was again being accused of producing atomic bombs, proved erroneous. Regrettably, the absurdity of the latest rumor seemed to exceed by far that of the earlier one, causing Gurnemann to assess the chances of refuting it as slight. In any case, it would require considerable effort to refute the claim that a female staff member of his institute was walking on air across town twice a day on weekdays. The abuse of scientific staff time for purposes alien to institutional goals incensed the professor. He did not smoke, occasionally drank wine until midnight, ideally, and then withdrew, regardless of the occasion. In general, he paid great attention to consistency. His institute conducted research from 7:35 A.M. to 4:45 P.M. five days a week. The delegation asked Gurnemann to devote special attention to the section of the document describing the role of this apparition as a threat to public morality. Gurnemann thought of the two-room apartment that Dr. Hill occupied with her son. The son was three years old, the apartment furnished with two beds, a table, three chairs, a wardrobe, a rug, and bookshelves. Walls not papered with a printed pattern but palpably of stone. Whitewashed originally, since then turned gray beneath the dust which the wind still blew in through the window cracks from the nearby gasworks and which the heat of the stove lifted to the ceiling. Vera Hill seemed not to mind. Gurnemann knew a gifted Hungarian physicist who attended international conferences with a paper bag in which he kept toothbrush and pajamas. At any rate, Gurnemann considered the charge of walking on air ridiculously slanderous. The ability to speak while reading, acquired in the course of his tenure as director, was once again of benefit to him. He had large eyes, with a conspicuously wide space between them, behind bifocal lenses. As he read through the lower lenses, he spoke: "Since the study of the structure of particles is carried out essentially by means of scattering experiments, we must also know the exact nature of the particle emitted. Thus the hydrogen bubble chamber which contains only protons as scattering centers is the best-suited detector of particles and particle tracks in scattering experiments. The disadvantage in the fact that neutral particles leave no tracks, and that the mean free path of the gamma quanta in liquid hydrogen is very great, is more than compensated by the fact that the hydrogen bubble chamber allows measurements of extraordinary precision. Thus, one can infer the existence of neutral particles by violation of the momentum and energy balance of all charged particles. The most favorable initial energies of the incident particles lie in the range 3 to 15 GeV. Only here are measurements still precise enough; second, it is possible to produce kinematically all recently discovered particles or particle resonances of interest." The amount of written material spread out before Gurnemann—among other things citing charges of disorderly conduct, of posing a threat to public health and [materialist] ideology, causing power blackouts due to short circuits, endangering youth, and creating a traffic hazard—required so much of the professor's attention that despite having gained time by talking, he had not yet thought of a convincing argument. This annoyed him and softened his judgment of brothers in the profession who refused to employ female scientists. Perceiving that the delegates' faces were contorted with respect and suspicion, he continued: "Frau Doktor Hill's department is studying films of the interaction between positive pi-mesons with 4 GeV energy in hydrogen bubble chambers. Currently she is dealing with two-armed events. First, she calculates the geometry on the computer. Then the events are studied for completeness with the help of a probability test, using the so-called Fit-Program. In this way the elastic interactions can be distinguished from the inelastic ones. In the cases where only one neutral particle is present along with the charged particles in the final state, we can determine the nature and characteristics of these particles. In this way the cross sections of the channels with two charged particles can be determined. In addition, the individual reaction channels are studied in detail, especially with regard to the excitation of mesons by nucleons in the different channels." Professor Gurnemann could no longer resist the charm of these detailed claims and pursed his handsome lips. While he did refrain from whistling through them, instead doing so through his teeth, he nevertheless ordered the secretary to bring coffee—although he was already in an excited state from the absurd report, because it was logical in and of itself and hence not lacking in a certain elegance. What pleased him most was the supernatural aspect of the alleged phenomenon. Involuntarily, Gurnemann remembered Vera Hill's mouth, the full, arched lips threaded with make-up in their creases; the skin looked puckered. A couple belonging to a sect had believed this woman to be the Holy Mother and interpreted her presence as a sign of the town's divine election to be spared in the event of a nuclear holocaust. But even those complainants who protested against disturbance of the peace and violation of privacy, blaming Vera Hill for possible or real glances into their windows and balconies—as well as the defenders of morality, traffic safety, and dialectical materialism— all the undersigned testified unanimously that Vera Hill crossed town twice each workday, namely at approximately 6:15 A.M. and 6:00 P.M., traveling southwest and northeast, respectively, walking on air. Statements regarding height and speed of movement differed. An orchard owner claimed in her damage suit that Vera Hill had knocked down yellow plums and broken branches of sweet cherry trees with her briefcase. Likewise, a short circuit at 5:50 P.M. on the third day of Christmas, which had caused a blackout of more than two hours, was blamed on Vera Hill. The tavernkeeper found exposure to the sight of black lace nylon underwear and garters intolerable for morally sensitive citizens and children. Gurnemann thought tenderly of long legs and slender thighs, put the document in a file folder, had coffee served to the visitors, and, rubbing his hands, promised he would investigate the matter. Sipping the foam of his coffee, he asked if he might keep the paper. The delegates reminded him of the list of recipients attached to the complaint; his institute was one of seven named. Then the professor dismissed the men with a handshake. Shaken, for he feared he would not get approval of the hard currency he had requested in order to purchase an English computer. Without it, his institute would not be internationally competitive. The computer building was planned, its funding secured, and the oaks had been cut down; Gurnemann left his coffee, threw his overcoat over his white lab coat, crossed the courtyard with long strides, and kicked open the door of the institute building. It smelled of charred condensers. The laboratory, workshops, library, and mainframe computer were on the ground floor, the experimental physicists' cubicles on the second floor. Each cubicle had a blackboard with a chalk tray and sponge; a desk with scissors, ruler, and protractor hanging up on one side; a chair, bookcase, coathooks; a typed inventory of equipment and furnishings in a clear plastic cover; a rectangular window, the lower half of frosted glass; a blue floor covering, two meters by four meters forty-six; and a door that distinguished itself from the others by its color, each as unique as the entry hole markers on beehives. Ms. Hill was assigned a cubicle behind a pale green door. The door was locked. Gurnemann knocked with both palms, assuming that Vera Hill had earphones on and a tape recorder running, a machine she characterized as an instrument of perception, since, as she put it, true learning and true music are rooted in the same thought process. To be sure, Gurnemann did not deny a poetic element to scientific thinking, but he did not think Hill any more gifted than himself, because neither could get along without the assistance of sensory constructs, which is why he insisted on discipline and chalked his initial on the still locked door. The laboratory workers felt this form of reproach an insult to their honor. On the third floor, where theoreticians had their studies, the corridors were decorated with portraits of the saints: Copernicus, Galileo, Giordano Bruno, Newton, Cavendish, Coulomb, Ampère, Galois, Gauss, Minkowski, Maxwell, Planck, and Einstein. In response to Gurnemann's inquiry, the theoreticians Hinrich and Wander informed him that Dr. Hill had received a call from the kindergarten and had left the institute about an hour before, the son apparently having gotten sick or something. Gurnemann, himself a father of small children, wavered between principle and compassion when he asked, as a joke, by which means she had left. "By air," replied the theoreticians. For a short while Gurnemann doubted his sanity. Although he was steeled against such things by now—the head of the mathematical engineering section was a fanatic hangglider, an electronics specialist had married his fiancée's mother, there were two sleepwalkers among the second floor theoreticians—airwalking was something he had not yet been faced with. And he was as convinced as ever that it was a figment of the imagination. A malicious invention, he had felt recently, that could—or was even intended to—harm the reputation of science in general and his institute in particular. Obviously, his research team had been infiltrated, and their materialist method was being undermined by mystical teachings without his having been informed of such scandalous developments. Was he being excluded from the institutional grapevine because of his position? Were staff scientists posing as sect followers in order to ruin him ideologically? Or, it was possible he was being double-crossed. Intentionally or not, for the same reason. Plagued by dark premonitions, Gurnemann withdrew to the villa located on the grounds of the institute which served as the director's residence. He spent the rest of the day there in front of the television set. Late that night it came to him that the rumor was Hill's plot to take revenge on him, and he swore he would henceforth refrain from extramarital intimacy. He awoke in the morning with a headache but in a mellower mood, for he had realized again with pleasure that Hill was one of those rare women who did not want to be taken in marriage. He also respected her manic working style and her habit of not forcing conclusions but of letting them evolve. Filled with confidence that the confusion would take care of itself, as it were, in some rational, natural way, Gurnemann set out once again, after a hearty breakfast, to Vera Hill's office, where, much to his delight, he actually found her. He offered greetings. Holding her hand in his, he felt his concern to be absurd, whereupon he became embarrassed and inquired about her son's health and the progress of her postdoctoral research. The information was encouraging. And concisely delivered; if Gurnemann had not been asked abruptly about the real reason for his coming, he would have kept quiet about it. He named the reason in a subordinate clause; the main clause was a compliment. Vera Hill brushed back her bangs by running both index fingers over her eyebrows from the center outward. Even under normal circumstances it seemed to be an effort for her to close her mouth, although her bite was normal. Gurnemann suspected, too, that she always had something in her cheek, at the very least on her tongue. He therefore took the precaution of apologizing for the silliness of the allegation, which obviously neither he nor any other sensible person had believed even for a moment. "Why?" asked Vera Hill. Gurnemann requested her practical assistance in disposing of the matter as soon as possible. An institute like his, he explained, was so financially vulnerable that any delay in the hard currency flow, even one caused by such absurdities, could inestimably diminish opportunities for scientific work. "The absurdities increase the opportunities for scientific work," said Vera Hill. "Of the competition," said Gurnemann. "Do you regard me as a competitor?" asked Hill. The question irked Gurnemann. Vera Hill saw it in his face, so she explained to him that without the timesaving shortcut on the tightrope, she would not be able to complete her postdoctoral study by the agreed date, since, unlike him, she did not have the services of a housewife or maid at her disposal. After work, when she had done the shopping, picked up her son from kindergarten, fixed supper, eaten, drawn pictures of cars and other items requested by her son, bathed him and tucked him in bed with a fairytale, also done dishes or laundry, or mended a hole or chopped wood, and had carried coal briquets up from the basement, then she was able, with the tightrope trick, to be back at her desk thinking about invariances by about 9:00 P.M. Without the trick, an hour later. Had to get up an hour earlier without the trick, too. After less than six hours of sleep, she explained, nothing useful occurred to her. Gurnemann spoke earnestly and at length with her about the unreality of this means of transportation. On the following day Vera Hill lost her balance on her way home. The lamplighter discovered her body, shattered on the lawn in front of the public library.

Translated by Nancy Lukens

Helga Königsdorf

Photo by Roger Melis, Berlin, courtesy of Aufbau Verlag.

Helga Königsdorf is unusual among the authors of this volume in having continued to pursue a career outside of literature. Born in Gera in 1938, Königsdorf studied physics at the universities of Jena and Berlin. After taking her degree in 1961, she joined the Institute for Higher Mathematics of the Academy of Sciences. She completed her Ph.D. in mathematics in 1963, became a full professor in 1974, and continued to research and publish as a mathematician under the name Bunke until 1990.

Königsdorf began writing fiction in the mid-1970s and published her first volume of short stories in 1979. It was followed by two more volumes of short stories, a novella, and in 1990 an epistolary novel based on authentic documents from the fascist period. In addition to her literary and scientific careers, Königsdorf became a political figure in the winter of 1989–90, appearing on countless talk shows and televised discussions and writing political commentary for the major journals. A collection of her letters and essays and a volume of interviews were published in 1990.

The following story is taken from her 1982 anthology *Der Lauf der Dinge*.

Meine ungehörigen Träume (My inappropriate dreams). Berlin/Weimar: Aufbau, 1979.

Der Lauf der Dinge (The progress of life). Berlin/Weimar: Aufbau, 1982.

Respektloser Umgang (Bad company). Berlin/Weimar: Aufbau, 1986.

Lichtverhältnisse (Light conditions). Berlin/Weimar: Aufbau, 1988.

Ungelegener Befund (Inconvenient findings). Berlin/Weimar: Aufbau, 1990.

1989 oder Ein Moment Schönheit (1989, or A moment of beauty). Berlin/Weimar: Aufbau, 1990.

Adieu DDR (Goodbye GDR). Reinbek bei Hamburg: Rowohlt, 1990.

Gleich neben Afrika (Right next to Africa). Reinbek bei Hamburg: Rowohlt, 1992.

The Surefire Tip   (1982)

IN MATHEMATICAL DEFINITIONS, emotions are irrelevant. Results are crucial. Thus, the probability of a random event is described by numbers between zero and one, regardless of whether we would have preferred a more optimistic expression of our chances of a stroke of luck, as .99, for example.

Otherwise, mathematicians behave more or less like everyone else. When His Eminence reached the point "Other" on the agenda, the feelings of the gathered section heads of the Mathematical Institute were in no way different from the feelings that participants in meetings invariably experience when the point "Other" has been reached.

It was once again time, said His Eminence, to take stock at the Center and determine whether results had been achieved which could be recommended for the Karl-Egon-Kuller prize. Of course, very strict standards would have to be applied, for the Center could not risk an embarrassment. Only truly outstanding achievements would be considered. His Eminence reserved for himself the judgment of what constituted outstanding. He didn't need to emphasize this. They all knew it.

If it had been up to His Eminence, the whole presentation of prizes would never have taken place. There were always numerous difficulties with the winners afterward, because they inevitably believed that they were in fact outstanding, for a while. It took an effort to reestablish order and to bring those recently lauded back down to solid ground. But His Eminence did not have his way on this question, and it was about time to produce another prizewinner; otherwise, rumors suggesting a lack of productivity at the Center would not fail to materialize.

In this case, the choice was nearly unavoidable, and her name was: Dr. Cornelia Froehlich. Froehlich, a probability theorist, was about to receive an appointment in K., where she wanted to move to join her husband, a biologist. Dr. Froehlich had essentially reached the end of her career path at the Center, His Eminence had said earlier. New discoveries of fundamental importance were hardly to be expected of her. But he valued her highly as a dedicated, reliable worker. A post at a small university was just the right thing.

The choice really was inevitable. His Eminence drummed his fingers on the tabletop with satisfaction. An institution that produced a prizewinner didn't look bad. Imagine how much better an institution that could afford to give a prizewinner to someone else would look. He decided to ask his academic secretary to prepare an evaluation of Froehlich. Multipurpose. It was fine to lay it on thick.

After the meeting His Eminence bumped into the editor of *Aha*, the popular science television series, in the hallway and wondered irritably why this person was still snooping around the building. Considerable time had passed since the first point on the agenda, which had concerned cooperation between the TV series and the Institute. He felt a deep dislike for the editor.

PR is part of the business, and not just his. That was how the editor had begun his remarks. But he wasn't about to let them bore people with mathematical facts. His show had a reputation to protect. He was thinking of a lot of music, a little fashion, the TV dance troupe, and in between the achievements of "our scientists"—preferably with domestic economic applications. And at the end the viewers must have discovered that mathematicians are just the same as ordinary people. Thus the "aha" effect. So to speak.

Thoroughly embarrassing, thought His Eminence. But one really couldn't leave beating the drums of publicity entirely to the other branches of industry. And besides, just as everywhere else, there were people at the Center who enjoyed the limelight. One could let them. It certainly would not reap them any recognition in serious scientific circles.

Cornelia Froehlich did not belong to this group. Her name was the result of an expedition which, much to the disapproval of His Eminence, the editor had undertaken through the Center.

In the small meeting room at Studio C, the editor was explaining the mathematicians' ideas. They want to ruin us, groaned the producer.

We can hardly do "Preschool Sexuality" again, the editor replied. And there was this woman. Women and mathematics—it had just that little twist of perversity that the show needed.

That, however, assumed a minimum of sexiness, commented the cameraman skeptically.

Did they think he was a beginner? He had taken a close look at the lady. Naturally, she was no debutante. But makeup. One should never underestimate makeup.

The editor's assistant already had a title for the show: "Is There a Surefire Tip? The famous probability theorist, Dr. Cornelia Froehlich, calculates your chances." The editor once again congratulated himself on his choice of assistants.

When the name Froehlich appeared in this connection on His Eminence's desk for the addition of his "approved," he experienced a distinct twinge of annoyance without, however, reflecting on its cause.

Things moved right along. The assistant not only had what it took to come up with a catchy title but also wrote a lively script. Kiddies, do me one favor, said the editor, who really wasn't a beginner, leave the state lottery out of it. Whereupon Cornelia and the assistant invented a game that you practically always won. The probability of winning is .99, said Dr. Froehlich on camera.

Now there are editorial offices which, lacking ideas of their own, rely on attaching themselves to the ideas of others. When filming was in full swing, a reporter from a well-known magazine visited Studio C and heard about the "photogenic little mathematician." Soon thereafter a multipage photo-essay on Cornelia Froehlich had been planned for the magazine. In a short interview, the reporter asked His Eminence to praise Cornelia's achievements in language accessible to the general public. His Eminence was now seriously annoyed, and his remarks emerged accordingly lukewarm. With only a little cutting and pasting, a minor heroic epic emerged from the manuscript, which His Eminence had specifically requested be submitted for approval.

His Eminence had this manuscript and the listing for the *Aha* show, which was featured prominently in the TV program, lying on the desk in front of him. He was thinking. Of course, anyone with any experience knew how this sort of article was produced. Nevertheless, these tabloids did have their effect.

What exactly were Froehlich's special achievements, thought His Eminence. The longer he brooded, the more clearly he realized that he had fallen victim to an error in judgment. Things like this might happen to other people. He, however, was man enough to take the consequences of his insight. He placed a call to the chairman of the prize committee and asked whether he could still withdraw his nomination without causing a major sensation. It was possible.

The TV program's advertisement for "Is There a Surefire Tip?" lay not only on His Eminence's desk but on the desk of a department head at the Ministry of Finance as well. At whose direction an assistant at the Ministry called an assistant at the television station. The Ministry very much hoped that there would be no difficulties with the program. The giant New Year's raffle was next on the agenda, and the television planners should take a look at their latest ratings.

When the editor found this news on his desk, he had a screaming fit. He wasn't about to let anybody tell him what to do. That would be just terrific. Just because somebody sneezed somewhere, they didn't all have to run for cover. He screamed and howled, pounded his fist on the table, and clearly realized: it was all for show. The director and the cameraman knew it too. And the editor knew that they knew. But that didn't spoil it. It was a good performance. The only disturbing thing was his assistant's admiring gaze. Which made him even more grateful when the director offered him a way out. Well, we could take a look at the ratings in any case, said the director.

That night the editor lay awake brooding. It was nothing. It was ridiculous. But how many people did he know who had been tripped up by something ridiculous. Two or three faces rose before his eyes. Puffed up, jealous, pompous asses. Ever ready to inflate some trifle into a major issue. And waiting in the wings, the ranks of the next generation. Still faceless. Without a public image. With clenched fists in their pockets. Innocent of the hardships of the early years. They want to move straight to the top. They can't wait for it. Objectively, they can't wait. Damned rotten age pyramid. By the time he retired, his assistant would be fifty. Could you expect him to wait that long? You couldn't. Suddenly, he had a completely different interpretation of his assistant's encouraging glance. At about 2:00 A.M. he swallowed his third sleeping pill.

Looking over the ratings the next day, the director said the colossal New Year's raffle could also be a colossal failure.

Exactly, responded the editor. And then they'll look for a scapegoat.

Then the game will be just the right thing, suggested the assistant. With such a fantastic probability of winning. If that's not advertising!

How high is it then? Asked the editor.

Point ninety-nine.

What, only point ninety-nine! Man, are you crazy! That's a surefire shot in the foot, not a surefire tip. Just to make it perfectly clear. If anybody around here gets to play scapegoat, it's me and not you. And I'd prefer to decide for myself whether I feel like doing it.

That evening the *Aha* program "Preschool Sexuality" was rebroadcast in response to repeated viewer requests. The editor did not see the program. He was in a state of total inebriation at the time.

The next morning he received a phone call from the editor-in-chief of the magazine, a college classmate. He could only stammer: What did he mean, what's wrong? They can kiss my . . . The two of us, you and I, we've both survived worse. "Worse" appeared to him at that moment in the form of reddish-green coils of fog in his brain and a choking nausea. He was incapable of providing further information and hung up.

Whereupon the editor-in-chief dropped the article on Dr. Cornelia Froehlich at the very last minute.

Naturally, Cornelia's colleagues also began to have their doubts.

The personnel director of the Mathematical Center was engaged in a long-standing feud with His Eminence, in the course of which his hair had visibly grayed. His Eminence didn't take his position seriously, made his work more difficult, and, in addition, accused him of incompetence. That was the situation, at least as the personnel director saw it. His Eminence saw the causality as flowing in the opposite direction. Each was ready to substantiate his version at a moment's notice in any given case.

In the case of Cornelia Froehlich, the personnel director accused His Eminence of having informed him neither of the fact that he had withdrawn his nomination nor of his reasons for doing so. His Eminence responded vaguely that anyone could make a mistake. But the personnel director, as usual, hadn't been listening to people. It had to make you wonder, the way Froehlich had suddenly been pulled back out of the limelight. Say what you want, there had to be something behind it.

His Eminence said all this to his administrative assistant as well. Who had a long chat with the economic director. The economic director saw the head of the Central Supply Office at a meeting. He, in turn, usually had lunch with the head of the Information and Documentation Department. Who had a consultation with the deputy director after lunch.

The deputy director saw it as his duty to report to His Eminence. Which went more or less as follows: Froehlich had caused a huge scandal at the television studio. There had been a session at the highest level. It was being hushed up.

His Eminence was not surprised. He had suspected something along those lines. He canceled Froehlich's planned trip abroad with the comment that it was no longer appropriate.

The personnel director, who couldn't allow the accusation of being poorly informed to rest, carried out a thorough investigation, which contributed not insignificantly to spreading the impression that something was wrong with Froehlich. Finally, he betook himself to His Eminence and informed him that there was no evidence against Froehlich. Who growled: I already know—and brusquely dismissed the personnel director.

The rumor about the withdrawn Karl-Egon-Kuller prize nomination also reached the dean of the university in K., who took another look at the two evaluations he had requested to support Froehlich's appointment. The first one, written by a colleague at the Technical University, was fairly noncommittal. The second, on the other hand, signed by His Eminence, went a bit overboard. Attempting to make sense of these facts, the dean arrived at the conclusion that this was a textbook example of praising someone out the door. He decided to cover himself by requesting a third evaluation. He found it quite convenient to miss the deadline, delaying Froehlich's appointment for a year. The dean informed the biologist Froehlich. A few problems had arisen at the Center which needed to be cleared up.

Whereupon the biologist appeared in His Eminence's office and demanded information. His Eminence responded with a long, foggy exposition about troubled relationships of personal trust in general and in particular, about staff members who failed to find the path to their superiors, about rifts that extended even into marriages; he dismissed the biologist more confused than comforted. Six months later Cornelia Froehlich's marriage ended in divorce.

The insolence with which the woman tried to act as if nothing had happened convinced even the last holdouts that she was a shameless hussy. Not only that, she positively blossomed. And without any makeup. It was rumored that she was living with the assistant from the *Aha* show, who in the meantime had become the editor. The problem of the deformed age pyramid, which had tormented his predecessor with sleepless nights, had in this instance been solved by a heart attack.

In any case, Froehlich showed no further inclination to accept the appointment in K. Whenever she crossed His Eminence's path, happy and carefree, he thought bitterly that the labor laws gave him absolutely no legal means of proceeding against her in the manner she deserved.

Translated by Dorothy Rosenberg

Rosemarie Zeplin

Born in 1939 in Mecklenburg, Rosemarie Zeplin grew up in north-eastern Germany. Following high school, she studied drama in Leipzig and, after finishing her degree, worked as a producer for the city theater of Eisleben in 1961–62. She then moved to Berlin, where she worked in the drama section of the state radio service. In 1967 Zeplin moved into the area of information science, first in a large trade organization and after 1970 at the Humboldt University. She has been an independent writer since 1978.

This selection is excerpted from her novella, "Schattenriß eines Liebhabers," published in the anthology of the same name.

Schattenriß eines Liebhabers (The shadow of a lover). Berlin/Weimar: Aufbau, 1980.

Alpträume aus der Provinz (Nightmares from the provinces). Berlin/Weimar: Aufbau, 1984.

Der Maulwurf oder Fatales Beispiel weiblicher Gradlinigkeit (The mole, or A fatal example of female consistency). Berlin/Weimar: Aufbau, 1990.

The Shadow of a Lover   (1980)

1.

PILGRAM AND ANNETTE could trace the beginning of their love back to a specific day. They frequently talked about it and reminded each other of all the details. This day remained an inexhaustible topic for some time, even though the facts had been established the first time they discussed it—by Pilgram, naturally, the final authority for the judging and naming of things. They had been beside themselves, he had concluded, satisfied to have now understood this expression in its essential meaning. It certainly was true that both of them—having slipped out of their customary self-control—had operated in a condition of limited self-awareness. What had happened, though it demanded an explanation, could not be credibly subjected to analysis because, as Pilgram concluded, it had been a miracle, and miracles cannot be explained.

Annette, in her inarticulateness, had no version of her own with which to counter. She was convinced that Pilgram was better able to judge these things. Of course, she could have contributed a few inessential and probably petty details, and did once try to, but realized that her additions were superfluous to Pilgram's clear and compelling vision. She didn't even challenge the premonition that Pilgram claimed to have had on that morning, January 20, 1967. Although she did at first object to his attributing one to her as well, in the end she did not insist. It didn't really matter. Had she not, unusually enough, had a very clear recollection of her own impressions during those hours, she would hardly have been able to resist the temptation of letting him convince her.

What she felt had in fact been panic, because an examination awaited her at 11:30 A.M.—the panic of someone hopelessly unobsessed by the science in question, with only a limited capacity for diligence, ungraced by any particular brilliance, but unable to withstand the urge to fulfill obligations. The fact that her fear remained within tolerable limits was due to Annette's lack of ambition and to a sense of fairness that helped her to accept the examination, in her heart of hearts, as an atonement for years of neglect. Contrary to all logic, she drew hope from this act of submission. Integrating herself circumspectly into the course of the inevitable, she had survived examinations unscathed until now, and the approaching one threatened no more than the ordinary dangers.

In the alphabetically ordered sequence of names, Annette was among the last of the seminar's examinees, and she had made extensive inquiries during the past few days among those who preceded her. She had listened, attentively and sympathetically, to the graphic descriptions of survivors relieving themselves of the terrors from which they had been released. Each vicariously experienced panic reduced Annette's own by the degree to which she was able to identify with it. She also knew that practicing answers to the questions passed along to her was a good method of furnishing the seas of her insecurity with islands and passable fords.

Premonitions, as Pilgram understood them, had been out of the question simply because Annette had concentrated all her mental and emotional capacities on a procedure which, when she later tried to explain this kind of meditative closing to Pilgram, she called centering. She did not mention that the utmost attention to her outward appearance was also a part of this process. How should she allay the suspicion that she decorated herself because she thought that looking pretty was advantageous in this situation? She found this belief, widespread among girls, to be ridiculous, fallacious, and inconsistent with her own observations. She did more than make herself up: she fully attuned herself to the approaching event and retouched her physical appearance according to her deepest intuition. The results of this process were quite possibly not even visible to others. For her, however, it was fruitful and stimulating because it channeled her diffuse energy reassuringly.

Annette still hadn't recovered from the shock with which she had entered puberty: the shock of what she looked like. It had hit her in pieces over the course of weeks, every day if she wanted, in any case as often as she saw her face in a mirror. A sight that was alien to her and almost unbearable—its discovery had ended her childhood sleep of peaceful ignorance. Her much older sister took the thirteen-year-old's long motionless lingering in front of the mirror for undue vanity, and her teasing reinforced Annette's suspicion that flaws which she herself could not yet recognize must be visible in her appearance, at least in the appearance reported to her by the mirror. Identifying these flaws was Annette's responsibility alone. Other, invisible defects did not seem so bad to her; they could be reserved for later treatment.

So if Annette concerned herself with her outward appearance, she did so in order to clothe her face, to darken the mirror through which anyone who knew how could penetrate her being. Nothing was better suited to cover this nakedness than beauty, which Annette wanted to surround her like a smooth, opaque shell which betrayed no later intervention and no previous effort—which, instead of attracting, would arouse disinterested neutrality in the observer.

On that morning there was no room for premonitions in her exalted concentration, nor, even if she had allowed her thoughts to stray from the problems of accounting and statistics while pinning her hair into an ostensibly severe bun at the back of her head, would they ever have arrived at Pilgram. Even as she stood by the bulletin board in the hallway, before what was later called "our meeting" took place, she certainly was not thinking of him. She had no idea who, in fact, was coming out of the rector's office and walking toward her, beaming and elegant, a public figure of university life at his side in whom Annette recognized the famous Professor Schwarzenberg. It took her breath away for a moment when this figure of dread was led directly toward her (and appeared to be no less irritated by this than she was).

Pilgram took Annette's hand and said—a little hoarsely: Hello.

Still holding her hand, he turned candidly toward his companion.

We know each other! he cried to Schwarzenberg, who had made no attempt to introduce the two in any case. Instead, he stared at Annette and appeared to be waiting only for the moment when he could continue undisturbed his guiding, indeed loving care of Pilgram.

The progress of this little scene was facilitated by additional participants. Annette's examiners, on their way to lunch, were energetically beckoned over by Schwarzenberg and replied eagerly to his: Well? with: We're in the middle of examinations!

They laughed and sighed and shook hands with Schwarzenberg (not with Pilgram, because his hand was still not free) and said again: We're still testing!

Well, said Schwarzenberg, and how does it look?

Now the examiners could also introduce themselves to Pilgram, whom they had been observing with great curiosity from the side or the rear. They murmured their names and allowed themselves to be contemplated from his superior physical height.

So, you are giving examinations, he inquired weightily, the way one speaks to children when one wishes to please their parents, but then immediately turned back to Annette as if that were enough small talk.

Were you also tested? he asked.

His look of amused disbelief as he said it was such that they all suddenly agreed that being tested was a great joke. They smiled, and the head examiner said something that did not penetrate the roaring in Annette's ears.

Congratulations, said Pilgram to Annette formally. I'm pleased! I'm really very pleased.

Even Schwarzenberg pulled himself together and congratulated her for successfully passing the examination, while Pilgram didn't let her out of his sight—smiling, with his arms folded, his head cocked mockingly a bit to the side. Before more of this could make unnecessary demands on his patience, he made a general announcement: Miss Warning was my apprentice. She did an excellent job, didn't you?

He did not, however, demand that Annette confirm his judgment; instead, he informed Schwarzenberg that he had enjoyed the visit, thanked him especially for his constructive suggestions, and assured him that they would hear from one another.

When? he concluded.

Schwarzenberg then had to think quickly and carefully, since he too had an appointment book and did not have it all in his head. A little, very harmonious negotiation was required before Pilgram, who kept glancing quickly at Annette, had managed to complete the farewell ceremony and to assure himself that Schwarzenberg was headed off to lunch in the company of the examiners.

Still within earshot of the obediently departing group, he said to Annette: The two of us are through here now, aren't we?

He touched her arm, a small symbolic gesture of support demonstrating that he had now assumed responsibility for her welfare. On the way to the parking lot he said: We'll eat in the city, shall we? Or do you know a place out here where one can eat?

Those were just about the last words that Annette could later vouch for having heard exactly. Later ones, including her own, danced back and forth between them, sounds free of meaning. Reception and transmission proceeded according to rules which, innocently unconscious, were directed by a simple principle. Unobserved for the seconds of their brief purposeful existence, they also remained undistorted. Annette, for whom words and their auras possessed a deeper attraction than any other sensory experience, found the loss of these midday and afternoon hours painful. Whether she wanted to or not, she had to be satisfied with Pilgram's summary, who decreed the language to be used for these events in a rarified exalted atmosphere: We had fallen in love. He said it, to be sure, like someone who had believed himself incapable of ever experiencing the power of these worn-out words directly. He enjoyed this act of nature again in retrospect by calling it by its name over and over, thus accustoming himself to the idea that it was perfectly possible in the normal course of events to fall in love. Falling in love, to be sure, then meant completing an activity that included the approach toward a goal and the assurance of reaching it: love. He had fallen in love, light as a feather and without resistance. Astonished and delighted, he made himself at home in it.

Naturally, a few of the most important pieces of information were also exchanged on this first day. One hardly knew where to begin, and Annette, in particular, had no idea how. She didn't even know his name, while he knew hers—a piece of knowledge with which he had just been able to lay claim to her so convincingly. Pilgram had the chief examiner to thank, who always spoke in complete sentences, particularly when he was announcing something as important as an examination grade and who, as a polite person, would never refer to someone who was present with a third-person singular pronoun. That was the explanation. Pilgram did not deny it in the end, although he didn't explicitly admit it either. The presence of mind with which he could listen was astonishing enough.

That she had been his apprentice was actually as good as a lie, although Annette really had completed an apprenticeship the year before and during that time had in fact once spoken with him. She and Doris Pruetting, another student, were diligently researching the market demand projections for quartz oscillator production. As a sideline they also concerned themselves with how they could escape from the Planning Section trailer now and then. Doris was the more resourceful. The excursion to the administration office, where they had to clear up a few questions, was one of her most productive ideas. There, in the receptionists' offices, the girls plagued a series of irritable people, one after the other, in search of someone available to consult with until Pilgram suddenly appeared. The receptionist, having already been repeatedly interrupted, was about to break off Doris's stream of words for Pilgram's benefit when he stopped her. He indicated agreement with the request presented and took the girls with him into even more remote chambers whose interior breathed soothing graciousness and contained a much prettier secretary. Her name was Ingeborg, as became clear when Pilgram gently requested that she see about some coffee.

After this audience, when Doris and Annette turned in their passes to the concierge and set out for home—before quitting time—they actually had to regard their mission as a failure (they later left the entire role of the laws of economics out of their extensive written report, because they had not learned anything useful about it).

Since it wasn't worth going back to work again, they talked about what they could do with the rest of the day.

Wasn't he great? said Doris.

She was obviously referring to Pilgram, charming and confidential, and the things he had revealed to them. (To you, the next generation, for you will, after all, assume this position someday, won't you?) He had let Doris babble on but actually answered only Annette, when she occasionally threw in a question, answered insofar as he made unconventional and witty references to things too familiar to him to be worth taking the trouble to explain them: that is, insofar as this incomprehensible extemporizing could be called answers at all. Annette also took pains with the impression she was making, with even greater effort than Doris, who made it very easy for her—to her subsequent shame—because all she had to do was provide a contrast to Doris's determined simplemindedness. She won this dubious competition against an unsuspecting innocent, and on the way home she wanted only to blot out the memory of it.

Terribly arrogant, she said, and was even more annoyed with herself as she, opportunistically repentant, offered Doris this beloved epithet. Doris, however, insisted that she thought it was great, what he had said.

They also realized that they had failed to read the nameplates on the doors on the way out. They had talked to a very high-level manager, in any case, and they had no use for what he'd said anyway.

Annette had fifteen minutes to relive these events, because Pilgram—after enjoying a noble aperitif—had to make a telephone call.

The wonder of these hours, by the way, would have been unthinkable without the incredible effortlessness of the external arrangements that surrounded Pilgram and Annette. (Annette, for example, had never before experienced having only to look up inquiringly for her wishes to be immediately ascertained.) They ate in a small room, the back courtyard extension of a once elegant restaurant the front rooms of which, along with the magnificent hotel facade, had been bombed away. Annette, in her ignorance of the history of the city, had never heard of the existence of this establishment. It seemed to her as if the world had forgotten it, especially because as long as they came here, no matter how often, Pilgram was never disturbed by anyone who knew him. Only solemn headwaiters observed their love with averted eyes. About half an hour after Pilgram's telephone call, the one who was serving them that day bent down toward the couple and informed Pilgram—clearly emphasizing the title preceding his name—that he was wanted on the telephone.

Annette heard this name in astonished disbelief; to her it stood—only as a name, of course—for an entire discipline (and a certain order of magnitude for the names of disciplines per se); in any case, it was something of a byword.

When Pilgram came back, he said: That was Ingeborg. I told her to go home. What have you decided on?

Pilgram took a small case out of his suit jacket, removed a pair of glasses and read the menu, quickly and decisively folded the glasses together again, and said: Are you engaged?

He lit a cigarette at the same time to avoid watching Annette as she labored at an answer.

No, said Annette (fortunately, she wasn't engaged), and you?

He had to laugh out loud, swallowed smoke and, snorting with laughter, coughed up the smoke again with tears in his eyes and responded: No, my child. At my age one is married.

A piece of information that Annette did not understand until the next day. She had, in fact, been thinking of Ingeborg—Ingeborg, his secretary at the headquarters office and still his secretary, although he had long since left and was now at the Ministry. Not directly in the Ministry but on a Commission (or Working Group, as she later noted, and attached to the Council of Ministers, to be precise)—but that was only temporary, an assignment that could not be refused, nevertheless not permanent. Not permanent and not for much longer! With these words he raised the second noble brandy and then willingly explained to Annette why this certainty was so gratifying. Namely, after completing this assignment he would be given The Journal; that had been approved, a firm promise.

They can't go back on it, even if it doesn't suit some people!

While Annette suppressed perfidious questions about Ingeborg, Pilgram continued on about The Journal.

You passed an important examination today, with honors (honors wasn't quite true), but I achieved an important result too, he concluded with some emotion. They were more than a little surprised at your Institute. They didn't expect it, those . . . !

He kept the insult to himself, although Annette was now wide awake and would have given anything to have known what was going on with whom at the Institute.

Schwarzenberg? she asked, her curiosity piqued.

Oh—him, said Pilgram (by now the third round of aperitifs had been delivered by the industrious headwaiter). He's just afraid, isn't he?

That Schwarzenberg could be afraid, just afraid, thoroughly delighted Annette. She laughed—not at Schwarzenberg. She felt infected by a freedom, light as a feather and completely secure. Without being shocked, she heard her own laughter, in which Pilgram joined, and she laughed until she had to wipe the tears from her eyes with her finger, and Pilgram took her hand and put her finger to his lips.

That was the only physical contact he allowed himself that day. During the short ride through the early evening crowds in the streets, silent and unapproachable, he controlled the tension between them. He followed Annette's sometimes impossible directions, which kept leading the wrong way down one-way streets (a characteristic of streets that Annette had never noticed before). He calmly said: That's not possible! when Annette, excited, suppressing a tremor in her voice, tried to tell him: Now left! He got out with her so that she could show him the window of her room, looked around carefully, indicated a slight bow, and withdrew to his automobile. He waved to her once more, quite unbelievably conventional, before he roared off and disappeared.

2.

What followed obeyed the laws of the progress of such events in the greatest imaginable compression. The collapsing of necessary phases to barely a week was Pilgram's achievement, directed by experience, concentrated observation, and discipline. It exhausted his entire capacity for feverish activity. And it had to be seen as a joint achievement—not merely a one-sided responsibility—because everything he did was complemented by Annette's response, a reflection out of apparently pure passivity.

As confidently as Pilgram acted, Annette reacted. She had been prepared from birth for what was supposed to happen, for as long as she had nursed the anticipation of a real, not simply tolerable life as an incessant, powerful, ever more amorphous hope. Now, after all, she knew that she alone had been chosen to experience complete happiness. An army of reserves—transferred from tolerable daily existence—stood ready. Annette needed precisely as long as Pilgram artfully drew out what looked like a seduction to be completely sure that this happiness had arrived. How and in what stages of psychological process, however, Annette was later unable to clarify.

In fact, she later forgot nearly everything, the first week with Pilgram and the months that followed. Props that she tried to draw into the amorphous mass of pallid fragments of memory failed to give it clear contours. Annette possessed a few data, excerpts from Pilgram's appointment calendar (or formal abbreviations of diary entries), which he had woven into one of the letters that he had recently written her as a reminder and admonition. Six dates, including the first Friday afternoon ("12:30 P.M., Meeting at the Bulletin Board") all with the time, place, and a reference to the setting. The following Saturday was called "Breakfast with You" (that was when Pilgram had gotten Annette out of bed at nine-thirty in the morning, unpacked bags of food in her room, and cleaned the glasses from which champagne was to be drunk in the washbasin where Annette was brushing her teeth when their eyes met in the mirror and they forgot washing and brushing, but didn't kiss because the self-control of Pilgram the virtuoso conductor was more intense than the immediacy of the moment). "Meeting at the Woodmarket Bridge" was Monday; Tuesday, "Coffee in the Forest Cafe." Wednesday was missing and Thursday was called: "The Night we Searched for Your Key"—the blackest hole, which Annette could refill only with fragments of all the other nights, all the days, all the hours of these days and nights.

In between she had also lived, somehow. She went to the Institute and had to spend an incredible amount of time there. She must have cut everything imaginable (and therefore have been rushed and terrified) to have been able to keep the dates on Monday and Tuesday, and she had had to eat Sunday dinner at Wolfgang's parents' in Falkenhagen, a misery that was stored in her memory in precise detail, sharper and more permanent than the hours of ecstacy with Pilgram. Afterward—in a little room under the eaves with a view of a phosphate fertilizer factory surrounded by fir trees— she had managed to make clear to Wolfgang, to whom she was not engaged, the irrevocable end of what had been until then, had managed to rouse his ponderous mind with repeated declarations and give him the most necessary information. That guy! he cried, but immediately lowered his voice because his parents were taking their after-dinner nap in the next room. He turned the key in the door and made a futile attempt to rape Annette. His pain was greater than his rage. Annette was able to turn back the key without long-term obstruction and run back along the path to the subway in pure, free flight.

Two or three weeks later the semester was over. The old order dissolved itself in an interregnum, four months of freedom which could not be enjoyed because one had to return at the end with five copies of a dittoed, bound, or artfully stapled senior thesis. The old class schedule still applied but created only chaos and general, silent rebelliousness because it had already become pointless. The students still met but only to wait for the end—hectic, morose, isolated by the oppressive and seductive prospect of paths about to separate. They talked—if not about tests and theses, then about the housing bureau, driving school, and maternity counseling (not about jobs; those had been settled long ago). They arranged small wedding celebrations: whoever hadn't yet married now hurried to do so.

Annette, who had difficulty hearing and seeing, intervened tempestuously in the conversations, became unreasonably upset about a newly decreed examination format, participated in a colossal argument about how the graduation party was to be arranged. She used all available excuses as outlets for her exaltation. Attacks of frightening fatigue when she suddenly could hear nothing but her stubbornly, steadily beating heart were followed by a feverishly surging need for expression. Trembling with impatience, she sat through the last classes, crouched in the middle of the confused busyness in which the old school rhythm culminated before it stopped forever.

Then she disappeared from the order of the world—provided with a topic on which she was to write a senior thesis. She re-emerged in the summer, as June began with a heat wave. Not all at once. The awakening was the result not of any event but of its absence, the failure of an all-encompassing change to materialize. While she still lived in blessed certainty, Annette had known only that it would most definitely happen. It had never occurred to her that Pilgram could have saved her from having to punctually deliver her investigation of the process of production forecasting in the chemical industry to the reception room of the appropriate rector's office. Nor had blaming him for the inadequacy of this thesis, although it certainly would have been logical, since the hours available for her to apply to it were only the remnants of their daily-nightly embraces. In any case, Pilgram would not have been able to do anything about her finally having to turn in her room key to the Student Housing Office, and not only one, but two, because she had occupied a room in a rundown villa in the north of Berlin all by herself since January, even though it had been intended for two same-sex students or a married student couple. Her roommate, Lydia, had followed the pull of the times—marriage before taking the step into a hostile world—and moved in with her husband, more precisely into his parents' living room. Pilgram had had possession of the second key for three months and had forgotten to return it when he left for Yalta. And Annette, overcome on the last evening

by the thought that he (who had invariably spoken in the singular of the im-
manent annoyance of a stay on this overcrowded multinational peninsula)
would, of course, not be traveling alone, and thus forgot far more important
things than the key. And so, Annette took her leave in discord not only with
the Student Housing Office but also with her friend Lydia, whose departure
was thus discovered and reprimanded, because Lydia had concealed a free
dormitory space by failing to report it; her senior thesis adviser who, in a
surge of sympathy for his pallid advisee, only cried: Why didn't you come
in for a consultation! (which meant: Why didn't you ask, if you didn't know
something!); and Doris Pruetting, whom she had told one day on the way
to the subway what had happened to her. Doris knew Pilgram, after all, and
Annette at least had to try out the news on someone.

In my opinion, said Doris, whose name was no longer Pruetting (her
face was broad and swollen and covered with pale yellow blotches), I really
don't know if you've thought it over carefully.

It was said without thinking—in the heat and the clouds of dust and
exhaust-spewing traffic—more absently than unkindly, but its effect was
that Annette's sandal, which had an odd wobbly heel, got stuck in the soft
Karlshorst asphalt, right in the middle of the road. Annette fell on her hands
and knees, pulled herself up again, and, reaching the other side of the street
with one bare foot, burst into tears as a hot wave of pain from the blackened,
grimy scrape wounds reached her heart. Doris, who could bend over her
swollen abdomen only with difficulty, collected the objects that had flown
out of Annette's purse and retrieved the shoe as well. The surface wounds
hurt so badly that Annette did not notice the more modest signals from her
injured foot until a few hours later. It was swollen and blue and would not
allow itself to be moved. The next day it was put in a cast, following a five-
hour wait in the emergency clinic. Without ceremony, with one suitcase,
two duffle bags, a string net, and a cardboard carton, limping through un-
abated, unspeakable heat, she left the city which, with all its overwhelming
ugliness and excitement and its wall-torn deformity, she had loved with her
entire heart from the very first day.

Translated by Dorothy Rosenberg

Daniela Dahn

Photo by G. Linke, Berlin, courtesy of Aufbau Verlag.

Daniela Dahn was born in Berlin and grew up in Klein Machnow, a suburb of Berlin also known as an artists' colony. After finishing high school, she spent a year as an assistant in the state television studios before going on to study journalism. Dahn finished her degree in 1973 and returned to GDR television as an editor and reporter. She has been a freelance writer since 1983 and lives with her husband, also a writer, and their daughter in Berlin.

Dahn's first independent publication was a volume of essays in 1980. It was followed in 1987 by *Prenzlauer Berg-Tour*, an exploration of a traditional Berlin working-class district which enjoyed a renaissance as the center of East Berlin's "alternative culture" scene. Dahn used interviews, text, and pictures to approach both the history and the contemporary cultural mix of the district in a series of "expeditions." She has also written a number of radio plays and the film *Liane*, which was produced in 1989. As a freelance journalist, her work appeared regularly in major East German cultural and political journals. She was also actively involved in the political changes of the winter of 1989–90 as a member of the citizens' committee investigating police violence during the October 7, 1989, demonstrations.

In the title of the following essay, taken from the anthology *Spitzen-zeit*, Dahn plays on Goethe's concept of the "eternal feminine," a quality of innocent suffering and wisdom that "exalts us and leads us onward" (*Faust, Part Two*).

Spitzenzeit (Peak Time). Halle/Leipzig: Mitteldeutscher Verlag, 1980.

Prenzlauer Berg–Tour (Touring Prenzlau Hill). Halle/Leipzig: Mitteldeutscher Verlag, 1987.

The Contemporary Feminine   (1980)

ASKED which quality he most admired in women, Karl Marx confessed: weakness. In a man: strength.

Oddly enough, I have yet to hear an opponent of Marxism dismiss this opinion as thoroughly antiquated or use it to attack Marx. Perhaps this is due to the fact that these critics are always men. No matter how hard they search for weaknesses, even Marx can be accepted as an ally in the defense of masculine strength.

But why haven't at least a few emancipated women complained?

Probably because it's Marx. Or because no competent authority has yet determined what virtues ought to be admired today. Word has gotten around by now that emancipation doesn't mean turning into a man or doing away with difference. Only the "but" isn't quite clear yet. What, besides the fine points, is the actual difference? What of the *eternal* feminine still exalts us today and always will?

At the moment, motherhood alone hardly makes a complete woman. Of the three Cs, "Children, Cooking, and Church," the last has been replaced by "Culture." Equal demands are made at work, measured according to masculine production standards. No separate teams in this league, even if the winds of change are blowing for women. Except for one day off a month for housework, generously decreed by men because it clearly marks—her territory.

A wife today has to be pretty, clever, attractive, always agreeable, and never aggressive. At cultural events she reveals herself as socially adept, well read, witty, and always well informed. As a hostess, she entertains with housewifely expertise, shows pedagogical skill when displaying the children, and is charmingly amusing in conversation. On vacation it turns out that she is active, athletic, and—on top of everything else—in excellent shape. Visits to a spa are actually quite unnecessary, for of course she must be healthy. Emancipation, short and not sweet, has shifted the scale rather one-sidedly in the direction of higher performance: that is, more pressure, *strength*.

Well, what do you want, for heaven's sake? I can hear the men exclaiming. Do you want to quit working and go back to the kitchen? No. (Absolutely not, out of the question, we want to show what we can do.)

Are we supposed to take over *all* the housework? No. (God forbid, where would that lead!)

Would you rather that we paid no attention to your appearance? No. (Why be a woman at all?)

Are we supposed to take over childbearing too? No. (Impossible offers are easily made. What do you know about it! And it's not just the nine months, it's the little childbirth every four weeks. But never mind, we can manage it.)

So, what do you want?

To be allowed to be weak. Among other things. But, only as long as we're still strong. Not just when we can't help it anyway, not out of exhaustion, but deliberately and for fun. To be able to be weak also means to be irritable sometimes before our nerves are completely shot, and ugly now and then as long as we're still really pretty. And simply weak. That ought to be possible without everything immediately falling apart. And we also want this demand not accepted with a generous gesture but understood, empathized with, maybe even appreciated. By our men, our strong men!

*   *   *

One thing remains unclear: Is this desire for weakness within strength, for safety, comfort, protection, for belonging, yes, sometimes even for unconditional submission along with unlimited equality—is all of this the contemporary feminine or is it just basically human? Do men feel this way too?

There are many indications that they do. But after being buried for centuries, masculine weakness is probably barely able to acknowledge itself. Most men are too vain.

Even Marx . . . (was a man).

Translated by Dorothy Rosenberg

Irene Böhme

Photo © Jürgen Junker-Rösch.

A native of Bernburg on the Saale, Irene Böhme was born in 1933. She held early jobs in bookstores, as an editor, and as a dramaturge. From 1961 to 1969 she was an editor for the East German cultural-political weekly *Sonntag*. She spent the next decade (1969–79) as a dramaturge at the Volksbühne am Luxemburgplatz in East Berlin, before moving to West Berlin in 1980, where she was dramaturge for the West German national theater, Staatliche Schauspielbühnen, from 1981 to 1985. She continues to live in West Berlin as a freelance journalist and writer, contributing to various West German literary publications; for example, her text "Entschuldige, daß ich dich geboren habe" (Forgive me for bringing you into the world), appeared in the 1984 *Kursbuch* titled *Mütter* (Mothers). Böhme's radio plays "Das Wesen" (The creature) and "Die erste Nacht" (The first night) aired on West German radio in 1986 and 1987, respectively.

The volume from which these selections are taken, *Die da drüben*, is a series of first-person biographical narratives by East German women of diverse generations and backgrounds, based on Böhme's interviews with her subjects. For her West German audience, she included introductory essays from the perspective of an emigré from the GDR to West Berlin in order to bridge the cultural, social, and historical gap that she saw between East and West Germans. We have chosen to let her subjects speak for themselves.

Die da drüben (Those "over there"). Berlin: Rotbuchverlag, 1982.

Women and Socialism: Four Interviews (1984)

Regine R. (b. 1935)

AFTER LEAVING SCHOOL I began an apprenticeship at Peulicke's Fish Market. My mother arranged it, she was a cleaning woman there. I thought being a store clerk was pretty neat, and you could take home a fair amount of money in the food business, which was important in 1949. But it wasn't so terrific after all. The store was always cold, my hands were red, and old Peulicke was always on my back. As a girl apprentice you had to keep your mouth shut and do what you were told: sweep the street, can cherries, chop wood, help with the laundry. For fun I went dancing. Every Saturday and Sunday at the dance hall. I was really crazy about dancing. In 1951 the Peulickes left for the West, and the district management took over the shop. Egon became store supervisor—that's what I had to call him because we're both in the union. Egon had been resettled from Poland, had lost one leg, sold stockings for a while, and didn't know the first thing about business. That was nice—I was my own boss. The management knew what was going on, which is why they wanted to send me to supervisors' training. But I wasn't interested in going to school.

In 1954 I got pregnant. I tried everything to get rid of the kid: red wine with pepper and hot baths, wild motorcycle rides, and who knows what kind of pills, until I threw up. My father beat me, he wanted to know who the "guy" was. I still say I didn't want Ralph, Marina's father, because he was no good. Actually that's not entirely true. If Ralph had said back then: Let's get married, I would have married him. But he didn't. I always did have my pride. When I told him I was pregnant, I said right away that it didn't have to be his problem. I cried every night. Not because of Ralph, but because of another guy I'd have no chance at now. I dreamed this guy would come into the shop one day and take me and the kid to his place. He was a college student and only came to town on weekends. He didn't know I was in love with him. For years I couldn't get him out of my head. While I was in college I would still say to myself: Now would have been the time for us to meet, as equals, so to speak.

Things seemed easier after Marina was born. I felt grown up at the ripe old age of twenty. I played mother and shopkeeper, since I considered the fish business with Egon as my own. I brought money home and refused to listen to Father's griping whenever I went out dancing. Then I got pregnant again, and Father ordered me out of the house. I left immediately. As I said, I have my pride. First I lived with a friend, then with an aunt. Marina was at my parents'. I knew that things couldn't go on this way. I was furious with men, and with myself because I enjoyed love so much. Sleeping with a man I like is part of life for me. Was I supposed to give it up forever? I was really at the end of my rope.

There was an old Party member in the payroll office I got to chatting with whenever I picked up my check. He liked me. For years he had been telling me I could do better than selling fish. Now that things were such a mess, he talked me into it, and I went away to take sales management training. That got me out of the line of fire for a while. All of a sudden I was having fun learning. You were in another world and weren't just dealing with trivia. When I got back three months later, I was seven months pregnant and like a new person. The company had found me a furnished room, so I moved into it with Marina. When I returned to work from maternity leave, the company found day-care spaces for Marina and Frank. It was the company that sent me on my first vacation to the Baltic. All this was thanks to the old Party member in payroll. He died last year. I went to the funeral. There were plenty of fine words but nothing about what he was really like.

At twenty-two I had two children, no husband, the first shop I could call my own, and my first apprentice . . . I had an uncontrollable desire to go back to school. First came night school for my high school equivalency, then business correspondence courses. Nine beautiful years. Not every day was beautiful, of course, but on the whole, it was. My landlady, Widow Schleede, was a terrific help. She gave me a second room, often took care of the kids, and didn't pry into my private life. There were some things she did set me straight about, though. I didn't want to accept alimony for the children. Widow Schleede convinced me that was stupid. I didn't want to have anything to do with men any more. Widow Schleede just laughed at me. Though I must say, not much was going on in the way of men, I really didn't have the time. Once, it was serious. He was married, couldn't make up his mind between us, and I broke it off. I didn't have the nerves for that.

When the first supermarket in our city was built in 1966, it was clear that I would take it over. After all, I was the Trade Organization's pride and joy—female and with a degree. Our class's graduation party ended up in the Leipzig Eden nightclub. Were we ever happy! For me, it ended in bed with a fellow student. After that, two days with him in Weimar, Hotel Elephant. It was all wonderful, and I was pregnant again. I wanted this one. It was part of my student years. That's how romantic I can be sometimes. The guy never found out he had a daughter.

After that, everything went like clockwork. I was manager of the supermarket. Later we were designated as a training center for apprentices. My first vacation in Bulgaria, a new high-rise apartment, problems with Frank in school, the usual. At thirty-seven I got married. My husband is a truck driver who's been making our company's deliveries for years. Surprised everybody. A man, independent, healthy, and what's more, younger, settles for a woman with three children.

Karin A. (b. 1937)

I met my husband at seventeen. A year later, high school graduation, marriage, and the birth of a son. One thing right after another. My husband was still a student. I was living with my mother and working in an office. We had agreed that I would start college when he had finished. It didn't work out that way. He took over a construction project, and I found myself sitting in an office again. For ten years we moved from one construction project to another and lived in villages, never more than three years in one place. Just when I'd gotten used to the new job and begun to make friends, it would be time to move. Socialist construction sites are only romantic in the movies, maybe for construction workers, like my husband, for example. I was unhappy and took it out on him. He was understanding and put up with me. He did what he could: made breakfast every morning so I could sleep fifteen minutes longer, always washed the windows and did the vacuuming. Outings on weekends, and once a month we went downtown for an elegant dinner out. I regarded these as cheap bribes. I started an affair with a colleague because I wanted to do something of my own, because I was fed up with everything. My husband understood even this. He acted as if he didn't notice anything, so I told him to his face. He calmly told me couples have to go through this kind of thing together. I thought he was the biggest egotist. He could deal with anything as long as he had a piece of barren land to build on. Once there were high-rises and shopping centers on it, once the wilderness had become a little more human, he was ready to move on. But in the middle of his desert of mud, he wanted a family. This is someone who only thinks of himself.

After ten years of this I had had it. My firm gave me time off to take a continuing education course in engineering economics. So I stayed and he moved on. I soon realized that I am not made for a commuter marriage. Every Saturday, obligatory lovemaking. Every Sunday afternoon overshadowed by the feeling it's time to leave. Lonely evenings. I let the boy sleep in his father's bed, and often crawled in and joined him right after eight. And still I overslept in the mornings. I never felt like doing anything, I got sloppy, I rarely went to my classes. My favorite time to study was on weekends, when my husband was home. I'm actually an outgoing person, but suddenly nothing interested me anymore. At some point I had to admit that I missed my husband, that by myself I am not even half of what we are together. It was all his fault, he had crippled me. Finally—a chance to discover myself. I followed a strict plan: Mondays and Fridays housework, Tuesdays union meetings, otherwise studying, movies, visiting colleagues. I was not enjoying myself, I just made myself do it. When I found out that my husband was shacked up with a woman with two children, my carefully constructed house of cards collapsed. I thought Manfred should be spending the evenings with me again, falling asleep in his armchair, for all I cared, which actually drives me mad. We made each other miserable for two years. My husband couldn't find his way back to me; the other woman meant something to him. I was not understanding: sarcastic insinuations every weekend, crying or suicide threats; a desperate vacation trip with a lot of alcohol and desperately wild lovemaking. I can't explain how we got back together again. It was a matter of convention. We moved to another construction project and had a "reconciliation kid." I gave up my dream of getting a degree and started learning languages. There are adult education courses everywhere, and every construction project needs people with language skills. I am already certified in Russian and Polish, and now I'm beginning Czech. A lot is the way it was before. But it means something different to me now. I am not living according to my husband's expectations; now they are my own. It isn't important whether someone foisted them onto me at some point, because I haven't found anything better for myself yet.

Ingeborg T. (b. 1940)

At twenty-two I entered the Workers' and Peasants' University in Halle. I had been a dressmaker's apprentice and worked as a supervisor in a ready-to-wear shop. Now I wanted to finish high school and go to college. I fell head over heels in love with Heinz, we got married at Easter, and Andre was born in June. Everything went smoothly; I hardly missed a class. We took Andre to Dresden to my mother-in-law's, who was happy to have a little boy to take care of again. This was fine with me too, because it was nerve-racking for parents and children alike to have infants in the dormitory. I had seen that with my girlfriends. My husband had a lot of trouble with school. He flunked two big exams and dropped out after his third semester. He went back to work as an electrician at his old firm and lived at his mother's. I went to see him and the baby almost every weekend. Heinz never asked how things were going in Halle or what his old friends were doing. If I talked about it, he acted indifferent. He had erased this chapter from his life. It was the most important thing in mine. All we had left to talk about was the kid. Anything else embarrassed us. When Andre was three, we separated amicably. The court gave Heinz custody because the child was living at his mother's house. A court ruling in the child's interest, a precedent for equal rights—the mother pays alimony. The judges were pleased with themselves. I was not happy about it, although nothing really changed. I continued to visit Andre regularly. It was probably the best thing for him. Later on, I never had the strength to challenge the ruling. Heinz remarried and had two more children, so Andre is growing up in an intact family. At that time, I did not know that I would not have any more children.

Marianne E. (b. 1938)

We came from East Prussia. In June 1945 I was seven years old, sitting on the curb and singing "Sweet Ann of Tharau." A woman came along and told us we could stay with her. That's how we landed in Mecklenburg, got some land through the land reform, and became farmers. After school I worked on the farm. At eighteen I wanted to marry a neighbor's son. About that time a new Swiss fellow arrived at the collective farm. He would play accordion in the evenings. I left with him for another cooperative. Gerhard was eleven years older than I was, and a Party member. We got married. I worked in the stalls with him. Work was fun every day; he loved to laugh and sing. In the evenings we would draw graphs or milk-production curves, or we'd just party. We fixed up a cozy corner in the barn for our breaks, and we started a village chorus. He was full of ideas and seldom lost his good humor. Two beautiful years filled with work and fun. Then a girl from the village had a child by Gerhard. I didn't want to lose him; six months later I was pregnant too. That didn't help. After our daughter was born, he moved in with the other woman, and we got a divorce. To this day I don't know what I did wrong.

I was twenty-one and unskilled. I didn't want to go back to the farm. So I stayed in the village and worked in the cooperative stalls. They needed all the help they could get. Everything I did was to get even with Gerhard. I wanted the cooperative stall to be better than the collective, so I went to school at night. That's why I became a technician, and later a brigade member. That's why I joined the governing board. The other reason was my daughter. I wanted her to be proud of me later. At some point my grudge against Gerhard evaporated; by now we're good colleagues again, almost friends.

I don't like to be alone. I need people around me at work and in my free time. That's why I moved into an apartment with Gisela, who works in the co-op office and also has a child. We set up a great women's household. The village grapevine was buzzing. One day we were lesbian, the next we were running a brothel. It didn't bother us; together we were strong. We didn't exactly live like nuns, but I wasn't looking for the man of my life either. I had become skeptical—less of men than of myself.

When my daughter started first grade, Ludwig joined the agricultural production co-op. Our animal breeding was famous, so we were assigned a university graduate. Things got serious between Ludwig and me right away. We found each other over our work; he had brains, and I had experience. I am impressed by men I can look up to; they motivate me. Ludwig is five years younger than I am; it's never bothered us. Ludwig liked to look the other women over. I was jealous but never really insulted. We wanted to organize a modern beef production plant. That welded us together. To be totally sure of him, I got pregnant. He was pleased, came to visit me in the hospital with a huge bouquet, and when I came home with our baby girl, he announced that he was going to the Academy for Agricultural Research and going alone. Again, two beautiful years, again total destruction, me thirty-two and two kids around my neck. Everything was exactly like the first time. Now I wanted to go back to school. At first the co-op didn't want to let me go, but then they sent me. My older daughter stayed with Gisela, and I took the little one with me to vocational school. She was a big help to me, too. Without children I probably would never have survived. They give structure and meaning to life. Three years later I returned to the village, this time as an animal production engineer. Now I am in charge of the large beef production plant that Ludwig had conceived of earlier. It's really rather strange: I owe everything I am to the men I loved and the children I've borne. Now I'm living with a man again, not a breeder but an agricultural engineer. Once again, everything is lovely, but I don't want a child with him.

Translated by Nancy Lukens

Christiane Grosz

Photo by Roger Melis, Berlin, courtesy of Aufbau Verlag.

Christiane Grosz has been active in a wide variety of art forms, from pottery to theater directing to writing children's books, poetry, and a novel. Born in the Berlin suburb of Mahlsdorf in 1944, she apprenticed for three years with a potter after completing polytechnical high school in 1960. As a housewife in the mid-1960s, she was involved in amateur workers' theater and cabaret productions while studying graphic arts at night at the Institute of Applied Arts in Berlin-Weissensee. Her first experiments with creative writing date from this period, when she wrote plays for amateur theater productions. From 1963 to 1965 she studied theater directing and from 1965 to 1970 directed plays for a children's theater. In 1979, she attended a course for writers at the Johannes R. Becher Literaturinstitut in Leipzig. Between 1978 and 1986 she published five children's stories before turning in her mid-thirties to poetry and, later, prose about women's experience.

Aside from her two volumes of poetry and a novel, *Die Tochter*, Grosz's work has appeared in short prose anthologies. This selection was included in an East German anthology of short stories by GDR women, *Das Kostüm* (The costume), published in 1982.

Scherben (Shards). Berlin/Weimar: Aufbau, 1978.

Blatt vor dem Mund (Mincing words). Berlin/Weimar: Aufbau, 1983.

Die Tochter (The daughter). Berlin/Weimar: Aufbau, 1987.

The Trick (1982)

THE COOL TOWEL covered my forehead and eyes. If I kept them open, I saw Karl walking back and forth across the room, filling the suitcase with the necessary paraphernalia. I would have liked to look at my watch but did not want to move my arms, which were crossed on top of my chest. The slight headache which had begun by moving across my forehead to my temples was now focused on a spot above my left eye which felt especially damp and cool to me. It was almost as if the cold towel itself was causing this pain. I was too lethargic to take the towel off my forehead. Looking through the little crack, past my nose, I saw the middle tiles of the white stove. Green shadowy spots. The trees in front of the window were reflected in the tiles, shifting. The sight made me nervous. I looked up, into the weave of the towel; its colors glowed blue and yellow. Sky and sun, I thought; I felt warm and contented and used my feet to pull down the blanket that Karl had put over me.

For several weeks I had been observing myself and had noticed that the only place I felt good any more was in bed. There were never crises. Beginnings of crises, to be sure, but since I recognized them immediately, I could easily avoid major escalations. If Karl was weak, I never showed my strength. If he was anxious, I would not let my courage show. If he was imprudent, I did not display my practicality.

One Sunday afternoon, a day habitually set aside for practice over the years, it happened that I—and fortunately I can now add the word "almost" —violated that principle. He was trying every way he could, except by magic, to get the four balls he had stuck between the fingers of his right hand over into the left one. The balls jumped out of his hands, rolled across the floor, and bounced under the dresser as if they'd been frightened. Karl crawled after them. I sat on the edge of the bed watching him, as was our custom. I reached up in the air with my fingers spread and instantly the balls flew toward me. They arranged themselves between my fingers like the spheres in a molecular model. He attributed it to magic, and that's precisely what it was. I had the touch. His head cocked at an angle above the floor and his arm still behind the dresser, he looked up at me, and I knew it was time for a decision. I could not compromise. I could either be alone and do magic or be married. I relaxed and let the balls fall to the floor. I was supposed to give him some tips, advise him how to do magic. I could just as easily have told a painter how to become talented. I pressed my fingertips against my temples and lay down in bed. Karl bent over me, quietly wished me a speedy recovery, took my limp hand and kissed it. I didn't resist.

Beside the bed was the stool with my things. My stockings hung out from under my skirt, my red shoes lay jumbled below them. If I opened my eyes just a tiny crack, I could see from the pile of clothes to the rubber tree and from there over to the sewing machine. I will never have to exert myself again, I thought. We can live fine without my money.

I could then devote all my time and energy to myself and my dreams. I dozed, resting from the strains of magic. A peculiar kind of lethargy came over me after I had levitated the bouquets out of their vases and across the room. Sometimes the power even left me in the midst of the magical process; I would lie down and the flowers would fall to the floor.

Half an hour before Karl was due home I would quickly straighten everything up, destroy the traces of my talent, and get in bed. Karl had gotten used to my being in bed all the time, and since household order nevertheless did not suffer, he did not object.

I had long since stopped going to Karl's performances. Before, I had never missed one. I always sat as far back as possible. The small auditoriums of the cultural centers were full of people in good spirits. Tired, dusty garlands of some bygone festivity were draped over the lamps, and reddish crepe paper ivy with matching fat clusters of glass grapes hung from the walls. Folding chairs were handed over people's heads to make room for those coming in from the bar. The mayor would button the middle button of his jacket and announce the magician. Karl had been doing the same routine for ten years. He would make water flow out of paper bags and one hoop jump through another, and pull money and cards from the noses of people in the audience. His routines always went over well. Even when he began to stretch his performances with little acrobatic numbers and fill them out with jokes. When he did handstands on a stool and his pantlegs slipped down his white calves, my palms would sweat. For years I believed it was a sign of sympathetic fear or stage fright. Only since I stopped going along can I name that feeling. At the time I called it a sense of responsibility; I perceived myself as him. I anxiously monitored the audience reactions, interpreted glances, waited impatiently for approval, for him.

For some time now he has been working with a new trick. A trick that has finally brought him the success he always hoped for. Now, with this trick, he has done it. Before going on he takes three members of the audience into his confidence. He asks them for their watches. In the course of his routine he invites these same people onto the stage, is applauded when he pulls playing cards from under their collars, has them pull long ribbons out of their buttonholes, and then lets them return to their seats. But at the end of the performance, to prove his immense dexterity, he takes the watches out of his pockets and asks the volunteers to come back and get the items deposited with him. Amid thunderous applause for the magician, the secret conspirators return to the stage and adeptly act amazed, which adds even more to the fun. They give a loud cry of "Here!" and recognize their belongings.

Ever since I stopped watching the show, since I've been lying in bed with a towel across my forehead, I have been more and more preoccupied with the question: What would happen if, for the sake of truth, someone remained silent?

Translated by Nancy Lukens

Monika Helmecke

Photo courtesy of Verlag Neues Leben.

An economist by training, Monika Helmecke is also a mother and, since her early thirties, a writer of short stories. Born into a working-class family in Berlin in 1943, she completed her secondary schooling and worked briefly as a stenotypist. From 1963 to 1966 she attended a training program for financial management, followed by university study at the Institute for Economics in Berlin. She married in 1970. Her interest in writing grew during the 1970s as she raised her four children, who were born between 1970 and 1982. After publishing her first short story in 1973, she became active in a local Writing Workers' Group, a GDR institution which served to encourage working-class people to engage in and talk about the process of creative writing.

This story is taken from Helmecke's short prose anthology *Klopfzeichen*. Since its publication in 1979, she has continued to publish short stories in multiple-author collections and magazines, as well as working in radio.

Klopfzeichen (Tapping Code). Berlin: Neues Leben, 1979.

September 30th

(1979)

IT'S EVENING, almost night. Beside me are a half-empty glass of vodka, the ashtray with cigarette butts. When I close my eyes, the dark world spins around me. My face is still smeared. It doesn't matter. There's no one here to notice it. So there's no one to wipe away the traces either, with soft fingertips or lips. No one. The evening of a day that began almost like any other, only a bit earlier.

The baby's crying. A glance toward the window: still night-gray. The clock has stopped. Maybe five-thirty. The pacifier, no tea. I reach to my left. The bed is empty. Of course. Business trip. Three more days.

When I reach my bedroom door, the baby starts crying again, loud, demanding, insistent. My bed is beckoning. It's warm. My eyes don't want to see electric light yet. But the crying. Up you go. That's the way it is. It might even be six by now.

I scrub out bottle and pan, still half asleep; I was too tired last night. Make baby food. The baby grins happily and is wide awake. What else can I do but talk to it sweetly, laugh with it. Even though my mouth will hardly open. Then the baby is back in bed. The radio announcer says: Six thirty-seven A.M. Too early for me. Much too early. The older one is muttering to herself: "The baby's been crying all night." It troubles me even though it's not true. But she goes right back to sleep. Soon I do too. I wake up from a nightmare and a noise as if toys are falling on the floor somewhere far away. The baby's crying.

8:05. No kindergarten today. So, it's "vacation" for my daughter and lots of time for breakfast. Cocoa, eggs, grandma's blackberry jam. And honey. Especially honey. She loves honey. It's like on weekends. But no toast. Father isn't here.

And then the day begins. My daughter knows there's no time to play in the early morning, at least not together. Mother has work to do in the mornings. Wash dishes from three meals, make beds, straighten up. Sometimes do some typing. Not today. She plays by herself. Building houses, each with a flower garden and a garage for the tractor. Now and then I have to come look. 10:00, the baby. Second bottle. Afterward it's on the carpet smiling and kicking about. The older one holds the rattle in front of it. A new game.

Until her arm gets tired, since the baby stares at it, fascinated, but doesn't reach for it yet.

Make lunch. Rice pudding with apples. No, there's nothing else to nibble on. An apple if you want. Then, clean, core, and chop a huge mountain of apples. The little girl helps. Hands me apples, gets mad, I reach for the fruit myself. The big juicemaker on the stove. In two hours I'll scrub the canning jars and boil the lids. But it's a while till then. Time to eat. Time for talking and asking questions. Also for making a mess. The vacuum cleaner never gets a rest in my house. If only you could get refill bags! Afternoon nap-time. The children sleep, or at least pretend to. My time. Time to lie down or sleep. Time to write. Today, only time to think and dream. Dream of things that never come true. As usual.

Walk to the phone booth. Try to reach the doctor. The older one's cough is really getting worse. Barks away our dreams at night. No success, no answer. Walk back. Stop by the greengrocer's. Tomatoes. I do need some. Recycling center. Return the glass bottles. Bakery. The drugstore, closed for months now. The tobacco shop.

Back home. The armchair. It's so nice to lean your head back. 1:30. Six more hours. My eyes are half closed. Still, I can see: dust. Dust. That's all I needed. Now? When else. It's clear how the afternoon hours will be spent. So, now: Pick up saucers, pots, candles, books. And the little pictures drawn by K. If I'm going to be thorough, I have to pick up every single picture, wipe it, put it back. A lot of pictures. A lot of motions. Too many for me today. So I won't be thorough. No. Another time. I get back in the armchair, pull my legs up, hug my knees, and put my head down. I have ten minutes left. Haven't written anything today. Lost time.

There goes the baby again already. Softly at first. Almost whining like a cat, at intervals. Be quiet, my child. It's too early. Your mother needs more time. A little more time to herself. I sit. Cruel mother. Try to conjure back my dreams. But the whine turns into calls of want, want. Hungry. And: touch, talk. I'm not alone. Be quiet. I want my dreams. But it's crying. When I open the door, the older one jumps back into bed and looks at me hopefully.

"Can I get up after the baby?"

"Yes, but after the baby."

After-nap rituals, repeated every afternoon. Cereal. I have to shove the spoon in three times before it goes down. The baby is so eager it spits every-thing out. And cries. Hungry. Hungry. But eventually the jar does empty and baby's full. It's a good thing there's none left. Who would eat it? The older one doesn't like vegetables when you can't tell what they are. Only apple with zwieback, or banana. Now quick, get the baby to bed. My big girl gets dressed by herself. Meantime I make the apple juice. Three bottles, for the winter.

Then out for a walk. Like every other afternoon. It's one of the few days this fall that's just the way I like. Gentle, slightly tired sun. We walk to the playground to play hopscotch. In the baby carriage net, the bucket for everything they'll collect, plus two cakepans. In my bag, the book and some chocolate. We don't need anything else. I'm told to sit on the red bench; I position the baby carriage next to the bench so I can see into it, put the little volume of stories in my lap, and dig out the chocolate bar. A piece for each of us, then my daughter is on her way. I open the book and gaze across the river. A party steamer without a band, far behind it a tugboat with three dinghies. Hardly a sound. I close my eyes partway and squint into the sun. I could purr like a cat, I feel so good on my red bench. Read a few sentences, look up again. Only a few people on the riverside walkway. Nobody but us on the playground. This is how a picture of peace should look. I try the pound cake with cherry rosehip jam. It's good. Needs a bit more sugar. Add a little. I am allowed to read again. And doze. The girl gathers chestnuts in her bucket. She finds a lot. She dumps them into the baby carriage net. They'll stay there until I throw them away sometime or other. But now I hold one in my hand. I like these smooth, brown little things. Could hold them between my fingers forever. Sometimes I build animals, little people, fantastic creations, too. But not every day. And not today. It's getting cool. 4:30. Time to go home, get the baby's bath ready. Three hours to go.

As always, the baby wakes up when I push the carriage into the dark entryway of our building. I would have liked to leave it in the courtyard for a while, in the overgrown grass. But baby will cry. So I carry the things upstairs first. All of a sudden there's screaming. I forgot the older one wants to win when we climb the stairs. I went too fast. She resents that. The worst name you can be called at kindergarten seems to be Slowpoke. I go downstairs, the baby's whimpering. I'm imprisoned by my children's crying.

I start a fire in the kitchen stove. The baby needs the heat. Thank God it doesn't smoke. And now the older one. "Please, please, mommy, play company."

I try to distract her, suggest all the games I'd much rather play, in fact would even like to play with her: dice, chess, dominoes, or picture lotto. Or better, clay. That's what I would like to do now. Form some things. Animals. The Bremen Town Musicians, or a little line of elephants that get smaller and smaller, seals balancing balls. That would be fun right now. But no. "Company, please, pretty please, play Company." I curse my friend who showed her this dismal game and obey, since the last half hour, at least that much, belongs to her. So:

"Knock Knock."

"Hello."

"Hello. What's your name?"

"Mrs. Doering."

"Oh, Mrs. Doering. How nice. And what is your Baby's name?"

"Yoga."

"What a pretty name." And so forth. Every evening, if my daughter had her way. Only the baby's names change, because she forgets the one from the day before.

Put the kettle of water on to heat, scour the baby's bathtub, cook baby food to fill the jars, get the baby and undress it. It lies there naked, kicks about, sometimes grins and watches me with big, now dark eyes as I adjust the temperature of the water. Bathtime. Baby is radiant. Tender pink skin, soft skin for stroking. Dry off, powder, cream. Dress again. Get both bottles ready. Both have one in the evening. The older one enjoys casting off her big-girl-ness for a while, being allowed to have a bottle, baby food very diluted with juice. The baby lies in my arms, smiling contentedly and full. I touch its thin hair with my lips. Owl-feather hair. Press my nose against it like every other night. And, like every night, I try to figure out what it is that baby hair smells like. I can't find anything comparable. Maybe a trace of hay and summer. The city kid. It looks straight ahead and has no intention of burping.

"Isn't Baby going to have a little burp?"

"No."

Shake it. Pat it. Put it over my shoulder. There it is. From way down deep. In bed, the baby cries for a while. It's dark and lonely in its room.

Supper for two. Then foot exercises with the older one to correct her flatfoot. I have to stalk around the room with her. As always, hitting the lamp with my too-long arms. Cramp my toes around the acorns. She loves it. Have to force things to a stopping point. The fairytale before bed. From the book that's almost a hundred years old. I don't like these point-at-things stories very much. But she loves them, without actually understanding everything. Brush your teeth. Wash up. Then she's in bed. Cough syrup, nosedrops, song, goodnight rituals of which you mustn't forget a word or she can't get to sleep.

"Give me lots of kisses." So-o-o-o many—she spreads her arms wide to show how many.

In half an hour my group starts. Glad to be able to get together with my friends today. After five years of marriage I can't tolerate being alone as well as I used to, even when it's only days at a time. I sneak into the children's room once more.

"Are you leaving now?" she asks with a penetrating whisper.

"Yes. Be good."

"You don't need to say that any more."

"And if the baby cries . . ."

"If the baby cries, I'll crawl under the covers."

"Right."

*   *   *

The two and a half hours of life with the group are over. Much too soon. I'm sitting in the car that will take me home. There are three of us. It's cold. Suddenly I feel miserable. The empty apartment. The question swirls around in my head, slips out of my mouth, almost involuntarily. I expect the NOs. And hear them. The first one, with a confident smile, makes a few friendly pirouettes before boring its way into my ears. The second a bit more hesitant but no less definite. So I'll spend the rest of the evening alone. Have no choice. The car ejects me. The waiting eyes push me to the door of my building. I would have enjoyed staying out a while, walking in the moist night air. It's so nice and dark already. I never want to see light again. Then the light goes on. My hands do not obey me. They know where the light switch is. Forty-two steps. How heavy my legs are. The light burns in my eyes.

12:30 A.M. I'm drunk.

Translated by Nancy Lukens

Helga Schubert

Photo by Barbara Koppe, Berlin, courtesy of Aufbau Verlag.

Born in 1940, Helga Schubert often writes about herself as a representative member of the first generation to grow up in the GDR. After spending a year as a factory worker between high school and university in Berlin, she graduated with a degree in psychology and began work as a psychotherapist in 1963. She completed further training as a psychologist in 1981. Schubert began publishing in journals and anthologies in 1973 and became an independent writer in 1977, but she continued to work in a marriage and sexual counseling center until 1988. She has published two volumes of short stories and a documentary volume on women in the fascist period, as well as writing radio and television plays, film scripts and children's books.

The following story first appeared in her anthology *Blickwinkel*.

Lauter Leben (Just life). Berlin/Weimar: Aufbau, 1975.

Blickwinkel (Point of view). Berlin/Weimar: Aufbau, 1984.

Judas-Frauen (Judas women). Berlin/Weimar: Aufbau, 1990.

Breathing Room (1984)

I'D IMAGINED a mother differently.

No, I wasn't a mother. My stomach muscles were so tight. How could a baby grow beneath them? And how was it supposed to get out of me? It would tear me apart. And then there would always be a baby there when I wanted to go out, take a trip, sleep late, make love.

But I got pregnant at nineteen. And the doctor who confirmed the pregnancy, who had known me for years and saw how upset I was, said to me, if you don't tell your mother today, I'll call her. No responsible physician would perform an abortion on you.

She was Catholic and had four children. And we didn't have legal abortion yet. I didn't know anyone who would have done it.

The father of the child had never been involved with such an inexperienced woman and suggested marriage if I wouldn't reconsider having the child. I had no father, no big brother, had never had a boyfriend. I was so grateful for anyone showing interest in me, masculine interest, that I thought it was love. I ignored all the bad signs. And we got married. The other women's apartments that he had to paint, the other women's records he had to listen to in the evening. I really believed it.

I brought my child into the world at 6:25 on a Saturday morning. I was in the hospital, a midwife carefully pushing on my stomach with her knee to help me. The woman doctor listened with a stethoscope to the weak heartbeats growing weaker. Urged me to hurry. I was awake to the very last moment. To the very first moment: a little wrinkled bluish baby, nearly choked to death by his/my umbilical cord. It had moved too quickly, it had already lived so intensely: my child. It could have choked to death on my/his umbilical cord. It would have been alive before and been born dead.

Twenty-one, twenty-two, twenty- . . . I counted as slowly as I could count. But my child didn't cry. It hung, head first, both feet in the doctor's hand, as if lifeless.

I had brought it into the world. And now it couldn't breathe in the world, couldn't cry.

I saw that it was a boy. I looked at him breathlessly. I saw them stick a long, slender glass tube down his throat, sucking out fluid. How they hurried. They didn't even answer me.

Then my child cried. It was alive. I had too much milk. They gave me my roommate's baby to nurse too. Two weeks later, examinations at the university, in between feedings. I was twenty.

When the child was three months old, I took him to the nursery every morning, pumped milk and left him there. When the child was three, I took him to the kindergarten. In the winter, through the snow to the kindergarten. In the evening, the tired child, the screaming child, the sick child. And my tiredness, my screaming, my illnesses.

The second child would have been a year younger. I didn't give birth to it.

My child was four when the divorce began and six when I finally moved into a new apartment with him. Since then, thirteen years have passed. And there was always a child. In the evening. In the morning. On the weekends. On vacation. I always had to think of bread, of butter, of milk, of homework, of PTA meetings. I cooked so many meals and washed so many sweaters and so many diapers that froze overnight on the line. And I scolded so much and begged for quiet and for cooperation and for consideration. And I oppressed the child with my expectations, my wishes, was disappointed and discouraged and loved him so tenderly when he lay in bed and slept. And I was ashamed of myself because I wasn't a gentle mother, not tender, soft, caressing. But this child was like my arm. I don't caress it either, I have it. The first time I left the child alone in the evening he was four months old. And we took the subway to the theater. He had fallen asleep at home, fed and freshly diapered. But in the subway I suddenly felt as if I were bound to the child by a long umbilical cord. A child—that tied me to the world. I was never again tempted out into the street by the glow of headlights.

The first time he got up on his knees in bed, the first time he walked, from his father to me, I thought, he already needs you a little bit less. And I was proud of him.

Once he almost died, at three and a half. He woke me up in the middle of the night, threw up, ran a high fever. We called the emergency service, called the pediatrician the next day, and every day we asked her to come again because the coughing kept getting worse until, tired of our phone calls, she finally arranged a hospital admission for an appendectomy. But it was a lung infection. And the woman doctor on the ward told us to hope that our child would survive the night.

His father had been given the child's things back: his red woolen cap, his little boots, his coat. He stood there in the apartment doorway and thought—no, he said it: He's dying and it's your fault. I was able to sleep that night, exhausted and calm, completely sure that he would survive. The next morning they told us we could see him. But only secretly. He can't be allowed to excite himself.

He was in a single room in an oxygen tent. The nurse put another sterile gown on over her uniform when she approached his bed.

His lungs had been aspirated during the night. They had drawn off the fluid. He had been given transfusions. And now he saw us through the glass after all. How much he had suffered during the night. And I hadn't sat with him, hadn't comforted him, had only put my faith in the doctors and nurses. He saw us, struggled to sit up, stretched his arms out toward us and cried. He was alive. Once, it was after he had started going to school, I came home and saw blood stains on the sidewalk leading to our door. A crowd of children was standing there, they were bent over, my child sat in the middle and held his head in his hands. Blood ran down over his eyes. A wound on his forehead. He had been riding his scooter when he turned to look behind him and crashed into a concrete lamp post.

The child took the train alone for the first time to visit his grandparents in the mountains. In my thoughts he sat in a train that kept getting smaller and smaller and traveled south, traveled all alone with sandwiches and money for a soda, traveled south on the map away from me.

His girlfriends: they went straight to his room. No, no tea. They'd rather have a cigarette. They didn't want to gain weight, you have to watch out when you're on the pill. Mother, why do girls I'm not interested in always want something from me? And why am I afraid to talk to the other ones?

Mother, why did you get a divorce? I think father's all right. He said it was your fault too. You know, really, it's better the way it is now. She suits him better than you did. And you and your man suit each other better too.

Have you ever met somebody that you can talk to right away for hours? The whole evening? The whole night? And then you sleep with them too? And wake up the next day and go out with them and eat lunch and could just keep on talking like that?

So, my son was grown up.

He learned to cut trees. He could clear the branches off a tree with an axe so sharp you could cut bread with it. During the day he lived in the woods and took breaks in a trailer that they heated in the morning. During the morning break they toasted bread on the stove.

He learned to drive a tractor, drag logs out, drive trucks. And he learned to trim crowns.

You have to climb up the trunk. You put your arms around the tree. You have the rope on your back. Then you have to secure yourself: you throw a line through the crown, climb higher and secure yourself with the crown line. When you're in the crown, you have to have both hands free to trim the side branches. If you've made a mistake with your lines, things can go wrong. You have to be able to let go once you're on top and you've secured yourself, do you understand? You've only got yourself to blame if you fall. The foreman stands below and says, now let go. That's quite a feeling. Up there in the air, all alone.

We took him to the army after he'd turned nineteen, on a Thursday at twelve o'clock: his father, his girlfriend, and I.

They all had short hair, jeans jackets, parkas, windbreakers. And when the officer in civilian clothes asked the young men: Do you have any more questions? a few called high-spiritedly: When's our first leave? When will we be discharged?

The officer spoke calmly to them: We're going to the train station now, from there we'll take the train to the next collection point. At ease, march. And the young men suddenly walked in pairs, in the street instead of on the sidewalk, along the narrow cobblestone street down the hill. He turned around and waved until they disappeared around the corner. And I thought of the centuries through which mothers and girlfriends had looked after their sons and boyfriends that way, again and again.

Ten days later he took his oath of duty: at a war memorial. All in steel helmets with pale faces. The path to the war memorial led through a cemetery. Past the graves on the way and back again past the graves. Past the women tending the graves.

I didn't recognize him among all the steel helmets. And he looked right at us out of the corner of his eye, facing straight ahead, until we recognized him. Then it was all right. We were allowed to stand with him for a while afterward. Touch him, pat him. We felt the material of his uniform, the steel helmet, freshly oiled that morning.

He looks so handsome in uniform, his girlfriend said to me quietly. It looks better on him than on anyone else here, doesn't it?

He stood there, tall and slim. With earnest gray eyes. Looked at his parents, his girl holding his hand, and said smiling: You didn't even notice that I was in the honor guard. I had to carry the flag to the front. That took some real practice.

A German soldier, I thought. I have a child who is a German soldier. My father was only nine years older when he died as a German soldier.

I could see the lack of sleep in my son's face, the worry about doing something wrong. And I also thought he looked handsome, as absurd as it sounds, and I was a little embarrassed by the thought. My grandmother had said of my father that he had looked very manly in uniform. How could I be thinking the same thing?

After lunch we were allowed to sit with them for two hours. Then each family gathered around their man in uniform: the wives with their small children, the siblings, the fathers, sometimes in uniform themselves, and us, laden with thermos bottles and fruit. When he stood up, he reached for his hat and his belt.

Then they had to fall in and march in step back to the barracks. We followed alongside him, ran, so as not to lose sight of him. Then they marched through the gate. I had unpacked his civilian clothes at home the day before. Now he has only his uniform, I thought.

When we couldn't see him any longer, we looked at each other, his girlfriend and I. My own vision blurred, I saw her smile through her tears: only 530 more days. He only has me and—she hesitated briefly and looked at me kindly—he only has me and you to care about him in there. After eleven days he wrote to me: Well, I've been here exactly three weeks. The worst is nearly over.

Last week a terrible dream woke me in the night. I was very old and was crying and telling a stranger that my child had been killed during his military service. I sat up in bed filled with horror.

Today I received two letters from him. The first was regular mail, the second special delivery. In the first letter he wrote that a rubber plug had stuck and sealed the filter of his gas mask during an exercise drill, and he hadn't been able to get any air. In his panic he'd forgotten how to get the mask off. The others had seen that something was wrong and hadn't helped him. Then he'd simply pulled everything off his head and was still alive. But there was no reason to panic.

In the second letter, which was more important to him, he wrote that he is coming home on leave for three days starting the day after tomorrow. And I should tell everyone, and I should give his regards to everybody, and his girlfriend already knows too, and we should expect him on the earliest train, and he doesn't have a key, heavily underlined, and he wants to be alone with her.

And for the first time he addressed me as: dear old mum.

Translated by Dorothy Rosenberg

Beate Morgenstern

Photo by Roger Melis, Berlin, courtesy of Aufbau Verlag.

Beate Morgenstern was born in 1946 in Cuxhaven, near Hamburg, and moved with her parents to Herrnhut in the Oberlausitz later the same year, where her father was a pastor for the Church of the Herrnhut Brethren. After studying German literature and arts education at Humboldt University in East Berlin, 1964–68, she held various jobs as a sales assistant, postal worker and office assistant. From 1970 to 1978 she was a photo editor for the foreign desk of the GDR news service. She also did volunteer cultural work in a large Berlin cable firm. Since 1979 she has made her living as a freelance writer of stories, a radio play, and, most recently, an autobiographical novel.

Morgenstern's writing reflects a concern for relations between generations and the particular traditions that shape them—in her own case, the patriarchal religious heritage of the Herrnhut Brethren.

This selection is the title story in her first short prose collection, *Jenseits der Allee.* Her first novel, *Nest im Kopf,* was published the same year.

Jenseits der Allee (The other side of the boulevard). Berlin/Weimar: Aufbau, 1979.

Nest im Kopf (Hinterlands of the mind). Berlin/Weimar: Aufbau, 1979.

The Other Side of the Boulevard   (1979)

THE WOMAN recognized it all: the shop belonging to the greasy-faced little furrier with fishy eyes who had looked her over; the ugly, dark red brick facade suggesting a collection of government agencies; the black-bordered sign listing the hours of worship and pastors' names and modestly pointing to a church. It occurred to her that the same building housed a school, a library, and a child welfare agency. Schoolchildren had painted huge, awkward figures of different races in glaring, gaudy colors in the gloomy entryway at the end of the brick wall. A short, broad street led off to the left and opened onto a large asphalt square, surrounded on three sides by tall brick walls, a kind of courtyard that echoed in the afternoon with children's shouting such as she had never heard anywhere else. The mighty sound of church bells was trapped here too. A narrow, barely visible street led out from the side of the courtyard. She remembered the greengrocer's with the large glass windows as well.

Ten years earlier, in the pubs she would later walk past, the woman had sat with a medical student she really would have liked to marry. But all he did was drink with her in the pubs or cook for her at his place, hot blood sausage with sauerkraut. He lived on the sixth floor right under the roof, so that the apartment got a lot of light; he owned a carpet and a rocking chair, which is why she felt at home there.

He no longer lived in the city but in some little town in the Harz, where he was bound to be married to another woman, perhaps to the one he had already set his mind on as a young boy, for whose sake he never touched another woman. At the time there had been no hope of his getting this woman. Now perhaps he was actually married to her. Or else he lived alone. The woman had been trying for years to remember his name, but all she remembered was that he was called Bernd.

It was not very far from here to her present apartment. But still, two worlds: this side and the other side of the boulevard that separated workers, delinquents, students, and artists from the middle-class population.

Now she was one of those who paid their rent by the second of the month or the fourth at the latest if it was due on the fifth, and who had at most two children, who, it should be added, were no trouble, and if they were, no one talked about it.

The woman was about thirty and wore a light sport jacket. She had her hands in her pockets. She was walking alongside a tall, thin girl with a pretty, somewhat immobile face framed by reddish-brown curls, a face reminiscent of an old porcelain doll or a handsome young boy little girls fall in love with and wish for as their prince.

The woman had to look up to the girl to speak with her. Perhaps that was why she stood so straight.

After finishing school, the girl had begun in the same office where the woman worked. That was two years ago now. Although the woman was only slightly older, it had taken her a long time to come to terms with the girl's lack of experience and make friends with her. Now she had been invited to go see the girl's first apartment.

The two of them went into the greengrocer's. The big freezer still stood in the center. It had always attracted the woman when she had been a student and lived here. Sometimes there were packages of frozen strawberries in it. But she saved her scant funds for shoes and sweaters, which seemed more important to her. Because of this and its large, clean windows amidst the gray buildings, to her the shop represented the quintessence of a world of cleanliness and moderate luxury worth striving for. It pleased her that the girl shopped here.

The woman stood to the side while the girl got in line and, with an inquiring glance toward the woman, took two ice cream cups from the freezer.

A young mother with two children walked into the store. She walked quickly and purposefully, but not hurriedly, and spoke with her two sons as if they were adults. The woman saw the austere, somewhat tired face of the mother, about her age, her dark hair tied back smoothly, a white sweater over her jeans; then she looked at the boys, who were wearing three-quarter-length leather shorts.

Suddenly she felt happy as she thought that there were a number of women in this part of town, and throughout the city for that matter, who were intelligent and self-confident and had their lives quite well under control, with or without husbands. The fact that she did not know any such woman seemed only the result of some coincidence that would certainly change.

The girl bought four pounds of tomatoes, which were still expensive. She paid from a tiny leather pouch that she opened and closed with long, slender fingers. I'm not going to scrimp and save like crazy just because of the apartment, she said to the woman as they left the shop.

There was a row of small shops that sold soap, paper, toys, meat, and

bread; resoled shoes, took in laundry, and advised tenants about simple repairs to sanitary facilities. Each shop looked more ordinary than the next.
Some had their blinds lowered, others were up: young married couples,
single mothers, and artists had moved into what had been shops. There
were colorful clay figures in the window of one shop-turned-apartment.

Pretty, huh? said the girl and looked at the woman.

Oh, yes, said the woman. She looked up at the buildings. The raw brick
showed in spots under the dark gray plaster, decorative balcony railings, an
occasional one freshly painted. Horizontal rectangles of bright stones and
corners of rusted iron girders under tightly locked doors leading into open
air showed where balconies had been torn off instead of being repaired.
They walked past the large paint store where the woman had still shopped
long after she had moved out of this section of town.

That's a really good store, she said to the girl. You can get everything you
need for your apartment there. And she added: You can get lamps farther
down this street.

Right, I need lamps, said the girl. She had drawn her shoulders slightly
forward. Although she took long strides so that the woman next to her had
to walk very quickly, her gait seemed slow and dragged irritatingly.

That's the good thing about this area, the woman said. You can get everything here. And if you can't get it here, you can't get it anywhere anyway.

And there's a bar or restaurant on every corner, the girl said, laughing.

There are only two where I live. Although it doesn't matter to me, of
course, we never go out to eat. Her heart stopped beating briefly as she
looked into the open door of the pub she had frequented with Bernd and
saw that everything was unchanged. She remembered having sat at the
table behind the pillar where a young man and a bald one were now having
a beer.

My sister still hasn't come to see the apartment. What do you think of
that? Either she's too tired after work or she's got something planned with
her boyfriend.

When you're preoccupied with a boyfriend, nothing else counts, said
the woman.

I have the feeling she isn't interested in my apartment at all. At least my
mother offered to help. But with her blood pressure, she can't. She wants
to make the curtains. That'll help. On the other hand, I don't like it when
she always says: If I were you, or, if I were in your shoes, and then suggests
something I don't want to do. If she had it her way she'd fix up the whole
apartment for me. According to her taste. When I want something one way,

she shakes her head and says: That's up to you, of course it's your apartment! And if we go shopping together, I already know everything will be a compromise. Not like I want it, not like she wants it. But of course she makes a lot of practical suggestions, too.

Why are you insecure? said the woman. Your mother's taste is different, that's clear.

It makes me think I'm not doing it right.

It wouldn't bother me a bit if my mother didn't like my apartment. But she generally likes it when I'm a little nutty. She used to want to be a dancer. Think of that!

You see, my mother has very definite ideas. She's amazed when someone else's are different. She can't understand.

I can imagine what she's like. The thing with your father, too. She thinks it's forever, and then he leaves. She can't get over it. Though I bet they didn't get along well, your father is certainly very different. Maybe she grew up in a very narrow environment there in the village.

Definitely.

Do you visit your father often?

No. We have to meet secretly, you know. And then one of us slips and gives it away after all. Then you can't talk to my mother for a week.

Why doesn't your brother help?

Oh, he's got his family. And on weekends everybody needs their time off.

And doesn't your mother tell him he should help you sometimes?

No.

But I think she should say something. Sometimes you're stubborn when you're young. Then at least the older one should keep an eye on things. After all, you'll resent having to do everything by yourself! I would. In any case, I would always remember that they didn't help me when I really needed it. It'll leave something between you that won't be that easy to clear up.

Of course I resent it. But am I supposed to ask 'em? When my brother got his new apartment, I helped them, too. But it wouldn't occur to him. My sister-in-law either. And what makes me angriest is that they're all meeting at the country place this weekend for a family party. Can you imagine how mad I am: I'm on the ladder scrubbing the ceiling while they're basking in the sun. If only my sister at least had to work the weekend shift. Then I wouldn't be so insulted.

It's just a good thing my relatives don't live here, said the woman. That way I don't have to get so angry at them. On the other hand, I think my mother would see to it that everything went smoothly in the family.

Oh, family, said the girl. We aren't a real family anymore anyway.

They turned into a street leading to the boulevard. The girl stopped and nodded toward the house opposite them: Here it is. She looked expectantly at the woman.

The building was no different from the apartment buildings on the street they had just come from. But the woman could see the tree-lined boulevard and the corner of a park on the other side. So she found the building and street a shade friendlier. Not bad, said the woman. Really, I've seen worse.

Wooden scaffolding had been put up on the building next door, but the girl said her building wasn't scheduled for sandblasting yet.

Someday it'll be your turn. You'll see, the woman comforted her.

They went into the apartment house. The girl pointed to her mailbox in the row of other tin boxes. She had written her name on adhesive tape on the mailbox in large, irregular letters that leaned in all directions.

It's open, said the girl. The man before me took the lock out.

What does he need the lock for, said the woman, shaking her head.

He took the light switches in the apartment, only the wires are still hanging there.

Are they insulated?

Dunno, said the girl. No idea.

When you've finished fixing up your apartment, you'll know a lot more, said the woman. I was just as ignorant as you.

There were shrubs and bushes in the little courtyard. Someone had just cleaned up the beds. The paved walk led through the center of the courtyard to the rear and side wings of the building.

I've never seen a rear wing like that, said the woman. It's really quite nice.

I've heard a lot of young people live here who care about the building, too.

You're lucky.

On the stairs they met a stocky young man with a full beard who looked them over.

When the sound of his steps had faded, the woman said: I wonder if that was your neighbor? He almost looks that way.

Could be. But these days they all have beards, artist or not.

The girl stopped on the landing to the fourth floor, took a large bunch of keys out of her linen bag, and began to unlock the door, right, left, trying the lower lock with another key, rattling on the door.

I've always managed to get it open, the girl said, a slight blush spreading across her pale face.

I don't have a knack for keys, the woman said helplessly, but tried it anyway, without success.

For a while they stood there not knowing what to do and stared at the door.

Wouldn't you know, the day you come with me, said the girl. She looked plaintively at the woman. That's my disappointment for the day.

You and your theory, said the woman. You're a real character. What if you said: Every day one little success?

At least I'm prepared for things like this.

You're a fatalist, said the woman. If you expect to be disappointed every day, you will be. The woman took the key once again and got the door open with no trouble. Well, there's your disappointment, she said, smiling.

You don't take me seriously, said the girl.

No.

They walked down a rather long, dark hallway that eventually led to the kitchen.

That's what bothers me, said the girl, first place you go is the kitchen.

I like long hallways, said the woman. As a child I ran down long halls and had the time of my life. We had halls like that in the children's home.

Were you in a home?

Not like you think. A kind of boarding school. Actually I always call it a boarding school so people won't misunderstand. I liked it a lot there and didn't want to go back to my parents.

Behind a door was another short hallway that led to the toilet on the right, a pantry on the left and a larger room straight ahead.

You have a lot of room. You could have a kid here, said the woman abruptly. It could sleep in the pantry.

You're always trying to talk me into having a baby.

Don't wait forever. Like I did. Then it'll be too late.

But you can still have one too. I'll take it when you want to go away.

Yes, I know, said the woman.

If only I could start all over again like she's doing now, thought the woman. A big apartment like this just for me. And whatever I did, I'd always have no one but myself to think of. Wouldn't be tied down. I'd get up early, the whole big apartment all around me. I'd wash under the faucet in the sink. The apartment gloriously empty. I'd have space for myself. Gradually I'd accumulate stuff, but only very slowly, here a bit, there a bit. If someone came, it still wouldn't be too crowded. *He* should come, too. He can sit in the living room, and I'll go into the kitchen and look out the window without feeling his presence. Be by myself. When I felt like it again, I'd go back to the living room, to him. But now and then he'd have to leave and go to *our* apartment. Then I'd visit him there.

So what do you think of the apartment, asked the girl. Both of them were leaning on the windowsill in the living room.

The woman's hair had fallen down across her face and her cheeks were red, so that she looked no older than the girl. While the girl's face hardly changed, only the expression in her eyes, the woman was visibly, almost breathlessly willing to listen. Beside the tall girl she appeared delicate and somehow in need of protection.

It's fine, said the woman. They looked down at the courtyard. It was different from the one they had walked through. Scaffolding extended to the roof. A young man was digging down below. A fat woman in a flowered smock was watching him with her arms folded. Dense, dark green bushes grew rampant in the black earth of this courtyard.

You know, said the girl, I never wanted anything for my future household, bed linens or anything. I got mad when my mother wanted to give me things like that. I was afraid that if I set my mind on having my own household someday, I'd never get an apartment. Because then whoever's in charge, God or Fate or whatever you want to call it, would say: What, she expects it? She's so sure of herself. Then she doesn't get one. That's why I acted as if I didn't believe I'd ever get one. Although if I'd consciously realized what I was doing, it would have been deception. And whoever's in charge can't be deceived. So I had to firmly believe I wouldn't get an apartment. Now I have one. Now I can talk about it.

The spell is broken, said the woman. It touched her that the girl made contracts with a power she didn't know, whose existence was more questionable to a person brought up without God than to her, who had grown up with religion.

First I only want to redo this room and the little one. I'll close the door to the kitchen when I have company. What comes later doesn't exist anyway.

Just give yourself plenty of time to fix up the apartment, the woman said.

I'm afraid you won't like it anymore when I've finished.

Why?

My taste is different from yours. I'm sure it'll all be too cool and modern for you. I've never liked old junk.

So what? After all, it's your apartment.

But I want you to like it, said the girl.

Well, you know, said the woman, trying to look indifferent.

Here, my first purchase, said the girl, pointing to two scouring pads between the double windows.

The woman laughed. I guess it rained in? What I don't understand, she added, you grew up in this city, have your family here, and only went away to go to school. Why isn't there anyone who'll help you?

In the city where I went to school there'd be somebody, he'd do everything for me.

You hardly know more people than I do, said the woman. And I'm not from here and besides, I'm so extremely shy.

It's true, said the girl. You can drive a person crazy the way you are.

Because I've never had you over?

Yes, that too.

I wouldn't have been able to stand it if you'd looked at my pictures and thought: So? What good are these?

I would never have said that.

But you can tell, said the woman. Sometimes you're so direct it's shocking. She remembered that half a sentence and a look from the girl had startled her as if she had suddenly been thrust out of a half-light into a harsh, cold glare.

Am I supposed to be a hypocrite?

No. The woman thought for a while. Then she remembered the incident with Chagall. Do you recall that I once told you I really like Chagall?

You may have.

And you responded by asking what was so original about him. As if it were a matter of originality!

Everybody loves Beethoven and Chagall and the rest. It's nothing special.

Well, I for one do not love Beethoven but do reserve the right to be so unoriginal as to like Chagall. And not because he's fashionable. That's what you mean, isn't it? And that's why I was so shocked every time. Because you didn't know me well at all. On the contrary, I find the obsession for originality in matters of taste a bit transparent.

You would have to remember that, said the girl.

I don't forget such things, said the woman. But in the meantime you've stopped saying things like that.

I've learned what to expect with you.

Maybe I'm too sensitive, said the woman. When we don't work together anymore, you can come visit me. I'll live if my pictures don't do anything for you.

You know, I'm sure I'll like your pictures. Actually nothing interests me more.

You'll be disappointed, said the woman.

No I won't. I feel it.

Oh, you and your feelings, said the woman.

But I do, I can trust them.

You're a modern girl and you claim to have premonitions?

Okay, you don't believe it. The girl shrugged her shoulders. You'll see.

You mustn't hold it against me, said the woman. It's simply too much if we sit across from each other day after day and you know everything else about me too. You can avoid seeing friends if necessary. But co-workers?

You're constantly making excuses, said the girl. I haven't been mad at you for a long time.

You've absolutely got to get a ladder, said the woman and turned away from the window. I'm sure the apartment will be nice. I can see it now.

Just not too much clutter, said the girl.

My apartment is full to the rafters. The rooms are awfully small. We really get on each other's nerves sometimes. When there's company too, you can hardly breathe.

There you go again making excuses, said the girl.

The woman smiled, embarrassed. I like the view, she said. You're up high enough to see the sky. And the buildings across from you are far enough away. And you know there's green down there. Later, if you like, you can install a shower in the pantry. I'm very pleased with your apartment.

Then I can count on your visiting me?

Yes, absolutely.

It's stupid that you want to go work somewhere else.

I'm counting the months, said the woman.

I've gotten so used to you, whenever you have off, it's pretty damn dreary, said the girl.

I'm happy when you're there, too, said the woman.

And then I'll be left. That's no good.

You shouldn't look at it that way, said the woman.

I like the job fine. But forever . . .

You mean, by then you won't be able to do anything else and you'll be scared to try, like everybody else.

You become one-sided, said the girl. You know all about that.

Yes, that's easy to do. Perhaps you should make a change in a year or two.

I can't manage all that, the new apartment and looking for a new job.

Why not? said the woman. Come on, the apartment isn't all that important.

You think I could do it? My mother says I should get the apartment fixed up first and then see.

On the one hand you know your mother's a little narrow, and on the other you listen to her. To look at you, you'd think you don't care what anybody thinks, that no one else's opinion matters. And then it turns out you're really very dependent.

Just keep telling me that. My mother and my sister are the only ones I ever listen to, whenever she manages to open her mouth. Besides, she's even less independent than I am.

I listen to what other people think, too, said the woman. Not about the apartment, but about certain things. On the job, for example. You're more self-confident there. But as far as your mother's concerned, I don't understand you. Although . . . on the other hand I do. I'd like my mother to agree with me all the time too. It's just that she's so far away that agreeing is easier. And when I get a stupid letter from her, I'm a complete mess. To be so attached to your mother. I don't think mothers are that attached to their children. Especially when they have more than one. Then they favor the one who's most like them, the one they understand the best.

I take after my father, said the girl. My mother was mad at me once and said something like that to my sister.

I know, said the woman, you told me. It's annoying when you take after the father your mother can't stand.

I could have parties here, said the girl, smiling to herself.

Could, said the woman. I just go to a cafe and tell people to meet me there. Or, one night I come home stone drunk with a horde of 'em.

And you drink such a lot, the girl said mockingly.

No less than you.

I could drink. I'm afraid I'd become an alcoholic if I started. That's why I don't drink.

Oh, said the woman, so you're afraid sometimes too?

My aunt is an alcoholic.

As long as you don't try to solve your problems that way, said the woman.

I have a will of iron, said the girl. But sometimes I really feel like ruining my life.

I know what you mean, said the woman.

They walked around the apartment a bit longer; the woman examined the condition of the toilet and the paint on the windowsill.

You don't need to paint anything but the outsides of the cabinets in the kitchen, said the woman. Maybe just around the drainpipes, too. Or at least grease them or something so they won't rot from the moisture.

Look at you figuring everything out.

Don't you want me to?

Oh, yes, sure.

If I get on your nerves, you should say so.

You aren't getting on my nerves. On the contrary. I wouldn't have thought you were so practical.

Oh, I do all right, said the woman.

Then they left the apartment and met the bearded man on the stairs again, this time with his wife and child. They stopped and listened to see whether he lived on the fourth floor. But he kept going.

Not your neighbor after all, said the woman.

When they were back downstairs, the woman looked for the neighbor's mailbox. She had already noticed the visiting card on his apartment door upstairs. I definitely think he's a musician. I've heard the name before. There aren't many people with that name. You'll certainly find out one of these days. Besides, all the telegrams on his mailbox. I'm sure he doesn't have a phone, so telegrams are the only way radio and TV can reach him.

What a tale you're spinning for yourself, said the girl, amused.

But you'd be pleased if he were a musician, wouldn't' you? After all, what matters is who lives next to you. Take me, for example, I don't know the woman next to me at all, and yet I hear everything she says on the phone and when she has parties. And she hears us. It's absurd. We're almost intimate, with the walls we've got.

It was quiet on the street; a few children stood by the front door. They looked directly at the two women and didn't seem at all unfriendly.

There's a restaurant on the corner, said the girl. Then there's a cafe and another restaurant nearby.

That's nice, said the woman indifferently.

I mean, as long as my apartment's not cozy yet, we could go have tea.

Yes, said the woman; the idea of going to a cafe or a bar again made her happy. We can do that. If we don't want to talk, or don't know what to talk about, in a bar it doesn't matter.

But we always have something to talk about, said the girl.

You don't know me, said the woman. If I have to talk because I'm with company, I can't.

Just like me, said the girl.

So we just won't say anything, and we won't make anything of it.

We'll see a lot more of each other, won't we, said the girl.

When I've gotten the worst of the housework over with.

They walked along the maple-lined boulevard. The sidewalk was very broad on this side, but full of people. Only a few at the outer edge were walking straight ahead. Most were making larger and smaller arcs, from one window display to another. Often the same people would meet in front of or inside a store and gradually become aware of one another before each one finally lost sight of the others at some point. Streetcar tracks divided the boulevard. On the other side were red brick buildings, hidden behind greenery and protected by armed guards. The boulevard narrowed at an overpass over the streetcar tracks.

The woman and the girl said goodbye, nodded briefly again, hesitated a moment but then did not shake hands, each walking in her own direction without turning around again.

The girl walked toward the elevated station, the woman crossed the boulevard at the crosswalk and was on the other side again. She seemed relaxed and youthful. She thought that there would soon be someone on the other side of the boulevard she could go see whenever she needed to. Until now, the woman hadn't known anyone there because her family lived far away, and she had no one else besides her husband. Though it is a lot to have one other person, it wasn't enough for her. And she was glad she could briefly reenter a world that was different in many respects from her own.

Translated by Nancy Lukens

Maria Seidemann

Born in 1944 near Leipzig, Maria Seidemann moved to Dresden with her family at the age of fifteen. After finishing high school, she attended college in Potsdam and received a degree as an archivist in 1967. From 1967 to 1972 she both taught at the library school and, beginning in 1968, took a degree in history at Humboldt University in Berlin. She also spent a year training at the Film School in Potsdam in 1977–78. Seidemann began writing fiction in the late 1960s and shared her first publication—a volume of poetry—with two other young writers, Christa Mueller and Reiner Putz-ger. In addition to two volumes of short stories and a historical novella, Seidemann has written numerous children's stories and biographies for young adults.

The following story is taken from her anthology, *Der Tag an dem Sir Henry Starb.*

Der Tag an dem Sir Henry Starb (The day Sir Henry died). Berlin: Eulenspiegel, 1980.

Nasenflöte (Nose flute). Berlin: Eulenspiegel, 1983.

Das geschminkte Chamäleon (The painted chameleon). Berlin: Eulenspiegel, 1986.

The Bridge Builder (1980)

ON FRIDAY the bridge builders visited the museum. As they left their duffel bags in the checkroom, Gregor thought: It's about time I settled down. At the end of each week, while his buddies were warming up with wives and children and homemade dumplings, a dreary Friday evening in a movie and a bar awaited Gregor, followed by two long days in a city which was still just as strange to him as all the others had been, and endless walks through streets and parks, trying to escape the empty dormitory. A night in a strange bed now and then always left him feeling lonely for days afterward, even when he was working on the bridge, which was usually an antidote to anything.

He almost looked forward to the tour through the rooms that succeeded one another like the centuries, even though the bridge builders visited the museum in every city, and Gregor always had the feeling he'd seen everything before.

Benita, in a dark museum uniform, greeted the bridge builders in the foyer and assured them she would be brief. The bridge builders concluded that she presented a pleasant sight and followed her gratefully into the first section. Gregor saw that she wasn't wearing a ring, and he was seized by the desperate hope of a cup of coffee for two. He didn't dare imagine anything more than coffee in any case, and knowing himself as he did, his nerve probably wouldn't even get him that far. He read her name on the badge she wore on her lapel and judged her to be about twenty-five. She'd tell him to get lost; he could hear it in her voice as she talked about hand axes and pottery. "And here's how a Stone Age wife lit her gas stove," said Benita. The bridge builders laughed obediently. Only Gregor thought with rising annoyance, which stemmed exclusively from his cowardice: She's making fun of us. Still, he liked the way she walked. Gregor imagined what she'd look like in long, tight pants or without any at all, with her hair down.

By that time they were in the Middle Ages, and Benita was explaining chain mail, which was unique because, except for two eye slits, it completely covered the head. Benita said: "Have you ever noticed that the battle dress of all ages exhibits two characteristics? It is intended to hide the wearer from his opponent and to make him invulnerable. Look at this armor here.

When the visor is closed, the enemy cannot see who he is confronted with, and he also has no opening for attack. These characteristics continued to be perfected in later centuries."

The bridge builders were struck by this and almost simultaneously thought of gas masks, helmets, and camouflage uniforms. Then they traded stories from their army days, and the museum visit ended up being quite enjoyable.

The bridge builders had hurried off to their buses and trains. Gregor was lying in wait for Benita at the rear entrance to the museum. A kid in jeans and a fisherman's sweater tried to bum a cigarette, but he refused to give him one; the kid was thirteen at most.

He almost didn't recognize Benita when she finally walked out with her hair down, wearing jeans and a striped pullover. Gregor immediately saw that the cigarette-bummer belonged to her. He grasped at the hope that they were brother and sister for a second, but his inner voice whispered sarcastically that Benita was obviously the mother and at least as old as Gregor himself and firmly in the hands of a family. He decided to sneak off.

But Benita had already spied him and called in her mocking voice: "Ah, the bridge builder. Would you like to join us for a cup of coffee?"

In the Crown Cafe, Benita introduced the cigarette-bummer as her daughter Caroline. Caroline declared: "Reuss said today that he's going to flunk me for bad conduct." Gregor could tell that Benita felt at a loss, although she said a few things to Caroline that he would probably have come up with himself in the same situation. Then they didn't say anything for a while.

"Your explanation about the suit of mail and the battle dress," Gregor began hesitantly, "I thought it was interesting."

"Do you think so?" Benita cried, pleased. "Unfortunately, I wasn't allowed to write my senior thesis on the subject. Instead, I developed a complex system for the classification of southern French jousting poles."

Gregor laughed tentatively.

"Can you imagine! Southern French jousting poles!" Benita repeated and laughed so hard that the waitress blushed.

Later, Gregor continued to be surprised at how casually Benita took him home with her without his even having hinted at his intentions. Her apartment consisted of a single room. Gregor's gaze immediately wandered to the two exotically covered couches. Caroline winked and said: "I'll sleep in the kitchen tonight." Gregor wandered around the room. He liked it even though everything was a little crazy. There wasn't a single closet, only pictures and bookshelves, nothing solid. As if temporary. But not to be compared with the dormitory, oh no. Benita laid out the contents of the refrigerator on the table, turned on the radio, and took off her shoes and later everything else. Gregor finally stopped being surprised and began to wonder how this Friday evening could be repeated. They lay together, contented, empty glasses beside them, a romantic piano tinkling on the radio. Gregor thought about Caroline, who was sleeping in the kitchen and was going to flunk. He felt guilty even though it wasn't his fault.

"When will the bridge be finished?" Benita asked.

Gregor muttered something indistinct.

"We could make a deal," she suggested.

He knew right away what she meant, it took his breath away. He rolled over toward her, and they immediately sealed the pact.

"But still," he said later, "even if it doesn't last, I want us to be honest with each other. No lies, no secrets while we're together."

"It's a deal," said Benita. "And now let's go to sleep."

After a while she sat up and told him.

Gregor laughed.

"It really does exist," said Benita.

He thought about her zeal in explaining the chain mail shirt and demanded: "Then show me."

Insulted, Benita said: "You don't believe me." Quickly running her hand across her hair she pulled off a blue hood and showed it to the astonished Gregor.

Benita said: "The amazing thing is that you can't tell by looking at someone whether they are wearing a hood. But there are a lot of them. Haven't you ever noticed?"

"How am I supposed to notice, if the hoods are invisible?"

"Don't ever ask me to give it to you," said Benita and put it on again. "My life depends on this hood."

"Tell me," Gregor demanded.

*   *   *

My father shot himself on the last day of the war. I lived with my mother in a big room in an industrial suburb. The room was in a side building on the ground floor, and there was a Catholic kindergarten in the main building.

I really can't say what my mother did during the daytime. In any case, in the evenings gentlemen of all ages regularly knocked on our courtyard window. I slept in the kitchen and would wake up and stand behind the dark windowpanes and watch the faces of the customers—I could have reached out and touched them—while they waited for mother to unlock the door. There were often several of them in one night, I wouldn't be able to get back to sleep and got rings under my eyes. Then I wouldn't go to school in the morning, would crawl out of bed at noon and go for a walk. School bored me, although I learned easily. The only thing I liked was the drawing lessons. I drew a lot, and Mother was touched and hung my pictures on the walls and didn't pay any attention to me.

At fourteen I had a boyfriend who came from a good family. Werner was seventeen and a machinist's apprentice. He tried to straighten me out, unsuccessfully. All his efforts ended on my sofa in the kitchen.

Without much work, I finished the eighth grade, although just barely, and was put into a children's home. The Catholic nuns from the main building had filed a complaint against mother and daughter for sexual offenses, and my mother lost custody.

My drawing teacher managed to get me into the middle school. I didn't actually care that much about it. I was much more interested in the drawing lessons that Lennartz gave me. Lennartz from the Academy. I think I was talented.

I met with Werner secretly. It wasn't hard, because I was allowed to go to school in the village, and they even let me go into the city alone, to Lennartz. When I realized that I was pregnant, I didn't return to the home one Saturday.

I found our room on the back courtyard sealed by the court. Mother had gone to West Berlin.

I went to my grandmother. I hadn't seen her for a number of years because she despised her daughter, my mother. She had a difficult life behind her and commanded a lot of respect. Thanks to her influence, I was released from the home and moved in with her.

I gave birth to my daughter Caroline without complications. Grandmother took care of the baby, and I got an apprenticeship as a seamstress in a clothing factory. Werner wanted to marry me as soon as I came of age. He had become a respected youth group leader in the meantime and had a positive influence on me, as the apprentice supervisor wrote in my evaluation.

When Grandmother died, I felt completely abandoned. It's true that Werner's mother took Caroline, and the Child Welfare Office found me a large room where a mover quickly unloaded Grandmother's furniture. But at work I was soon made aware that the consideration I had enjoyed because of Grandmother's reputation had come to an end. They no longer concealed the fact that they considered me a delinquent—a single mother who wasn't seventeen yet. Not to mention my landlady. Werner was getting a degree; he was going to school and never had any time. My apprentice wages and the child support were hardly enough for the bare necessities. I didn't know what to do.

I was about to make a little winter coat for Caroline out of Grandmother's old jacket when I discovered the blue hood in a suitcase. Standing in front of the mirror, I discovered that the hood became invisible as soon as I put it on. Not only that, but I found myself changed in a strange way without being able to define it more clearly at first. It was a while before I understood the unique qualities of this article of clothing: without being visible itself, it makes its wearer invulnerable and disguises her true nature. When Werner left me because my background and record would have been too great a burden to his future career, I took it calmly.

The hood saved me from despair and social decline. I registered for night school and proceeded to defy anyone who crossed me.

By the way, Werner became a politician. No, he's not at the very top but quite high up for his age. Since his wife can't have children, he now wants to adopt Caroline. The school and the Child Welfare Office would be pleased, because Caroline would certainly have a better environment than with me. To be fair to Werner, I have to admit: I don't think he has the faintest suspicion that the blue hood exists. If anyone were to tell him about it, he would think it was metaphysical nonsense because, after all, it can't exist.

I, on the other hand, began to observe my surroundings more carefully after coming into possession of the hood and soon could recognize fairly reliably who, like me, was equipped with a second skin. Voice, gaze, and interaction with each other provided clear indications. Since I found all the suspected hood wearers without exception unattractive, I swore without thinking that I would use my hood only until I'd gotten my life together and was on my feet again. I took Caroline back from Werner's mother and put her in a children's home. I finished my apprenticeship and passed my high school equivalency exam. When I applied to teacher's college I was turned down. I wanted to file a complaint about it with the Child Welfare Office, but they didn't consider themselves responsible for me any longer because I was of age. So I turned in my resignation at the factory and started working in the museum as a technical assistant.

Thanks to the hood, things were looking up for me. I was assigned as an assistant tour guide and given time off to go to night school. Thereafter, history tied me to my desk five nights a week. I got an apartment and a kindergarten space for Caroline, who now lived with me.

I'm sure that I would gradually have accomplished much more, but I met Lagulat.

Lagulat was an unsuccessful poet. His hopelessly honest verses brought him nothing but trouble. We fell in love at first sight—I loved him for his weakness, and he loved me for my presumed strength. He moved into my apartment, and before the first week was out I'd banned the hood to the lowest drawer. We would draw enough strength from our life together, and we didn't want to conceal anything from each other.

We lived this way for a year and a half, and then I ran out of energy. Work in the daytime, then Caroline, who exhibited the same kind of problems in school that I'd had at her age, history classes in the evenings, and Lagulat at night. He had given up writing poetry and spent his days waiting for me.

It wasn't long before we began to fight. I reproached him for his parasitic existence and unfairly attacked his lack of success. After days of hostile brooding, Lagulat suddenly began to write with grim determination. That was fine with me, but he also lost interest in my problems, pushed Caroline away from him, and seemed indifferent to all our vague plans.

When I was about to collapse, I looked for the hood and couldn't find it. My suspicion was soon confirmed. Overnight, Lagulat became a successful author. Newspapers praised him; he was invited to receptions, to round-table discussions, to conferences. He joined several organizations, received a prize, and wrote his famous trilogies in rapid succession. At his side, I gained entrance to a world in which I had wanted to arrive under my own power and which I now realized wasn't mine. I did Lagulat more harm than good. Skinny, nervous, and irritable, I stood out at a disadvantage from the spouses in whose circle I was henceforth supposed to move. My clumsy if earnestly intended attempts to contribute to the conversation were met with amusement, annoyance, or boredom. I suspected that I had landed in a circle of hood-wearers. I accused Lagulat of hypocrisy. A year before he would have harshly condemned what he wrote now. Without even deigning to argue, Lagulat left me. That is, he moved into one of our rooms, Caroline and I lived in the other. I felt the ground slipping out from under my feet again, and thought of dropping out of school and leaving the city with Caroline. I was overwhelmed by chronic fatigue.

I asked Lagulat for the hood. He would certainly succeed in finding another. He gave it to me, but I had to let him have the apartment in return.

Caroline and I moved into this room. I received my bachelor's degree with honors. In a few years I'll have a new apartment, and when a professional position opens up in the museum, I will have a more challenging job.

I'm still young enough to arrange my life to suit myself.

*   *   *

Winter followed fall. Gregor spent every weekend in Benita's room and bed. Troubled, he watched the bridge grow and with it the approach of his unavoidable departure. He admitted to himself that he had invested years of repressed emotions in Benita and her daughter—yes, in Caroline too, who wasn't like her mother and brought the two of them little pleasure.

"What do you want to be?" Gregor asked.

"Who cares?" Caroline shifted her gum to the other cheek. "The main thing is to get hold of a hood fast."

Gregor, troubled, said nothing. He had realized some time before how dangerous the existence of Benita's hood had to be for the child.

That evening he tried to talk to Benita about it. "Your indifference," he said. "Wouldn't it be better to do without the advantages of the hood?"

"I never want to be an outsider again," Benita replied. Then she accused Gregor of self-interest. When he thought about it, he realized that she was right. Because even though they lay skin to skin on the sixth and seventh day of every week, Benita remained distant and he knew why. Gregor wished she would open herself to him completely; nevertheless, he never again asked her to take off the hood. As a temporary lover, he probably didn't have the right to.

Benita's birthday fell on a Friday in April, and Gregor wasn't waiting in front of the museum. Her happy anticipation of the weekend together having instantly vanished, Benita sat alone in the Crown and treated herself to a double cognac with her coffee, then another one and thought about Gregor, the bridge builder. But that didn't get her anywhere, so she strolled morosely across the street to the bookstore to buy herself a birthday present just like every other year. Just then, Gregor came out; he didn't see her and hurried by. So, it's not work on the bridge that's holding him up; he's running around and has forgotten me. Her browsing spoiled, Benita trotted home and bought a bottle of vodka at a kiosk along the way.

At home, Caroline lay on the carpet reading with sparkling eyes, what an unusual sight. The table was set with flowered china that Benita didn't recognize. Gregor lit three candles, one for each decade.

"What are you reading?" In a sudden rush of embarrassment, Benita bent down toward her daughter and turned back the title page of the book—*Ships and Bridges*.

"From Gregor," said Caroline.

Benita handed Gregor the bottle of vodka. He poured two glasses half full. Benita felt the vodka join the cognac in a glowing sphere that began to spin.

She let herself fall into a chair and laughed in relief. "I thought you'd dumped me," she said to Gregor.

He handed her a filled-out form. "Departure," she read out loud and looked at him, mystified. "I moved out of the dormitory," he explained, and Caroline said gleefully: "He hung up his shirts behind the curtain."

"Don't we have anything to eat?" said Benita, confused. She was dizzy. Gregor had even thought of cake, but then they fried sausages instead.

"You haven't said anything," Gregor burst out expectantly.

Benita stretched out her arms until the joints popped. "I think I'm drunk," she said, took off the hood and held it over the candle flame. Gregor and Caroline watched her in silence. Then Benita opened Gregor's present. Twelve tubes of oil paint lay in a wooden case.

Caroline asked: "What are we going to do when the bridge is finished?"

Translated by Dorothy Rosenberg

Angela Stachowa

Few observers are aware of the fact that the German Democratic Republic had two official languages, German and Sorbian. The Sorbs are a Slavic national minority whose traditional homeland lies in the southeastern region of the former GDR. Although the government supported the preservation of Sorbian culture, German attitudes toward Slavic peoples, and a concentrated attempt by the Nazis to destroy the Sorbs by outlawing their language and oppressing its speakers, continue to affect relations between Germans and Sorbs today.

Angela Stachowa, who grew up in the GDR, is Sorbian and bilingual.

She was born in Prague in 1948 and attended the Sorbian secondary school in Bautzen. After completing high school and an apprenticeship, she attended the Technical University in Dresden, graduating with a degree in economics. She then moved to Leipzig to continue her study of economics in the graduate program at Karl Marx University. She has lived in Leipzig as an independent writer since 1976.

Stachowa's first volume of short stories was published by the Domowina Press, a state-subsidized, Sorbian-language publisher, and then translated into German. She had also written articles and short stories for Sorbian-language magazines and anthologies. Since 1976, Stachowa has published three anthologies in German, another in Sorbian in 1985, a volume of fairy-tales in German, and several children's books and radio plays.

This story is from her collection *Kleine Verführung*. The reference to the "Tribe of Asra" recalls an Islamic oral tradition of love tales introduced to German literature by Heinrich Heine in which lovers are fated to die.

Stunde zwischen Hund und Katz (Hour between dog and cat). Halle/Leipzig: Mitteldeutscher Verlag, 1976.

Geschichten für Majka (Stories for Majka). Halle/Leipzig: Mitteldeutscher Verlag, 1978.

Kleine Verführung (Little seduction). Halle/Leipzig: Mitteldeutscher Verlag, 1983.

Talking about My Girlfriend Resa   (1983)

OF COURSE her name isn't really Resa. Who's called Resa these days? On the contrary, her name is lovely and resonant, one of those first names that sound the same in every language and refer to divine beings.

All right, Resa. If I only knew what makes me want to talk about Resa— she certainly didn't give me permission to, and I really hope she doesn't recognize herself in this description.

Resa is what is referred to as a young, single woman.

The reader who is so inclined will stop reading at this point and skip the following pages. Because there are as many stories about young, single women as there are stars in the sky, perhaps not as fine and clear and exactly alike, but it has become fashionable to curl one's lip, yawn with boredom, or wrinkle one's forehead when someone suggests a story about a young, single woman.

But this isn't going to be a story about a young, single woman. I'm just gossiping a little about my girlfriend Resa.

Some people find her pretty but definitely not cute; a few, attractive, which I believe is the result of a misunderstanding; a lot think she is little and sweet; some friends think she is venomous and much too direct, not to say tactless; on the other hand, some find her a pleasantly reserved person, perhaps a little too quiet in her verbal participation at Party and union meetings; others and others and still others—see if you can figure it out.

Resa is officially described as of medium height. Which is a slight exaggeration. She's short. Which she subtly conceals through her choice of heels.

She used to be very thin; she still looks thin, but she has to put a bit of effort into that, too.

By this point she's a year over thirty. But for once everybody agrees on something: she doesn't look it. She looks like she's in her midtwenties or a little over twenty-five. This usually doesn't bother Resa; on the contrary, her response is: It's going to happen anyway. She's insulted only when she notices that some people equate knowledge and experience and perhaps what's called wisdom with age and a wrinkled brow.

In the days when she was still very thin, Resa almost invariably wore long pants and, if possible, something over them with pockets to stick her hands into. At the very most a denim skirt now and then or an equally casual dress. She didn't make a fetish of it, it was just the way she was. But now, slightly over thirty as I said, situations inevitably arise which require dresses; Resa has mastered that too, but she still looks best in pants. Feels best in them too. Corduroy, for example. Navy blue.

In addition, Resa discovered her love of evening gowns. Among other things, she looks good in them. But much more interesting and important, each one of these evening gowns has a story. And each story is lovely. Not a single tear has fallen on these dresses, which all come from different countries. Something you can't say about other pieces of clothing. I mean mostly about the tears.

Now and then, drinking wine with someone intimate and close, Resa tells about one of the evening dresses. Maybe she conjures up a Scheherazade mood. Maybe; I haven't been included yet.

People who love Resa, or call it that, discover two beautiful things about her: her eyes, which are a true blue-gray without even a hint of any other shade, and her unbleached, undyed hair, which is composed of different colored strands from very light to dark blonde. Recently, after two totally miserable years, Resa discovered in the mirror that the fine soft hairs just in front of her ears had a gray shimmer. But no one else has noticed yet. Or knowing Resa's vanity (which of course stays within bounds), people want to be tactful.

But why have I been going on and on about Resa? Even giving a lot of superficial details. Which, I believe, Resa wouldn't like at all. After all, her opinion of herself is that she's a shy person; now and then she says so, too. Only life and her career force her to appear confident and sure of herself. To form opinions and hold opinions. And what's most difficult: to express opinions. Anyone named Resa should wear a dirndl, loden, and shoes with buckles. Resa has a horror of all such articles of clothing. She hated dirndls even as a child. Unaware of this, her mother once bought her one with a little green apron, which was the only part of the outfit that Resa accepted and wore. For reasons still incomprehensible today. Resa should stop trying to find reasons for everything in any case, always trying to have things and herself under control. She should take life as it is. Resa envies people who can do that, from the bottom of her soul.

Soul she's got. Much too much of it, she thinks. It's one of the reasons she finds life difficult most of the time. Often too difficult. Soul. Who can afford a soul? At the very least you have to hide it. Disguise it. Resa doesn't live sheltered and protected either in a cloister or in a large house with a high whitewashed wall around it. Resa doesn't have enough money for all that much soul, either.

I regard Resa as a handicapped person. Not in the currently literal sense. And I hope I won't be thought dull and tactless for using this term. But it does come to mind.

Emotionally handicapped. I would like to write something about the tribe of Asra, but I can already see Resa refusing with a gesture of displeasure. Resa can't stand pathos in connection with her own person. But just between us, I would say Resa belongs somewhere in the vicinity of the tribe of Asra.

Once she just made it by the skin of her teeth. Just barely. And it took years before she had pulled herself together again, patched herself up, and so on, even longer before she could give the outward impression of being a generally contented and harmonious person. But Resa never talked about it. Just once with me in great detail. But I'm sworn to silence about that too. That time and those years produced Resa's frequently repeated statement: "There's one thing that will never happen to me again. I will never accidentally land in another *farce-à-trois* where women appear at night angrily, histrionically, weeping or whatever, demanding that I give back their lawful wedded husbands. As if I had tied them up and was holding them prisoner. And the little men, weeping and lamenting and swearing eternal love, crawl back pointing out that, after all, the women had always done everything for them."

Resa never quite manages to give her voice the appropriately cynical or at least nasty edge; sometimes her eyes turn sad, and she puts on a pair of glasses with slightly tinted lenses for a while.

The experienced reader may notice that we are approaching the point of the story. Although it wasn't supposed to be one. The way Resa wanted it. And for many years she regarded herself as a strong-willed person.

Recently, Resa sometimes asks herself at night, for she awakens with great regularity at two in the morning and then only falls asleep again before six if she's lucky: How many times can a person die? Sometimes she gets up and looks out of the dark room into the moonlit park. She thinks: Maybe I should do it. And maybe it would be the best thing. But then little Resa grits her teeth and forces herself to think about sin and responsibility. I just touch on the theme of responsibility here, I won't go into it: it's a matter of Resa's daughter from, as one says so nicely and clearly, her first marriage, still not all that big and still not all that grown up.

At this point we don't want to fail to mention: Resa, a perfectly cheerful and lively person, has certainly not been spared the attentions of younger or older men. (She'd be insulted if this weren't the case. See vanity). The ones who say you only live once and should live life accordingly. And not be so provincial, prudish, ridiculous, and whatever. And Resa, sometimes to her own regret but mindful of the evenings and weekends that would still be spent mostly alone, has to refer to the more or less dear wifey these men have at home. And those being rejected do not always react politely.

But to the point, finally to the point of the story. How can I say it best, most discreetly? How can I satisfy Resa's obsession with managing her private life as well as daily conversation without pathos, yet on the other hand not offend the possibly very delicate sensibilities of this or that reader? After weighing the range of options, all that's left is the simple and direct approach: Resa, without wanting to, without even thinking of it, and above all without wishing to, simply out of high spirits and *joie de vivre,* which was how it started, has fallen again into one of those affairs which she had sharply and disdainfully referred to as a *farce-à-trois.*

Resa is in love. And the man has a wife. Not just a wife. The man has a Mommy.

Naturally, Resa is vicious enough to call her a Mommy—the second, the stranger, the other woman—to herself (less often in front of others, since she really doesn't like exposing her private relationships) and, of course, to me. As well as calling her other things, after the man applied this term once in the heat of an argument. In all fairness I would like to add, however, that in the last year of her marriage Resa had frequently caught herself and her lawfully wedded husband calling each other Mommy and Daddy. Primarily because of their daughter, to make learning these and other words easier. Perhaps this was the unspoken but real reason for the divorce.

So, the Mommy. During the past three weekends spent alone—or should one say left alone (for it has been claimed that the love on the other, male, side is just as great and strong and true as Resa's)—Resa worked out a number of ideas and theories about Mommies. Was also specially provided with information about this one. Even enjoyed the doubtful pleasure of hearing Mommy's voice in its full emotional register from hate, to attempted motherly understanding for the oh-so-ridiculous situation, to whining (at any rate, very flexible and adaptable). Resa wondered whether she shouldn't immediately sink into her friendly embrace and thereafter lead a life *à trois,* minus the kiddies.

Mommies have usually been along from the very beginning. In this case since age eighteen. A bitter comment on this by one of Resa's friends who has been dragging along under similar conditions for years: My god, as if you had a choice at that age. As if you ever had a lot of choice in life.

Mommy's great advantage now is that she has thoroughly convinced her spouse of the idea that he is incapable of taking a single step without her supportive presence. And don't forget: Mommy controls the family bank account.

In fact, Mommy has gotten the man (Resa avoids calling him Daddy even in her thoughts; after all, he's only left her alone for three weekends) used to a lot of things. Let's call them supportive functions. For after the first few years of love and the care and management of two children, it became obvious that it was completely impossible for Mommy to remain in her job in industrial sales. And at the time they were in complete agreement: it didn't pay that much. If the man really wanted to continue working on his research project, then he should.

Because Mommy wanted that most of all. After all, she could then be proud of him. (I'm not talking about the goose that laid the golden eggs.) They could get by on his salary, and it would get better, quite a bit better. They both foresaw that, even back then.

In the meantime the children are nearly grown up, Mommy is still typing her husband's manuscripts (which Resa couldn't do; she finds it more efficient to send her own research reports to the typing pool), heats the house, makes applesauce from the little apples that fall from the little tree in the garden of the little house that they bought a few years ago, learned to drive with difficulty and some apprehension and, and, and. And reminds the man at least three times a week how dangerous life can be (using periodic gallbladder attacks as evidence) and how comfortable they both really are, after all. Of which the man is not entirely convinced when he is outside her sphere of influence. He often gets quite animated and lively then.

Mommy has gotten the man accustomed to things. Above all to the idea that she has made sacrifices for him. Sacrificed herself. Which naturally gives the man a permanently good conscience. Mommy is supported in this effort by her two sisters; the man's mother died years ago. He had no one but her.

Does it require any further explanation? Well, maybe this: of course, Resa is unfair. Simply unfair. She completely fails to take into account the good things that bind the man to Mommy; at the least common memories, in the best case mostly good ones. (Except, when is that ever the case?) But, Resa asks, does Mommy take into account that inexplicable thing called love?

Resa displays no generosity in complaining about Mommy. Resa, try to show generosity. Suffer quietly. Hide your own gallbladder attacks. Do without. Become Mommy's friend. Resa, dear Resa, you always were in favor of dignity and generosity. No matter how everyone else behaved. Oh, Resa.

The man says he can't leave Mommy so soon, everything takes time. Has to develop. He has responsibilities. Who, if not a woman as clever as Resa, could fail to understand? (Resa once again refrains from asking how he feels about his responsibility toward her, since he has already barged his way into her life.) Resa should give him time. Why the devil doesn't she understand his situation? Why in the name of all that's holy is she acting so juvenile and stubborn? Another girlfriend says: "You know, Z. put up with it for eight years." Resa doesn't answer that she isn't Z.

Meanwhile, the man is busily continuing to rebuild the house, which was begun before Resa's time. When Resa asked him about it, he said without thinking that after all, he had to plan for the future. He goes to the theater with Resa now and then, or out to eat. But only during the week, of course. Sometimes quite innocently he mentions attending Saturday concerts with Mommy.

Resa is a fool. Why doesn't she react to his "plans for the future" regarding house building? For herself. How, she naturally asks herself, does that fit with that strange thing called love? It is the beginning of the thread. And objectively speaking, that's where Resa should start to unravel the tangled mess.

Why does she banish these thoughts the moment they occur to her, quick as lightning, and why in heaven's name does she still rejoice whenever she so much as sees him? Resa is a fool. I'd be glad to give it to her in writing.

Resa would like to meet someone nice some day.

Like just about everyone else, Resa sometimes has bad dreams at night. And wakes up filled with horror. And then reaches next to her. And no one is there. Then Resa takes several deep breaths and swallows. After all, she is an adult. Or is considered to be one. Sometimes Resa then gets up and goes to the window. Looks at the houses and the trees for a few minutes, because to be fair, the area where Resa lives can't be described as anything but pleasant. And finally, Resa goes back to bed and tries to fall asleep again. Of course Resa knows that the next day, or the day after, someone will certainly call again who, on demand, will declare that he loves her and that he is the one who is the unhappiest that things are the way they are, that they have to sleep in different places, but she understands all that. Resa is really the most understanding person in the world . . . but at night things are often very difficult.

So, Resa would like to meet someone nice. Someone who wakes up when she reaches for him and strokes her dark blonde hair and looks into her frightened blue-gray eyes and asks gently: "Another bad dream?" Who then gives her a real old-fashioned hug and murmurs: "Everything's all right." Who goes with her to the window, arm in arm, and pulls her closer to his side and repeats: "It's really all right, it's all right." Oddly enough, Resa has found most things pretty bad for some time now.

Translated by Dorothy Rosenberg

Angela Krauß

Photo by Roger Melis, courtesy of Aufbau Verlag.

Angela Krauß was born in 1950 in Chemnitz. She studied at the College for Advertising and Design in Berlin and worked as an advertising editor after finishing her degree in 1972. From 1977 to 1979, she attended the Creative Writing Institute in Leipzig—named after the GDR's national poet, Johannes R. Becher—a common pathway into literature for the younger generation of GDR writers. She has lived in Leipzig and worked as a freelance writer since 1979. Her published work includes a novella and two volumes of short stories, as well as contributions to a number of anthologies.

The following selection is from the first chapter of her novella, *Das Vergnügen*.

Das Vergnügen (Amusement). Berlin/Weimar: Aufbau, 1984.

Glashaus (Glass house). Berlin/Weimar: Aufbau, 1988.

Dienstjahre (Service years). Berlin/Weimar: Aufbau, 1990.

Work

(1984)

A DAY, a transparent day in September.

In the southern lowlands, the fields of stubble shine like gold spun out of straw. On a day like this the eye can penetrate even the rural mean sulfur dioxide level in the lower atmosphere and touch bottom.

The earth lies in a gentle curve, flowing here and there into a hollow where dry bushes rattle their last leaves; the land stretches under the sun to the horizon where a group of chimneys stand sharply outlined against the blue sky, cheerfully waving from the distance, hardly to be taken seriously, a miniature copy of the ones that stand for the ages, protected in the valleys in the fissured center of the land.

This is the factory.

The Rosdorf briquette factory.

Carl Sendmayer & Co.

Founded 1912.

The tattered black letters of the past fading into the gray plaster above the vaulted red brick arches of the factory windows, arabesques in the wrong place at the wrong time; where were the eyes that had looked upon them?

On the roof, eight short chimneys release clouds of white steam, eight white pennants over the factory and above them two long banners of soot, the village below lies in the lee of the chimneys: Rosdorf, with its gardens in luxuriant bloom.

Under the factory roof a light bulb glimmers in a wire cage over eight coal bunkers. It takes six adult steps along a narrow metal catwalk to cross each one of these little abysses. A slight figure stands there in the light of the bulb.

This is Felicity Haendschel.

Her work area reaches lengthwise across four bunkers. It is an arm's breadth wide. By pressing buttons, she moves the coal conveyor belt across her bunkers, one after another, checks their level, adds more, moves on.

She hardly notices the noise because her work doesn't require conversation.

Felicity Haendschel's responsibility consists of seeing to it that none of her four bunkers, through which the coal falls into four giant dryers, is allowed to empty completely. Her attention is centered on a phrase passed along with the job: Don't let one run empty.

Nevertheless, three numbers are written in chalk on one of the iron girders in case of emergency. Felicity Haendschel can call the brigade leader, the foreman, or the safety inspector. She has to know whom to call for which kind of trouble. Felicity Haendschel has stood up here for three years.

She hasn't called anybody yet.

*   *   *

No two days are alike, the food in the canteen is different, or now and then someone has a birthday. It's something to think about, waking up in the morning. Her own birthday, for example. It has a smell. The penetrating smell of floor wax. Marianne has spread this pungent odor of unassailable virtue over the entire apartment, the wooden staircase, and the finished attic.

Because Felicity Haendschel will be eighteen today.

She had figured out some time ago that this day would be the last of four day shifts, which follow a cycle of three times four work days on, twice with one day off between and once with two days off.

Since Felicity began working here, she's known where she has stood. She had been fed up with school. Of course, this statement, in contrast to just the thought, would require far more self-confidence than Felicity Haendschel has ever possessed. She never expresses herself like that. After vacation, she had simply begun getting up every day at four-thirty in the morning and had adjusted to her new life without difficulty, sleeping soundly at night and quickly learning to find the advantages of this life. In this life, disadvantages are compensated for. If someone suffered an inconvenience, compensation was paid. Starting tomorrow, seven marks for a sleepless night.

Who had ever compensated her for her sufferings in school? The daily, casual humiliations: *Girl, have you lost your tongue?* She had stood wordless beside her desk until she lost all feeling for time. School seemed to be the wrong place for her. Her tongue was simply too long. So she paid attention to what she said. No more than necessary.

After she had finished the seventh grade, she stood under the caged light bulb in the coal-drying loft over the four bunkers and she knew: she could find herself here. Around the clock, later on, sleeping at different hours. She felt secure. And there was compensation for the darkness. Days off add up for shift workers; with the extra day off as shift compensation they get a three-day weekend once a month. It's like a little vacation.

Since Felicity is working the last of four first shifts today, she'll be able to go to the party tonight. The factory is celebrating its seventieth anniversary.

So there's a good side to everything, thinks Felicity Haendschel at four-thirty in the morning in her bed in the finished attic, while pots and pans clatter in the kitchen below.

*   *   *

That is Mother. Marianne Haendschel. She just dropped the lid onto the kettle, on purpose. The child has to be up at four-thirty when her shift begins at six, even on her birthday. She'd better get used to it. Punctuality is the most important thing of all, Feli! You don't know how long life is. It's longest between two and four in the morning, my dear child, and Marianne sets the lid gently back on the pot. The coffee water bubbles and boils. Marianne Haendschel is washed and dressed. She was at the hairdresser's yesterday and had her hair touched up. Because her daughter was turning eighteen? Maybe. You have to take advantage of every occasion, there aren't as many of them in a year as a woman of Marianne's age needs touch-ups. She has put on a fresh apron and is waiting for the day finally to begin. She has been waiting for five hours; she knows exactly what the alarm clock looks like in the dark: a phosphorescent green face. When it has gotten completely quiet outside and her eyes are wide open, she hears the coal trains clanking in the distance. And that is how she falls asleep.

Your internal clock is out of adjustment, the doctor says. It doesn't surprise her, says Marianne, she's spent a lifetime resetting it.

Marianne had already worked in the factory, on the drying ovens at 210 degrees Fahrenheit, when Kurt Haendschel had appeared, no longer exactly young. He came straight from the mine. Down from his bulldozer, which he was not allowed to drive anymore. Because of a few incidents. Everyday events in the years after the war, after prisoner-of-war camps and hunger in the cities, when everyone came looking for work here, when the mines took anybody. Kurt Haendschel was looking, too, and was offered coal as payment-in-kind and tax-free brandy. But what was he supposed to do with a thousand pounds of coal in his furnished room? He had preferred to trade a thousand pounds of coal for a hundred liters of brandy. After the incidents, he was offered the assistant driver's seat on his bulldozer, but it wasn't for him. He left. And he ended up where Marianne stood by the hot dryers and said: This is a family operation.

They moved into an abandoned farmhouse together, where they lived in two rooms, a hallway like a tunnel, and most often the large kitchen.

Marianne, twenty-nine at the time, hoped that this Kurt Haendschel, her husband, would reveal himself to be the one she had been waiting for. And nothing makes the years go faster than intense hope.

*   *   *

And Father is sleeping. If anybody sleeps, then he does. And when he's had his fill, then the whole world can kiss his . . . He snores like a burly giant and makes the plains tremble and the leaves of the dry poplars ring. Passersby outside hear him and think: There'll always be a few like that. Poor fellow. Damn drunk.

But he's been well beyond caring for years. It doesn't even register anymore. But someone like him hears certain things even better. Because once they stop listening to what people have to say, when they don't care, then they truly begin to hear. Their ears actually turn inward. They listen and listen. And suddenly there's the clock. Like a spring winding down, tick, tick, tick . . . and then they recoil from themselves again. In pure terror.

Who suspects any of this? The neighbors in the farmhouse who've been watching this go on for twenty years? When somebody snores that loud, people think there's enough noise to keep anything from happening to him. And how somebody makes his noise is his own affair. It's healthier for everyone.

He's the only one who's sick, and he's just realized it again.

He hears too well.

And his face looks like a piece of crumpled paper when he looks in the mirror in the morning. Had the rosy Marianne's hopes had anything to do with that face? She isn't what she used to be anymore, either. Dried out by her dryers, inside. Outside there's nothing to disturb him. But he can't see his liver when he looks in the mirror. Outside okay, inside rotten, and the other way around, its hardly anything to lose sleep over, this night has passed and so will all the rest, calm and as deep as the bowels of the earth. He can thank the bottle for that.

Did somebody say something? He doesn't want any noise! Not any rattling pans early in the morning either. He wants to spend his days off sleeping. The next shift is as far away as judgment day. Lying there, he's not waiting for anything. Nothing at all. Just lying there, and below the rattling in his throat rumbles the bucket chain, the conveyor belt bounces, trips, and rattles forward, nice and steady, all night long. Suddenly it snags, dead silence for seconds, the old man has hit a stray boulder in his dream. But the bulldozer catches again, and now he's even whistling as he digs in deeper and deeper . . .

Into what?

Into the dream of another life?

It smells of alcohol there, too. Into his chances in the great might-have-been? There never was one. Maybe there had been a chance instead-of? But it's over. Missed. Slept through. Drunk up.

But what did it look like, that chance? That's the question. It digs and eats away. Deeper and deeper into the silence, into his sensitive hearing. His ears turn inward all over again.

But there! There's a sound, very faint. Delicate and faint. A tiny voice, delicate, faint and small. And later, when they've all gone out, when he's alone in the house, then he'll go upstairs. And if somebody like him still has a wish coming, then he wishes that the fellow who knocked her up never shows his face again. Because he wants to be a father now.

Start all over again from the beginning.

What does he care what people think. He has the child, his daughter's delicate, pale, illegitimate child. He's a father all over again.

But nobody needs to ask him about it.

Because when he sleeps, he sleeps.

*   *   *

Not to be forgotten: the child. It was born without complications when its mother was fifteen years old. It has her thin reddish-blonde hair and her clear, remarkably steady gaze. It doesn't talk much for a three-year-old, a few sentence fragments in the local dialect with its characteristic grammatical peculiarities.

If it weren't a boy, you could say: It's the picture of its little mother. As it is, however, it can be assumed that his life will proceed somewhat differently.

*   *   *

First attempt to make a speech. Marianne quietly opens the door to the attic room; she stands in the doorway, small and neat: festive order. Orderly festivity. To wring a meaning out of every day requires discipline and a bit of good will and maybe not all that much imagination. A fresh apron with a snow-white collar is enough for Marianne. So every day of the year has its requirements, and satisfaction is within reach; it works as reliably as the plastic kitchen clock that she winds up every morning.

From the doorway Marianne reaches to the right, where the chair draped with last night's clothes always stands. The room is dark, a dark gray morning. Through half-closed eyes Felicity is watching the wind moving the curtains. The child is sleeping next to her. Its mouth is open in a little round hole, like a fish.

Marianne knows how to prepare for days like this: a clean house, hairdresser, fresh linen, flowers, and a gift. Now she stands in the dark room and holds onto the chair which she knows always stands there draped with her daughter's clothes in a very specific order. She's also sure that the girl is awake. Only the little boy is asleep, his small face flushed. Suddenly, Felicity's eyelids shut tight, like double doors closing against everything coming from outside.

Something ought to happen now.

The moment in which all the preparations culminate. The moment for the right word. It comes and goes.

Embarrassed, Marianne smiles, helpless before her daughter's closed face. Disconcerted, she watches as her own hand reaches clumsily over Felicity's shoulder and grabs at the boy, ruffling his thin hair and waking him. He starts crying. And Felicity raises her arm and reaches for the switch of the light on the nightstand. The light bursts into the room; whoever had been about to speak isn't going to now.

*   *   *

The dreams that Felicity Haendschel dreams replay the little surprises of her day. It happens almost every day: Miss Anna steps out of the office. She walks over to the laboratory. She needs a number, the moisture content of the briquettes, for example. She's wearing a white blouse with full sleeves, a straight skirt and white shoes with high heels and ankle straps. Miss Anna has the natural gait of tall slender women. Her hair is a gentle blonde. Seen from the sixty-foot height of the coal loft, she looks like a golden coin skipping across the brown square. If Felicity leans far enough over the fire escape railing, she can see the straps dancing on Miss Anna's ankles.

*   *   *

A morning still life, almost, as Felicity stretches her legs under the kitchen table. The gas flame flickers and the fluorescent lights cast a cold feverish glare, a sweating pressure chamber where the coffee steams turkishly into Marianne's lacquered hairdo, and sticks. She spreads red and yellow marmalade, again, much too fast for this morning.

Well, drink up, girl!

Marianne rummages in the drawers of the still new, laminated kitchen cupboards as if she's looking for something.

Felicity waits, not drinking, what's she waiting for?

Go on, drink it, urges Marianne from the cupboard. Even there she senses the suspicious silence at her back; the lack of activity makes her distrustful.

Here we are, Marianne finally sighs.

She triumphantly pulls something out of its hiding place and lays it on edge of the table: a pinkish gray department store bag.

That's what happens to people with too much time on their hands, says Marianne lightly, they get old.

Felicity is young. She hears very well. She hears the heavy reproach beneath the light tone. Marianne hasn't worked in the factory since the baby was born. Over the past three years she has settled into the kitchen and talked baby talk, and the boy hasn't learned to speak properly.

Well, open it! Marianne urges, and closes the cupboard again.

Why don't you sit down? says Felicity.

Go on and open it. Marianne stands next to her, nervously kneading her fingers.

Perhaps it's an art, celebrating things as they come.

Well, if you don't dare, says Marianne, picking up the bag by the bottom and shaking out a pair of purple slippers. They're still on the shoe trees that the saleslady inserted. Marianne sets them next to one another on the kitchen table. So that Felicity can see the silver pompons.

They fit, says Felicity a moment later, with her head still down.

And this too! Marianne pushes a bill across the plastic tablecloth, leans on her hands and is pleased. She's not cheap. Money hasn't been the problem for years now. Times have changed, and she herself—yes, Marianne finally sits down—she has probably changed too. She sits at home while everyone else is having a good time at the factory.

Thanks, says Felicity, stirring her coffee and stroking the plush slippers with her other hand. As if there were anything more to say. I never asked you to stay home with the baby. That sounded different than she wanted it to.

Most of the time what Felicity says sounds different than she wants it to. It's her lack of practice. Practice makes perfect, they say.

What do you mean you never asked? Marianne inquires with ritual outrage. You're the one who wants to work rotating shifts.

So, it's the old argument again.

Absolutely, says Felicity. She doesn't use that word very often.

*   *   *

A memory of childhood. Our earth was a dead rock. Looking out of the schoolroom window this appears to be true: the factory is made of stone, gray with red brick arches over the windows. The fading, magic number 1912.

She sits in the next to the last row. In front of her is a large girl behind whom she can hide. Whenever she knows the answer, she slides silently to the middle. The girl in front provides cover. Seconds pass. A hundred years.

Our earth was a blooming garden. A tropical garden with palms, swamp cypress, cedars, and magnolias. Giant blue dragonflies buzzed through the air.

There's something for your local history notebook. You can spend some time on that. Time to look out of the school window over the gently rolling fields, shorn like a moleskin coat. The newly planted birch forest in the distance, the poplar grove on the slag heaps. Eight high-tension lines humming overhead.

And that was supposed to have been here?

With the help of the questions of the girl in front of her, she fills three pages in her local history notebook before the ocean crashes in and floods everything over and over again, burying the splendor in sand and gravel and clay.

What ocean? The Baltic?

No, the primeval sea. For millions of years.

What are millions of years?

That is time.

No, time is when the bell rings: long recess, short recess, that's time.

No children, time is what's outside the window: change.

Felicity doesn't reappear from her chair until the bell rings; she's heard everything. But she won't tell anyone, not even later when she's grown up. She can keep a lot to herself. Other people can't do that. On the other hand, other people can pronounce their names. Felicity can't.

There's a good side to everything.

*   *   *

Second attempt to make a speech. But first Marianne sits down, finally.

I happened to like going there. She sips her coffee, which by now has cooled off, it seems like a digression. Marianne's last job had been in the cafeteria. Once, someone brought back a bowl of fruit compote and slammed it down in front of her nose, he wasn't about to eat the bug in it. A spider sat on top of the canned fruit, one with long hairy legs. Naturally, Marianne had shrieked; the spider was a gold-washed one on a stickpin. Someone had noticed Marianne's passion for shiny things. It only occurs to her now, reliving the memory, how much that meant. She's wearing the spider on a pink scarf, half hidden under her apron. Who wants to know.

Well! She pushes herself away from the table, turns down the gas flame, takes her cup and sets it quietly in the enameled sink, picks up the dishcloth, and wipes broad strokes across the plastic tablecloth; there's something else.

You're of age.

The cloth circles Felicity's plate.

You have to show people!

The fingers grip the cloth tightly. So tightly that water squeezes out.

Show what?

The hands wring at the cloth, small, bony, unadorned hands that turn white across the knuckles from the strain.

You have to be somebody, says Marianne. Her eyes look sober.

Felicity swirls the dregs of her coffee, Marianne's hands begin to spread the cloth out over the water faucet.

When they can't do whatever they like with you, says Marianne, and doesn't complete the sentence, doesn't shift her eyes, her sober, insomniac eyes. Finally, her hands lie calm and firm on the back of the chair.

That's not true, says Felicity with an intensity that is directed inward, not true at all!

When they can't do whatever they like with you, Marianne continues speaking without hesitating, then you are a real person.

Absolutely not true, Felicity repeats in a monotone with her eyes closed, absolutely not.

There's a pause. Until the mother says to her daughter: You need to eat something, girl.

Obediently, she butters a piece of bread and chews for a long time with her eyes fixed on the tablecloth. Afterward, Felicity can talk.

She can finally say things that Marianne has known for years. That she's going to work rotating shifts in the coal loft because she wants to. What does Felicity care if Lucy wants her to work three shifts, too? Lucy happens to need Felicity. Doesn't that feel good? And for the first time, Felicity is doing something she wants to do. That's an even better feeling. Until the longed-for end of her schooling, she had done what others had wanted her to. She has a name that she doesn't want because her tongue is a few millimeters too long for it. It staggers clumsily against her front teeth twice and then withdraws completely, like an injured mollusk. Felicity Haendschel had withdrawn with it to the last row, hidden from her tormentors, and practiced silence even in her gaze. But anyone who says nothing, knows nothing; and someone who hears this over and over again in the end really doesn't know very much. *Girl, have you lost your tongue!* And anyone who only made it through the seventh grade can't know very much. But someday a person is grown up and has to show people that they are. And that's why Felicity Haendschel is doing what she wants now. She's doing rotating shifts.

Because it's shift workers that you hear about, not the mothers on the day shift. On the day shift she still wouldn't be taken seriously, would still be someone to be taken care of, someone who required special consideration. But Felicity Haendschel, finally, finally wants to be one of the ones you hear about.

It must be possible to be somebody, even if you want what the others want.

Those are the lucky ones, says Marianne.

But things like that can happen on your birthday, and she smiles as she says it.

You have to go, child, says Marianne.

Felicity puts her cup in the sink next to her mother's. Marianne turns off the gas, it uses too much oxygen. The kitchen cools rapidly, and they both shiver.

The mother follows her daughter to the front door. It's beginning to get light over the fields; it smells like fallen leaves and frost.

Felicity says something with her head turned away. The boy, her mother should take him with her later when she goes shopping. The boy shouldn't be left alone in the house. Promise! And her tongue strikes bluntly against her teeth again.

Marianne promises, of course he'll be with her.

Felicity steps over the threshold, her light step echoes across the silent courtyard, drowning out the hidden, muffled sound of snoring. Then she turns around again and looks into Marianne's small, aging face under the fresh, stiff hairdo.

You're wearing the spider today, mother. Because of me?

And Marianne blushes. She doesn't have an answer. She's not really too sure about it herself.

And then Felicity turns onto the path that she follows twice a day, that Marianne took in her best years, when Kurt Haendschel had come out of the mines because of a few incidents and stayed on with her and her family business. The path leads across the fields and then runs parallel to the tracks where the coal trains shuttle from the mines to the factory. She can't miss it.

Translated by Dorothy Rosenberg

Gabriele Eckart

Born in 1954 in Auerbach, a small town in the Vogtland region of the GDR, Gabriele Eckart studied philosophy at Humboldt University in East Berlin from 1972 to 1976. She began to publish poetry in newspapers and magazines in the mid-1970s and has made her living as a freelance writer since 1980, joining the GDR Writers' Union in the same year. Also in 1980–81,

Eckart undertook an assignment for the Free German Youth organization, documenting the life, work, and attitudes of agricultural workers in the Havelland fruit farming region. The result of this project was a collection of interview narratives, *So sehe ick die Sache: Protokolle aus der DDR*, from which this selection is taken. The book was first scheduled to appear in East Germany in 1984, but after a few of the interviews (including this one) appeared in censored form in the literary journal *Sinn und Form*, her publisher canceled the project; it was then published in West Germany. Eckart subsequently brought out three volumes of poetry and novellas in the GDR, the first of them appearing concurrently in the West. In 1987 she emigrated to the United States and now lives in Minneapolis.

There are references in this selection to the denazification process undertaken after 1945 in the GDR, whereby nonprofessionals were trained to fill civil service positions previously held by Nazis. Such persons were called *Neulehrer* (new teacher), *Neurichter* (new judge), and so on; a *Neubauer* (new farmer) received land under the land reform, as in the context described here.

So sehe ick die Sache: Protokolle aus der DDR (That's how I see it: Interviews from the GDR). Cologne: Kiepenheuer & Witsch, 1984.

Stoßacker (Shock field). Berlin: Buchverlag der Morgen, 1985.

Der Seidelstein (Seidelstein mountain). Berlin: Buchverlag der Morgen, 1986.

Frankreich heißt Jeanne (France's name is Jeanne). Berlin: Buchverlag der Morgen, 1990.

Per Anhalter (Hitchhiking). Berlin: Neues Leben 1982; Cologne: Kiepenheuer & Witsch, 1982. Trans. Wayne Kram as *Hitchhiking* (Lincoln: University of Nebraska Press, 1992).

Ilse, 56, Chairperson of an Agricultural Production Cooperative

(1984)

I WAS WARTIME, and we lived in Babelsberg. The bombing raids every day . . . finally it got so I didn't care if I died or not. I thought, it's not as bad for a young girl like me as it is for somebody who has a family. Like my uncle. He was an artist, a painter, and had two children with a third on the way. He often talked to me like a grownup, about sexuality and everything. He was killed in combat and I thought, why should I live instead of him?

After the air raid on Potsdam, Father and I went to visit my grandparents. When we got to the station, there was a munitions train on the tracks, grenades were exploding, everything was on fire, bomb craters everywhere, flames leaping over to the factory on the right, I was afraid my hair and clothes would catch fire, I stopped, my father kept going. Then a young couple came along, the husband threw his coat over my head, and we walked down the street that way.

The next day I had to report to the district headquarters where I worked. When I got to the top of the stairs I saw my co-worker, two feet tall and burned to a crisp. That's when something in me came unglued. I'm telling you this so you can understand what it felt like after the war: it doesn't matter whether I have a lot or a little, whether there's a light fixture or just a bare bulb, the main thing is I'm alive and trying to make the best of things . . . Then this feeling gradually fades. You get rather wasteful with your time and energy, like when you fight with your husband about petty things. Afterward I often think: What did you get so upset for?

Of course, I'm glad my children didn't have to go through it all, but I can't pass along my experiences to them, either. When I tell about it, it's a fairytale to them.

Now we're affluent. It's nice to have a refrigerator and washing machine; all I have to do is throw the things in . . . but a lot of it you don't really need. There are things in life that can't be measured in terms of affluence.

I don't understand why a lot of people here are so preoccupied with their own family farms that they don't have time for themselves anymore. So what's life all about? They've never given it a thought. I had jury duty at the district court for a while. After the war there was a new judge in Neufahrland, just as there were new teachers, and he recruited me as a juror. I was in family court. When you sit through one of those divorce proceedings, you can tell right away when someone's lying. The act they put on! I thought. After all, they must have been in love with each other at one time or other. Nope, I thought, there's no decency any more, not even in the family. And then when my husband said he was going such and such a place, I didn't believe a word he said. One day he said: What's gotten into you, anyway? We also had a lot of cases of people who work and work and lose themselves in the process. Then they've got their car, their summer place, their bank account . . . and suddenly they're faced with a vacuum . . .

I had gotten married in 1947. My husband wasn't my first sweetheart, we had broken up, but I'd heard a lot from him about my future husband, they'd been in the same company in the army. So I had a very high opinion of him without even knowing him. I was supposed to give him a message from someone, and there I found this very shy young man, very decent . . . He'd been given a farm here under the land reform, and he came with his tractor to get me and my things. After living in the city this was an adjustment for me. Visiting my relatives as a child, I had learned how to milk cows; my husband didn't know how. But I couldn't feed pigs. They ate when my husband fed them, not for me. So at first I was always crying. We didn't have much money, I was always afraid there wouldn't be enough when they came to collect for the gas or electric bills or when coal was delivered. I didn't know what I'd do for diapers for the first baby, either. There just wasn't anything. So I got some old bedsheets from my aunt. That's how we managed until '58. It was fun, when you think about it, except that I was really very tied down. When you have to head for the cow barn in the morning, and then out to the fields—I drove the tractor, my husband behind me on foot tending the attachments; I had the kids out there too, so I was too exhausted in the evening to read a book or listen to the radio. That's why I was for the cooperative. They divide work evenly among the members, there's more time left for your own personal freedom. I did the bookkeeping for the cooperative, the best I could. Then I went for an agricultural engineering degree. When I had finished that, I became chairperson of the cooperative.

What do I like to do? Read, watch TV, talk with friends. We have a boat moored on the lake, and we move there every May. Good friends live right next to us. She's a potter, he's a painter. They're interesting people! We discuss lifestyle questions, for example, and what can be done even with the little we've got. So people don't have to live in these big high-rises where the old people get isolated and the young people get aggressive because they're lonely too . . . This is more important to me than spending an evening dancing with music and booze.

I rarely have conversations like that in the cooperative, because of my position. That hurts the first time you notice it. But I try to reduce the distance between me and the others. I'm a person who'd rather say "Hey, Fritz" ten times than "Yes, Mr. ——" once. I always try to know what's going on with them at home, how their vacation was, and so on. I was really pleased yesterday. There's a co-worker who was along with me in Moscow recently, a very reserved person. As I'm starting for home, I see him coming toward me, and he says he'd like to thank me again for the trip. So I asked him a few questions: How was it? . . . In situations when I notice someone is pleased, I can take pleasure in it, too. We also stay in touch with the old folks in the collective, go see them on their birthdays—seventieth, seventy-fifth, every fifth one. A card is sent for every birthday. Now and then it's a bother; this year almost everyone's birthday fell on Saturday or Sunday, and after all, I do have things to do at home, too. But these are members I've known since the cooperative was founded, and we're still talking about things that happened twenty years ago, very personal things too, like children and I don't know what all. Frequently I even get kisses, and I have the feeling they like me. Maybe it's easier for a woman than a man to talk about everything under the sun.

I am the only chairwoman in the region. The men don't like giving up responsibility to women. They simply have more faith in themselves than in us. On our farm the Party secretary is a woman, the bookkeeper, and me. So now it's called "The Ladies' Club."

Young women miss work frequently because they have babies who are sick a lot. You can't get women seriously involved until they're over thirty-five. Until then, your family is more important than your job. It was the same with me.

My husband was always a braggart. He loved me the best when I was professionally or otherwise successful, when I was in the spotlight. But . . . he doesn't want to do anything to make it happen. He's very supportive when I have problems, talks things through with me and gives me a certain calm and confidence, but he won't help me with the housework. When he was chairperson here, he took steps to support women and even cooked and washed dishes at home now and then, but that's all over now. He can't drink coffee or tea, always has to have seltzer or beer, and if I forget to pick some up, he can ruin my whole evening. He has a store at his workplace, and a case of beer or seltzer is heavy; can't he bring one home himself?

Everybody has strengths and weaknesses, including us women. We have to be tolerant of one another. But tolerance doesn't usually come until later, at first you're pretty bullheaded. By now I'm old enough to say: Why get all worked up about such little things? You just do it, and that's that.

I have four children, the youngest girl is still at home, she's studying at the vocational school for inland fisheries.

My own childhood was no paradise. I do have some wonderful memories of my paternal grandparents; in fact, I moved in with them when I felt like nobody at home understood me any more. My father was very strict. There were three of us brothers and sisters, plus a foster brother. I was the oldest and had to help out a lot. My foster brother was very spoiled, he got chocolate from Mother and I didn't. But I was a kid, too. So I quit eating chocolate, out of spite.

The early childhood years are very important, and I took them especially seriously with my own children. Unfortunately, I have no influence over my grandchildren now. I have friends, a couple, who have a young boy. He gets a lot of love and is cheerful and uninhibited. My grandson, on the other hand . . . The little boy talked back, and my son beat him. Children can't take that. He became withdrawn; he needs a lot of time before he'll trust you. I had him overnight at my house once, and he wet the bed. In the morning he stood there and shook with fear. I said: It's no big deal! changed his clothes, and gradually he calmed down. He must have had bad experiences with bed-wetting at day care. And when I actually heard a few things, I had a talk with the director: This was happening with my grandson and the others too . . . I also spoke with a doctor about it. He said: Children should go ahead and wet the bed as long as they want, it's an important developmental stage. But those are views you don't run into here. You simply have to be toilet-trained by such and such a time. When her little boy was three, my friend fixed him a diaper at night, just so he could pee to his heart's content without worrying about it. And he's turned out to be a real little personality . . . Later, when my children were fifteen, sixteen, they complained that I wasn't like other mothers, who make breakfast and have more time for them. We were both very busy with our jobs, of course, and the only time we had for the family was Sunday, when we had a big, hearty breakfast, three or four hours long, and the children could bring up their problems, little ones at first and later on bigger ones.

Today they say: Mom, you did it right, you didn't meddle in anything. Our friends have stopped talking to their parents; with us, there is still a trust relationship. You can't be dictatorial with children, you have to talk things over, tell them all the background, the pros and cons, and then let them decide for themselves, you know? Still, they're all different, none of them turned out the same.

My motto was always: People can say whatever they want about me; it's my conscience I have to answer to. I want to have a clean record in my own eyes. I told my sons that, and now I say it to my daughter: You have to think for yourself about the whys and wherefores and not cave in to everything people demand of you. I wouldn't like it if she always fell into line.

But you can get in a lot of trouble in life with this motto. A few years ago we received instructions as to how cooperative work was to be done. I was against the extensive specialization of enterprises. My husband and I said publicly what would come of it. We tried to keep that from happening, and in the process ran right into a brick wall.

Today we see that what we said was right. That hurts.

A few enterprises here are simply too large and there's no accountability. People don't know anything about one another; all they see is, the other guy is doing a worse job! And so they think: Then I can work less, too. People don't have commitment any more, there's no common interest, no responsibility. I see it here on the next farm over. With pesticides, for example. They drive into the orchard from the front and the back, and don't spray in the middle. The main thing is to get your hours in and get your paycheck! In our co-op everyone knows: We can only distribute what we produce. During the first few years there was a common interest in making progress. We now have two hundred cooperative farmers; we had to reassign more than a hundred, including the fruit operation and the necessary basic tools and funds, to the interoperations organization, Fahrland Seed Production.

Our operation is easy to keep track of. At first I was very sad when we suddenly lost our fruit division. After all, the cooperative had been known at home and abroad as a fruit production operation. Now we only produce vegetables, do some grain production, and keep cows, since nothing grows without manure. We really need about 220 more acres. Since we had to give up a lot of our acreage, we no longer have any real crop rotation system, and the soil quality is suffering.

Our operation was supposed to be dissolved back then, but we prevailed. After all, people do need vegetables. Nevertheless, we are regarded as outsiders in the Association of Cooperatives; we never get invited to anything, but we have to pay up like everyone else. I think that for an association like this to function well, the individual farms should be more autonomous. They hardly have any say anymore as to the use of their land. Everything is decided from the top down. And you definitely shouldn't discount an operation out of personal dislike for its chairperson. I'm not working for myself, you know. The people want to eat, and we raise carrots for the whole county, for example, guaranteeing the production of baby food. The first few years, our operation didn't even get machines. Some things have improved in the meantime.

I also don't understand why the workers all live in Werder and are supposed to commute back and forth every day. If I were on the road one to two hours in the morning and again in the evening . . . It works best in Damsdorf, there the people live right where they work.

And the apple monoculture! The women just can't hold up for months at a time pruning trees. They get tendonitis and go on sick leave. And they don't watch what they're cutting anymore. Just a branch here, one there . . .

Since we grow different types of vegetables, our work isn't monotonous. First we plant, then comes the strawberry harvest, and so on . . . And in the summer, when we have seasonal help, our members act as work group leaders. That's very important for some of them, you can see them blossom. But not everyone enjoys their work more when it gives them more responsibility. So that isn't the solution to the problem. The solution would be a greater degree of mechanization. There's been a lot of progress in field agriculture; potato harvesting, for example, is fully mechanized now. Horticulture is always a little behind. The machines are very expensive, too; they're more often made to order, you know, not mass produced. But we're trying to make a lot of improvements ourselves, our innovators are working on all kinds of problems.

When I see how hard the women work in the cold or in the hot sun, the men on the tractor have it easier. So I'm looking for varieties to produce where I can mechanize the work in order to give the women a break. Carrots are good, we have harvesting machines for them. The women sit at the conveyor belt and scrub carrots, so at least their work doesn't depend on the weather. Then there are brussels sprouts. We rebuilt an old threshing machine to harvest them; the women sit in the factory at the coring machine and don't have to pick brussels sprouts in the ice and snow any more. The problem is partly solved for cauliflower and cucumbers, but not for leeks and celery yet. There the work is still very hard. When I try to imagine still having to do all that hard labor, I wonder, would I have the patience and tolerance for it? The younger ones don't want to do it any more, and I don't know what will happen when the older folks are gone.

I think the majority of the young people in agriculture are different from what people say about the younger generation in general.

The ones with the "right stuff" choose other vocations.

We get young people who haven't made the grade in other places, for whatever reasons. Some who've already been classified as troublemakers pull themselves together, but there are still others where it's just too late. A young tractor driver in our cooperative lives in Glienecke in an attic, his parents are dead; we wanted to bring him here, but he's afraid he'll lose touch with his friends. He has turned into a drunk and a rowdy. You think that's only because of his job?

Everyone has some idea about the work they want to do, of course. You want work you can take pleasure in. And a lot of what we do in fruit and vegetable production isn't exactly what you'd call ideal work. I don't have any apprentices here, but I can imagine it's very hard for them. Finding their niche in the collective after an apprenticeship must be, too. Our older colleagues judge the new people too harshly. They're biased; everything the younger ones do is criticized right off. I often get very angry. You can't expect as much from a young person right away as you do from older ones. When I was young, I was careless now and then too, and who knows what all I did. In any case you can be sure I didn't sacrifice every free hour to my job. As a young person you want to go dancing once in a while, and do this and that, so you just turn up at work a bit hung over. The older ones give them a hard time, whether it's out in the field or in the office. When a young group member starts in with us, I have to be so protective that some people think they're a personal friend, and then even more people get angry. But in this situation I follow my husband's example; he works a lot with young employees.

My second oldest son is a brigade leader. There's tension between him and the other members because we're mother and son. And I go out of my way to pay less attention to him than others. I hope he understands. After all, if he has problems, he can straighten them out with Father.

My husband was chairperson here for fifteen years before me. I was chief bookkeeper and had a much narrower view, somehow more inflexible, maybe that's a hazard of the trade. I was my husband's worst enemy, which affected our personal relationship, too. I had always thought to myself: If you were chair, you'd do everything totally differently. You have to be stricter here, and this is how it's done. Then when I was in charge, I suddenly got scared, because I'm an economist and not a farmer. For example,

I can't tell a tractor driver how to plow or anything. I thought it wouldn't work out and asked everyone in the cooperative to help. I'm also not as quick to grasp things as my husband, and I've lost a lot of my assertiveness in living with him. Often, when I'd worked really hard on something, he'd take it over. Like a report at an annual meeting, for instance. After I'd finished writing it up, I'd show it to my husband: Take a look at it, is it okay? And then when it was my turn to speak, half the time he'd already said three-quarters of it already. I often got very angry. So it's a good thing he says he's not going to mess with the cooperative any more. This way I had to learn everything for myself. And everyone has a different leadership style. Suddenly I stopped being so strict, got all sorts of new perspective on my work, and all of a sudden I understood my husband. You can't rush things or just push through with your own plans. You soon notice that everyone has to be treated differently; one person goes along with things right away, another not so fast. If you try to force something, you create resistance. I've become a completely different person, more generous in dealing with people. Sometimes people on the staff try to take advantage of it and get me in a corner. But I try to keep on talking things over first, instead of giving orders. I don't like to reprimand people anymore. A lot of the men at work accuse me of being too soft. Every time that happens I take it to heart and think things over a while, but every time I come to the conclusion that I'm not too soft.

For example, someone made a mistake, wrecked something or whatever. The Board decided the guy had to pay for the damage. But when you look closer, there were other factors that came into play, and you can't blame the man any more. Some think I should haul people over the coals more often. But the older I get, the less I can do that.

Maybe I have too much faith in people, but so does my husband. At the same time, he can be rougher on them. He doesn't mind hollering at somebody once in a while. I raised my voice once in my life and regretted it for years. I consider it a sign of weakness. It was an official from the district office that I hollered at. It was about reorganization plans for this region. He said his idea of Communism was the right one: From now on no more cooperative farmers, just one single social class, and presto, we'd have Communism. I had a different idea, but he didn't let me finish and kept interrupting, so I hollered. Afterward I was angry at myself. I shouldn't have gotten emotional. It's no use arguing with someone who has a preconceived idea. I never raise my voice with my staff.

At the moment I'm feeling very tired somehow. The only fields we have left to work with are unsuitable for orchard farming, but most of them aren't suited for other crops either. We're located right next to a military training camp and have to cope with damage from maneuvers. We have some low-lying acreage where the crops are flooded in bad weather, and we have small plots, a quarter-hectare and less, that you can't work with large machinery. Although we've proved we can live with all this, and it's even more profitable than some of the straight orchard operations, it's still stressful for me. We are ordered to cultivate crops for which we have no suitable acreage. Where are we supposed to plant the forty hectares of strawberries we were assigned to produce, for instance? In the fields that flood? That was outrageous . . . Then when these things come up at public meetings, people act as if the problem was with my leadership.

My husband tries to encourage me to stick it out. If he were in my position, he'd probably put up a fight with the state authorities, he's thicker skinned than I am. So are the other district managers, but these battles get on my nerves. I should take a vacation sometime. Normally I don't cry at all, certainly never at work. As a manager you have to appear emotionally balanced, of course. But to act confident regardless of my mood, that's something men can do better than we can.

I'm also worried about nearing retirement and not having found a successor yet. Our good younger staff people were assigned to the interoperations organization. I've just asked two others who I think could do it, but they have contracts with state organizations. Of course at some point my successor will face the same problems I have, so it will have to be a tough man who knows the ropes. The whole economic situation has become more difficult; there's more pressure everywhere, you feel it in a thousand ways. It's making things more and more complicated for the chair. My successor has to be clever but at the same time someone who thinks about people. Not a yes-man who has no credibility with the staff. He has to have a little imagination, too. A person with no imagination shouldn't be chair, I say. Only imaginative people move society forward. How would it be if we only had people with no ideas of their own? We wouldn't get anywhere.

You ask if I'll miss anything when I'm retired? You can't tell until the time comes. I had quite a scare once. I was sick for a long time, and the doctor said I should stop working. That would be lovely, I thought at first, but then it really gave me a little shock. But . . . you only live once, and there are some things I'd still like to do just for myself before I kick the bucket. Travel. And then, too: I wanted to be an artist, I'd taken some graphic arts courses in Berlin but stopped going because of the air raids, it was too dangerous. I didn't ever intend to get married, I wanted to be free to live and work as I saw fit.

In the early years after the war I painted a lot; later, I didn't get around to it any more. I wonder if I'll manage to get back into it?

I've been doing ceramics, there are a few nice pieces, and I always enjoy looking at them. Only I don't have a kiln to fire them. Maybe I can get my husband to build me a kiln. It's hard to get the materials. Of course I also want to do a little painting and glazing, and so on. So I'm actually not afraid of retirement. And my husband has planted a vineyard. If you have wine to pour, you always have company. And then, a little gardening and a few other things . . .

I have no illusions about old age. Although the children say: When you're old and get sick someday, we won't put you in a home, I can imagine that would encroach on their personal lives so much that they'd change their minds. And I would never want to be a burden to them.

My husband is very proud about these things, too, he'd never go to the doctor if something were wrong with him. He has a disk injury and it's an effort for him to put his socks on in the morning. If I say: Come on, I'll help . . . no, I'm not allowed to do that. Where does he get this strength? My daughter is exactly the same way.

It doesn't really bother me that my career as a graphic artist and the dreams of my youth never came to anything. After all, I've done a few things and can face my own conscience. And besides, I want to accomplish some things in my last two years with the cooperative. I wonder if it'll all be recognized? You can't expect thanks for anything, in any case. That's something you have to be clear about with yourself. I had four children and raised them to be decent human beings, that's something, too. After the third I wanted to call it quits, but now I'm glad to have a girl too. Although . . . maybe that was too many children. They do come first when you're their mother. There's not much left over for your husband. And our daughter was very complicated. She only wanted her mother. Even as a baby. When my husband would bend down to pick her up, she'd start screaming. Later, if we were standing together and kissing, she'd push us apart. She was my shadow. It kept up this way until she was thirteen or fourteen. Now she's interested in her father, too. But some of the intimacy you naturally want as a woman has gotten lost over the years. I can count on my husband absolutely, he's a good friend, but he's also very unemotional; I just miss affection. Sometimes I would just like to be a woman. I think I'm too much of a man. Personally, what I can't handle is that my oldest son no longer lives in the GDR. My father-in-law had died, my mother-in-law was all alone. I thought things might be easier if I had one fewer at home and sent her my son, who'd just finished with his apprenticeship. I didn't have much influence on him any more, and my mother-in-law, after all, was a child of the Prussian Empire. I think this is one of the reasons he left her. He was serving with the border police, had taken a radio along to guard duty once and was severely punished. He could see into the officer's window from his room and found him out: the guy watches nothing but West German TV! So he talks one way and thinks another. After that, we visited him one more time and talked it over, we thought everything was straightened out . . . But then they suddenly brought us his things. For me, it was like in the war, as if he'd been killed and they were bringing me his ashes. Not to be able to see each other any more! That's a wound that doesn't heal. You're still his mother, no matter what the child has done. He still keeps in touch with us, calls regularly, so something must be left from the early years, don't you think?

I'm alone a lot now. My husband has become an avid hunter, he never had time for that before. At first I was sad about it, now I've gotten used to it and really need the time. If he happens to leave later than usual, I get nervous and ask: Aren't you going hunting today?

I need that more and more now, time to be really alone and relax. When my daughter brings her boyfriend over on the weekends, it makes me nervous.

Having friends I can talk to about things is very important to me. If you just swallow everything, you don't deal with the conflicts in your life. We don't pay enough attention to people's souls. We pay attention to all kinds of human needs, even physical well-being, but what the minister used to do, that's missing these days. Nobody is responsible for the soul any more. If you can talk openly in your family today, you're very lucky. But what about people who don't have a family or the right partner for it?

When I couldn't cope, I used to think I was pretty much alone. But through the difficult experiences my husband and I have had, we've met people from all walks of life who've been through exactly the same thing in one way or another. That encouraged me somewhat, you can talk with them. And you can tell your real friends from the false ones. So now I value these experiences.

When he suddenly was no longer director of development, my husband was completely thrown off course. He always had a very "positive attitude," as they call it, often getting things through that he wasn't personally in favor of. I thought: You have to be true to your beliefs to the end! And suddenly I had a husband who was defeated, but gradually also one who was more human. I prefer him this way.

Models? As chairperson, that would be my husband, even though I often disagreed with him. My political mentor is Hans R. He's an old-time Communist who was First Secretary here in the district Party office. He had a good heart, knew how to listen, had the courage to stand up and be counted, and had nothing against anyone. Unfortunately, he's retired now, and we rarely see each other. I thought: If someday most people are like him, we'll have an ideal world. That's the reason I joined the Party.

You could ask Hans R. a stupid question now and then, too. I don't know any functionary today I could ask something that's not appropriate but that I just don't understand and need someone to explain to me, so that I can say: Yes. I don't dare to ask questions any more.

There have to be people in the hierarchy who can give you a good explanation of something and, where they recognize something isn't right, try to change it. I'd see a real hope for us if there were people like that.

The first years of the cooperative were the best time of my life. We younger ones went at it with such conviction that the old people went along too. Together, our drive and their experience made for good communication (though they often had different political views, they cooperated fully on the job). Well, things moved along, we got recognition, sometimes too much, you're embarrassed in front of the others who are working just as hard but don't happen to be quite as far along. We got more and more attention, until the Association of Cooperatives came along and we laid our reservations on the table. That's where the recognition ended. But I didn't want to be chairperson of a showplace operation, either, so I purposely slowed things down a bit on the official side. I worked quietly on what was important to me and didn't really run into trouble any more. If I knew I would run into my enemies somewhere, I didn't go at all but waited it out, and now the cooperative is stable again. That was another success. Or was it a failure?

Translated by Nancy Lukens

Petra Werner

A native of Leipzig (born in 1951), Petra Werner received the Art Prize of the Free German Youth in 1974. Her university studies in biology led to a doctorate in 1980, and her professional experience has included a research position at the Institute for Botanical Research; employment in the GDR Ministry of Health, 1980–82; and, since 1982, research associate at the Central Philosophical Institute of the Academy of Sciences in Berlin.

Werner's story collection *Sich einen Mann backen* was made into a GDR television series in 1984. As a scientist-turned-artist, she has written about the failure of scientists, in their concentration on detail, to perceive the whole picture or to be emotionally engaged while unbiased. Such concerns may provide a clue to her intention in creating the male protagonist of this selection, first published as the title story in her anthology of short prose *Die Lüge hat bunte Flügel*.

Certain cultural references may warrant explanation. The old working-class Prenzlauer Berg district of Berlin was the center of the "alternative scene" in the GDR capital; its population included "squatters," who occupied and renovated abandoned nineteenth-century apartment buildings as an expression of contempt for the inhumaneness of the modern high-rises. Arthur Schnitzler, a turn-of-the-century Viennese dramatist, is known for his depictions of love entanglements in plays such as *Reigen* (Love dances).

Poesiealbum (Remembrance album). Berlin: Neues Leben, 1976.

Sich einen Mann backen (Bake yourself a man). Berlin: Neues Leben, 1984.

Die Lüge hat bunte Flügel (Lies have bright wings). Berlin: Neues Leben, 1986.

Lies Have Bright Wings (1986)

ACTUALLY, I should be satisfied. I went to medical school, which had been my childhood wish. I can afford to dress well and drive a car. Once a year I go abroad on vacation. As far as my health is concerned, I have nothing to complain about other than a bit of bronchitis in the winter and hay fever in the summer. As a physician I see worse, as you can surely imagine.

I'm on the medical staff of a teaching hospital, I have a Ph.D., and tenure is as good as in hand. Sometimes it bothers me that I live alone, yet it does have its advantages. I don't need to take anyone else into consideration, and I can spend my money on myself. I know from friends how expensive kids can be. My supervisors love me because I don't mind working nights and weekends. I don't like spending holidays at home alone. Children squealing all over the place, especially Christmas Day when presents are opened. I'd love to ring the doorbell then and say, "Guess what, kids, there's no Santa Claus." And when it gets dark. It's not good to be alone then. On days like that I'd rather stay at the hospital. Children are born every day. There's something dramatic about a birth. The nicest part for me is when I put the newborn into its mother's arms. Women are gratifying patients. A lot of them come back when they've recovered and bring champagne or wine. I'd say I really understand women. No, not just their anatomy or physiology because I'm a gynecologist. I know when to give a woman which flowers, for example, or when to pay her a compliment. When you deal with women professionally for more than twenty years, you know.

I'm forty-three, but I look younger. I haven't found a single gray hair in my beard yet. My previous relationship with a patient ended at Easter. You're my last attempt, I told her. If it doesn't work out with us, I'm staying single. I remember it clearly. We were lying on my double bed with a green light shining in the window from the house next door. I still had the pine tree then. It's dead now.

Maybe I'm too afraid of being taken advantage of. I had a bad experience as a young man, and I still carry it around with me. It might also be that I'm afraid of the everyday life of a relationship. When she comes yawning into the kitchen the morning after a night of lovemaking, I think, no, this isn't it after all. There was only one time it didn't bother me. As I said, that was the bad experience.

It all began with a phone call. It was one of my first nights on call as a resident. It was about eleven o'clock. I'd just gotten undressed and into bed when the phone rang. I jumped up and grabbed my pants, because I thought they were calling me to the delivery room. A woman was on the line.

"Peter?" she asked in a deep, pleasant voice I didn't recognize.

"Yes," I answered, "who is it?"

"It's me, Susanna." She sounded a bit annoyed. I was embarrassed that I hadn't recognized her voice right away.

Susanna paused and said hesitantly: "I still have a book of yours. Should I mail it or bring it by?"

"Bring it," I replied. My voice cracked with excitement. We made a date for four o'clock Saturday at the Cafe Rendezvous.

*   *   *

The next few nights I dreamed about her. I'm sitting in the train again reading a humor magazine. A young woman is seated beside me. I don't notice her until she giggles and taps at a cartoon with her finger. I look up, annoyed: slanted brown eyes, slightly buck teeth, athletic figure—Susanna. Or, we're walking through a barley field. It's May. Susanna's dress is bright yellow. There are burrs stuck in her straight brown hair. Her face is flushed from bending over. She picks poppies, bachelor's buttons, and barley stalks. Later I find the bouquet on my desk. The poppies go first, then the batchelor's buttons fade. By the time the barley was ripe, she had left me for another man. She's probably realized her mistake by now, I thought, and was pleased.

Then I didn't have time to think about it for a few days. We had three new admissions one night, and one young woman died.

In the morning I went to the House of Fashion to buy a pair of white slacks and a navy blue shirt. Someone had told me once that navy blue looks nice with my eyes. I asked the salesgirl to pick me out a tie. After I'd written the check, she smiled and said, "Thank you, Doctor." I admit the smile did me good. I changed into the new things right away and looked at myself from all angles in the mirror until I noticed that everyone was staring at me.

As I walked up the narrow street toward the Cafe Rendezvous, I stopped and felt nervously for my heart, which was beating wildly against my ribs. But there was only one couple and an elderly gentleman sitting on the cafe terrace. I wiped off the chair and sat down where I could keep an eye on the street. When I leaned back and closed my eyes, I noticed an intense scent. The bushes were dripping from the last rain. I suppose it was spring. I was young, and the change of the seasons affected me. Now I'm too busy and always in a hurry, so I drive a car and all I ever see is the road in front of me. In any case, back then I was happy to see the couple looking straight into each other's eyes. Now and then he kissed her on the neck. More people came, only Susanna did not. Gradually the lovers started looking silly. I don't like people who exchange intimacies in public. The elderly man got up unsteadily. His suit was full of spots. I decided to wait for ten more minutes.

Just then a young woman came up the street. She was slender and stood very erect. The color of her raincoat matched her blue-gray eyes. She wore her blonde hair in a knot on her neck. She should wear her hair down, I thought, and finished my soda.

She hesitated a moment, looked around uncertainly and headed for my table. "Are you Doctor Adam?" Her cheeks flushed with excitement.

I nodded and looked at the birthmark on her upper lip.

"Susanna sent me," she began earnestly, "unfortunately she can't make it. Her mother who lives in the mountains has taken ill. I'm supposed to give you this."

She laid a wrapped package on the table. Then she took a pack of cigarettes out of her little blue purse. Her hands shook as she lit a cigarette. O God, is she nervous, I thought, amused. I noticed she had nicely formed lips, only her teeth were slightly crooked. Why don't parents take their children to the dentist in time?

"Susanna has told me a lot about you," she said, interrupting my thoughts.

"Oh, what did she say?" My question probably seemed a bit hasty, because she laughed self-consciously.

"Well, just that you're very intelligent and work a lot. Susanna thinks she isn't terribly intelligent."

Well, what do you know, I thought. A liberated woman like Susanna can't handle being with a man like me. She found herself a dumber one. Now I had it figured out. I leaned back. This chick appealed to me.

I waved for the waitress, who approached us, trailing the scent of expensive deodorant. I ordered champagne. It was served in large, shallow glasses; the bubbles tickled the tip of my nose like tiny fountains. The young woman—meantime I'd found out her name was Camilla—was drinking hastily but in small sips. The birthmark on her upper lip hopped up and down. Now and then she smiled, I didn't know why. She wrinkled her nose charmingly as she smiled but kept her mouth closed, probably self-conscious about her bad teeth.

"What do you do for a living?" I could no longer contain my curiosity.

"I'll be starting in African Studies in September," she replied quickly, and looked at me. One of her blue eyes was lighter. "African Studies," I repeated, drawing it out, and finished my champagne in one gulp. The cranes I could see over the top of the glass at a distant construction site suddenly made me think of giraffes' necks; the honking of passing cars sounded like elephants trumpeting. I'm not used to drinking. Africa—I always did want to go there.

She obviously hadn't been there yet, either. But she did tell me interesting things about her family. It turned out her father was a professor.

It had gotten dark. We were the last customers on the terrace. The wind had come up. The waitress had put on a winter coat and didn't come back to our table to give us our check until the end of her shift. I felt warm. I wanted to take Camilla home, but she insisted that we say goodbye at the Museum station.

It only occurred to me afterward that we had forgotten to make a date to meet again.

I ran down the subway steps, but her train was already gone.

In the next few days I caught myself at meetings, or when I was alone, writing her first name in my notebook. She was following me like a shadow. Sometimes I saw her smile and wrinkle her nose. There's something lovably vulnerable about her, I would think before falling asleep. Whenever I opened a telephone book, I would start leafing through it, but then I'd remember I knew only her first name. After work I drove slowly past the cafe where we'd sat on the terrace, and past the Museum station. I got the course schedule of the Near Eastern Studies Institute, but she wasn't going to register until September, and it was only May. In short—I experienced a feeling I would never have thought I could feel: love. I had an intense desire to share my feelings with someone, and said to a colleague as we were washing our hands after a D&C: "If you only knew what a wonderful woman I've met."

"It's supposed to rain today," the colleague replied and walked over to the window.

I was outraged by these banal words.

I had to work that night. Whenever the telephone rang, I jumped, hoping it was her. Around eleven the receptionist called up and said, "Doctor, there is someone here for you."

I dropped the receiver and ran to the lobby. Our basement corridor, with its steel doors on either side leading to the doctors' offices, seemed endlessly long. For the first time I noticed the ugly, rust-covered heat ducts on the ceiling.

She was standing in front of the glassed-in reception desk, her dented cardboard suitcase beside her. Now and then the receptionist looked up from her embroidery work and peered suspiciously through the window. I was taken aback at first. Camilla looked like a pitiful little waif. It must have been raining hard, because her hair was dripping rainwater into a puddle on the floor. I immediately asked the receptionist for a rag; I can't stand disorder. She jumped to her feet, saying, "I'll take care of it, Doctor."

Then I took Camilla by the hand and picked up the suitcase. We didn't say anything, only our footsteps echoed along the corridor. She stopped in front of the memorial plaque to our hospital's founder and read it to herself. Look at that, I thought happily, she's taking an interest in my work. When we got to my door, she said, "I've left home." Her voice sounded tired.

She huddled at one end of the sofa. She shivered when I started rubbing her dry with a towel.

"How old are you?" I asked.

"Nineteen," she replied. In that instant I felt infinitely superior, although at the time I was barely thirty. It's probably because I'd already been through a lot. I was born during the war. I remember writing on the wall of the air raid shelter when I was four: Whiter than White, while my father stared at the ceiling reciting lines from operas. My mother sometimes flinched because above us, what had been the chocolate shop in which she had worked as the head saleswoman was being bombed out.

I told Camilla I wanted her to meet my parents soon. She looked up, astonished, and seemed pleased. I told her my parents had started a bakery after the war. They were people with a lot of drive. Unfortunately, when I visit them nowadays, all they do is ask me about various diseases. It makes me sad.

Camilla sat in silence, only nodding now and then. That was different and it made me feel good, because as a doctor I'm the one who usually has to do all the listening. I often feel as if the patients only come to tell me about their troubles. I'm planning to write up my extensive experience in this area in an essay, "What It Takes to be a Good and a Bad Doctor."

Camilla was a grateful audience for my life story. I talked and talked and didn't leave out even the trivial details, like the fact that as a student I would bicycle to the Grossedlitz Castle Park to study. I remember that there was a chorus singing on the terrace there once. Later someone played the piano. The fountains rose and fell to the rhythm of the impromptu. The sphinx between the carved balustrade and the lawn terrace smiled at me as I mumbled to myself, reciting the names of the muscles of the human leg.

Camilla laughed out loud and fell asleep smiling with her mouth slightly open. Her face looked relaxed. Only the tiny hairs of her thinly plucked eyebrows stood out. I felt like touching her but was afraid she might wake up and look at me dumbfounded.

In the morning we drove to my apartment. She stretched out on the seat next to me and men driving past us craned their necks in her direction, since her long blonde hair was draped over the headrest. In the elevator I couldn't stand it any longer and kissed her, regretting that I lived on the fourth floor and not the thirteenth. Dazed, I opened my front door and immediately pulled Camilla over onto my couch. Her hair floated through the air like threads of light. Later, as I lay beside her exhausted, I gradually became aware of the noise of passing cars again and the old woman across the way shaking a dustrag out the window. With sudden resolve I got up, went into the kitchen, and washed the dishes.

The next morning Camilla tried to cook me oatmeal, which I have to eat for my nervous stomach. The oatmeal burned, and the smell in the tiny apartment was intolerable. Strangely enough, I already had the feeling back then that her parents had failed to instill a sense of order in her. Maybe she just wasn't used to taking care of a man, either. Still, she tried hard. When I got home from the hospital after work, the table would be neatly set and there would be flowers in the vase. Once she had mistaken a head scarf left by an earlier girlfriend for a tablecloth.

One evening when I got home there was a little girl about four years old sitting on my couch. The girl had very dark eyes and tight curls all over her head that made her look like a blackberry bush.

"My daughter," Camilla said simply. "My girlfriend was taking care of her for a few days."

She looked at me a bit anxiously.

I only nodded. The child did not resemble her; its skin was bronze-colored, it had black hair and looked foreign. When I inquired, Camilla said some of her ancestors had been gypsies. Not until much later did I hear the touching story of her first love, the Algerian student Riad, whom she had called "my little Berber sheep" and who had returned home while she was pregnant. I admit I was jealous of this Riad, especially when I found out he was the reason she had decided to go into African Studies.

"What the hell," explained Camilla, "he was lonely and I was lonely, even though I had parents. They always came home late and I hardly knew them."

I began to feel sorry for her. But back to the evening she brought her child with her to my apartment. The little girl sat on the couch, sipped on a soda, and looked at me with very big and very dark eyes. The radio was playing instrumental music. Suddenly the little girl got up, struck a pose in front of the built-in cabinets, and in a loud voice sang the words to the song about broken hearts. At the same time she danced with graceful, catlike movements, until her temperament ran away with her and she darted around the room like a young goat, bumping into a little shelf and knocking down some books. I was taken aback. How could this little snake desecrate something that meant so much to us adults! I liked that song, it had served as a theme song for a former girlfriend and me. How absurd the words sounded coming from a four-year-old: "Then I felt your blood, how hot it was as it ran over toward me."

"Isn't she sweet?" Camilla asked with half-closed eyes.

*   *   *

The little girl slept in my apartment's only room, which served as my living room, bedroom, and study. That is, about ten o'clock at night she would curl up in a corner on the carpet.

"This can't go on," I said to Camilla, "a child needs a regular schedule. Besides, I need to work at night."

I was writing my doctoral dissertation at the time. We put the child's bed in the hall. In vain: Camilla's daughter Jacqueline would come screaming into the living room because the footsteps on the stairway frightened her. It got to the point that I didn't go home at night but went to the library reading room instead. But that was not a long-term solution because after work I need to lie down for a while and have something to eat.

"Doesn't your child have grandparents?" I asked Camilla testily one night.

She didn't answer, and I remembered that she had in fact told me about her parents. Within two days she had found a place for the child, because she woke me up that night and said, "Peter, the little one'll be better off with my grandparents in Thuringia than in our concrete box, right? My grandma has a lawn out back, and rabbits and chickens."

"Uh-huh," I mumbled and went back to sleep.

"It's not that easy to find a new father for a kid," she began abruptly and earnestly one night as we were standing on the dance floor of the Seventh Heaven bar during a band break.

"He'd have to be dependable. That's the most important thing," she continued, "and patient with my little girl. She's a wild one. They say I used to be the same way, and that's why my father beat me so often. He was still in school and only came home on weekends. I'd go to my mother in the kitchen and ask her: When's Papa leaving again?"

Camilla stopped and looked at me expectantly. Frankly, I didn't feel like having any serious discussions just then. I thought Camilla looked especially pretty that night. The light reflected from the rotating ball of mirrors scampered across her face like little stars. Round glass panels, installed in the dance floor, were backlit by colored lights that were flattering to Camilla's legs.

"Think about it—you couldn't go dancing as often if you had to take care of her," I replied to placate her.

"Maybe," said Camilla loudly and threw her head back, laughing. I think she was slightly drunk.

*　　*　　*

The summer passed without my being able to take a vacation. I sat at the typewriter pretty much night and day and cranked out the second draft of my dissertation. Camilla went away to visit her grandparents and her child, as she said. I realized I had gotten quite accustomed to her by then. I lost weight because I found it easier to skip meals. I even had trouble picking out a tie to go with my shirts. How had I managed when I lived alone? When I got home from work, I would look around in the living room, bathroom, and kitchen for Camilla. Once I thought I saw her in a car driving past me.

Now you're beginning to hallucinate, I thought, amused.

Camilla returned wearing a white pleated skirt and a light blue angora sweater and looking gorgeous. She unpacked a T-shirt with a Marlboro logo on it for me and said her grandparents had given it to her. I explained to her that I couldn't run around in something like that.

September came. Camilla registered at the university.

"Don't you need any textbooks?" I asked her after a month.

"No," she replied. "All we have so far is Marxism-Leninism."

Two weeks later it occurred to her that she did need books after all, and I gave her two hundred marks.

You couldn't say she was a spendthrift, but for a student her talent for spending money was amazing. The thing that irritated me the most was that she couldn't keep track of what we had in the house. How many times I quietly threw out a dried-up head of cauliflower or a spoiled sausage I found in the refrigerator. "Why get so upset over nothing?" was her only comment.

In such situations I would patiently explain to her that having been born during the war, I can still see my mother weeping as she made vegetable broth out of nettles and dandelions.

Camilla would lean against the kitchen door and smirk. Although it irritated me, I also realized that she was still young. I had this thought frequently after that, and unfortunately, I kept thinking this way until well after the day of the awful incident.

It was on a dark and gloomy November 14, it was raining: in short, a day when anxieties and illnesses are felt more intensely. I had left the hospital early with acute shoulder pain. About to unlock my apartment door, I heard Camilla on the telephone. The phone was in the tiny entryway near the door, so I could hear every word.

"This is Ilona Mueller," I heard Camilla's voice say. "I just wanted to let you know that I'll take the subbing job on Wednesday. Three highlights, one coloring, one perm. Fine." It was followed by a long discussion of the new sweater of an apparently mutual colleague, about the colleague's daughter, men, and French champagne that she had drunk sometime with a girlfriend. I leaned against the wall and struggled for breath. I tried biofeedback but couldn't calm myself. I couldn't stand it any longer, turned the key in the lock and threw the door open.

Camilla jumped and hung up the phone, slowly turning around. Blinded by the light in the corridor, all I could see of her face was a surface with no mouth or eyes.

"Show me your ID this minute," I screamed at her.

She began to dig in her purse. Her movements seemed clumsy and helpless, like someone whose glasses have just been taken away. The thought kept hammering in my head: it can't be true. She's only a child. I must have heard wrong. When she reluctantly handed me her ID, the letters swam before my eyes for a moment. But it was true: her name really was Ilona Mueller, and the only word of truth in everything she had told me was her age.

"And that I have a child," she insisted, as we sat in the living room. It was one of the most grueling nights in my life. Camilla (I couldn't get used to her real name that quickly) sat up straight as an arrow on the sofa, her hands on her knees. I had gotten up and walked over to the window. Looking down at the street without being able to see anything, I questioned her.

She told me her parents had worked abroad for years, so she had been raised by her grandmother in a little village in Thuringia. When the grandmother died, she had been sent to a home.

"I still remember," Camilla said, sobbing, "my parents were in Africa at the time and couldn't make it back in time for the funeral. I stood behind the coffin all alone in a white dress with a black collar that the neighbor lady had sewn on. I cried so hard I almost fell into the grave. Somebody from the village held me. The old women screamed, they were superstitious. I still visit those village folks sometimes. You'll manage, my girl, they always said. I had good grades and always wanted to major in African studies, but then Grandmother died and I had to go to the Children's Home."

"But surely your parents were able to visit you?" I had become skeptical.

"They did come once in a while," Camilla answered, hesitantly, "but usually they just sent packages. I always wore the nicest sweaters and things in the Home," she added with obvious pride.

"Do you have pictures of your parents?" I continued my questioning.

Without embarrassment, Camilla dug again in her purse and laid a few color photographs in a row on the coffee table. One showed a woman with blonde hair piled high like a helmet. She wore a bright batik dress and stood on the palm-covered terrace of a hotel. Another showed the same woman surrounded by Africans on a sun-scorched field with a pointed hoe in her hands. This time she wore a perspiration-soaked T-shirt and a pony tail. The resemblance to Camilla was unmistakable. She was obviously telling the truth this time.

"And your father?" I inquired.

Camilla raised her shoulders and jutted her chin forward so that her face took on a stubborn expression.

"He wasn't my real father," she finally said. "My real father lives in Dortmund. They didn't tell me that till I was fourteen."

"That's not surprising," I replied gently. "You were so little, you wouldn't have understood anyway."

"But I could always tell," she countered defiantly. "Especially when Carla was born."

She was almost crying.

"Who's Carla?" I asked patiently.

"Oh, my stepsister." She looked at me as if I were a bit dense. "He'd always wanted children of his own, and my mother enjoyed having everybody think she was younger than she was with a baby in the baby carriage."

She snorted with contempt and pointed to her temple.

"And the little girl is with them in Africa now?"

She nodded. "I was already too old."

I now had all the pieces of the puzzle. Yet I asked innocently, "Do you have a picture of her, too?"

As I expected, she shook her head violently and looked at me with child-like outrage.

I sighed. I admit I felt sorry for her.

Then she told me that she had always wished her name was Camilla in-stead of Ilona. When she was fourteen she had tried to talk a police officer into changing the name on her ID. She described this so graphically that I could well imagine how helpless the young policeman felt.

She's only a child, I thought again and tried not to smile. I quickly changed my mind when she admitted to the trick she had used to get to meet me. My ex-girlfriend Susanna was a regular customer of Camilla's at the beauty salon. It's commonplace that women gossip a lot at the hair-dresser's, and Susanna had told Camilla all about me. Like most people, she needed someone to talk to now and then. And I knew from experience that Camilla was a grateful listener.

That is how Camilla learned a lot about my life, my relationship with Susanna and how it had ended. It was shortly after our breakup that Camilla called. So I had been right in thinking her voice sounded unfamiliar. Well, what do you know, I thought, what a clever hussy.

"Whenever Susanna talked about you," Camilla interrupted my thoughts, "it was as if you'd written me a letter. You know, there are pen pals where you never meet the other person. But I wanted to meet you." She reached for my hand.

"But surely Susanna must have told you that I'm a difficult person," I said gently, withdrawing my hand.

"Yes, she did," answered Camilla. "But that you're a good person, too." She began to sob. "Why shouldn't I finally get lucky too? After all, I had a difficult childhood. Besides, Jacqueline needs a good home. She doesn't have a real father. I thought as a gynecologist you of all people must love children."

She had picked up the part about the difficult childhood somewhere. But the last sentence really threw me off guard! I broke off the conversation and went into the kitchen, where I spent the rest of the night on a cot. That is, I tried to sleep but couldn't. My brain wouldn't stop working.

Finding a father for her child, I began, is an acceptable motivation, espe-cially for a woman. But why did she ever pretend to be in African Studies? I suppose because she thought I wouldn't respect her as a hairdresser. I tried to judge her fairly. I found no trace of disrespect in my behavior toward her, although I have to admit that I would have preferred a woman with an edu-cation because of the intellectual interchange. On the other hand, if it hadn't been for the phone call, I might never have found out the truth. Besides, a hairdresser brings home not only entertaining gossip but nice hairdos. Their problems also tend to be less complex: a little in-fighting at work, a new dress, a flirtation with the boss. An educated woman is different, she'll get in bed and keep right on discussing ideas with you.

I admit that my attitude was condescending back then. Besides that, I steered her single-mindedly in the direction I wanted her to go. For this reason: I never wanted to be alone again. So I counted up the advantages Camilla offered, not forgetting that she was younger and I could still teach her some things, that she had become quite a decent cook and was an interesting lover.

But I kept all these thoughts to myself and wasn't really convinced by them. Camilla's former life was something dark and mysterious to me; it repelled me and attracted me at the same time. I was afraid of a woman who could lie so well. I got into the habit of asking every question two or three times and watching her intently, as if I could see the truth in her soft, smooth face. At the slightest variation from earlier versions I would shiver; in fact, I began to make notes of conversations and compare them. Camilla noticed what I was doing and tried to smile sympathetically. Once, though, she raised her right eyebrow and replied gently: But I've already told you that.

In every other way she took pains to please me. I took it for granted, perhaps because I had gotten used to it, and I made her feel she owed me something. Once I even spit out some salad onto the rug because there was sand on the lettuce. She almost cried, and I apologized.

I came home late sometimes now. I had gotten to know a patient who ran a dancing school with her husband. She was forty but still wore a pony-tail, so she looked rather girlish. Her husband was twenty-five years older and would retire in a year. Because of her, I registered myself and Camilla for the Dancing for Beginners class and then went by myself later, because Camilla's feet hurt at night from standing all day at work. Besides, she kept trying—she claimed she didn't realize it—to take the lead when we danced, which led to constant arguments. How pliant Renate, the dance teacher, was by comparison when she nestled in my arms: she swayed like a feather during the Viennese waltz and my toes hardly touched the floor. I, who had never been very coordinated, could dance! Renate's Maria Farina perfume enveloped me and stimulated my imagination.

We met outside of class, too, in cafes and parks. I remember cutting my office hours short now and then, or even canceling them, to see her. It turned out that she had actually wanted to become a dancer, but her husband, whom she had married at eighteen, had been against it. In general, she did not seem very happily married, although she had probably had unrealistic expectations. She lent me a photocopy of a "Marriage Design" that some writer had concocted, and seriously expected me to be excited about it. But after all, you can't dance the Viennese waltz all day! And then, she looked pretty old in the glare of daylight. But it didn't matter, I hadn't made her any promises.

I don't know if Camilla had noticed anything.

Sometimes she wasn't there when I got home at night, but I didn't give it a second thought. Though I did always check the living room, kitchen, and bathroom for her. I don't like to come home to an empty apartment at night. Camilla didn't talk about work much but asked all the more questions about mine. I answered monosyllabically. The first draft of my dissertation had been rejected, and I blamed Camilla in part. Since she'd been living with me I hadn't been able to concentrate on my work. She obviously felt this, because one day she told me she wanted to go spend two weeks in the village where she'd lived with her grandparents. I nodded. She seemed fond of this village.

During that time I saw Renate even more often. I thought our dates were a welcome change from her life as a dance instructor. One day in the park, however, while standing in front of a sausage vendor's stand biting into a frankfurter, she admitted that she was feeling guilty toward her husband. Besides, she said, she preferred the less intense but dependable pleasure she had with him to the stronger but undependable relationship she had with me. And finally, she couldn't leave him; who would carry him to the toilet when he got old? I shrugged. We said goodbye, promising that we would never forget each other.

The day before Camilla had said she would be back, I cleaned the apartment and bought groceries. I even used the cookbook to surprise her with dinner, and lit a candle. Nine o'clock came, ten o'clock came. She didn't. I can still see myself sitting facing the table with the white tablecloth and turning on the TV in desperation. An old film with Henny Porten was playing and I watched the whole thing, although I usually can't stand old films and especially not with Henny Porten.

Camilla didn't come back that night or for the next seven days. She simply wasn't there when I got home. My restlessness and desperation wore off after three days, however, and when she stood in the doorway on the eighth day, a Saturday, I jumped, because I had stopped expecting her.

She looked like a tramp. At least I thought I noticed bluish circles under her eyes, and her tangled hair smelled of smoke. It's possible that my rage was interfering with my vision and hearing; I saw what I wanted to see and heard what I wanted to hear. I had made up my mind and all I was looking for was evidence. I led Camilla into the living room like a stranger and pushed her into the armchair. Then I put paper and pen on the coffee table and demanded that she account for every minute of her absence. She never even got around to taking off her jacket or shoes. When I was certain she had not been in that infamous village but at a local campground, supposedly with a girlfriend from Berlin, I went to the closet and threw her things on the bed, along with the cardboard suitcase she had brought with her when she moved into my place. It was about eleven o'clock at night. She packed her suitcase lethargically. As she walked out, she left the door open. I watched out the window how she walked across the poorly lit square in front of my house. The suitcase banged against her legs as she walked. Now and then she put it down and looked back. I quickly ducked.

A month later I received a postcard. There was a picture of a basket of young kittens on the back. The message read: Dear Peter, I'm expecting and you're the father. Signed: Camilla-Ilona. The return address was a back street in Prenzlauer Berg. I laughed, decided the whole thing was another trick, and tore up the postcard.

The next few months I worked furiously, though with little success. It took me a while to forget Camilla. You know how it is when a woman has lived with you for a long time, you find a barrette or a comb when you least expect it, and suddenly they're back, the memories.

It was November when she called me at home.

"This is Camilla. I'm due in a month. Can you deliver it—I'd be less afraid with you . . ."

This time she made no attempt to disguise her voice.

"No, no," I stuttered in horror. "I'll get you a bed in Friedrichshain Hospital."

I called a colleague and told him about a friend's cousin I was concerned about. That obviously wasn't a very good cover, because I noticed he was suppressing his laughter. Meanwhile, I was seeing a divorced woman colleague at the hospital.

As Camilla's due date approached, I found some reason to call Friedrichshain every day. I was overcome by a strange restlessness. How often I, the gynecologist, had been asked if I had children of my own. Some people gave me a strange look when I said no, and once in a while I had the feeling I owed them an explanation. But what would I say?

* * *

"His name is Peter, after you," were Camilla's first words two days after the delivery. She looked pale and almost transparent but still very beautiful.

"He's got your straight nose." She smiled. "He wasn't red and wrinkled at all, but looked really cute right from the beginning. But I didn't feel that well after he was born. I lay alone in my room and thought: Well, so this is it, the famous joy of motherhood. I felt so isolated . . ."

She laughed, turning red with embarrassment.

"But then the nurse brought in our son, and when she left, I used my pocket mirror to compare: my eyes—his eyes; my mouth—his mouth; the nose wasn't mine, I saw that right away . . ."

I was hardly listening. I left the room and had them show me the baby. He looked like every other newborn. Although Camilla was right about the nose.

So I legally acknowledged paternity and paid my child support on time. Actually, I authorized automatic payments from my account. If only because I didn't want to be reminded every month. I had no desire to see Camilla or the baby. I can't stand children making noise, I think I said that already. Although I once heard that it's different when they're your own.

Once, it was four months later, I happened to run into Camilla on the street with my son. She looked great, she'd filled out a little, had rouge on, and her crooked teeth had been corrected with caps. In a word, she looked like a young woman any average working man would have considered himself lucky to get. I suggested going for coffee. She looked at her watch in embarrassment and finally said: "It's almost one, I have to put the little one down for his nap." When she noticed the irritation in my smile, she explained soberly: "The director of the day-care center says a regular schedule is very important for a young child."

Fine, I thought, disappointed. She still had ten minutes. So we stood on the street and chatted about nothing in particular. As we talked, she rocked the baby carriage to quiet the baby, who was obviously hungry. Then she'd straighten the blanket and shake the rattle as my son reached up for it, cackling.

I stood there, stiff as a board. I didn't feel like a father, more like an uncle from America. To make things worse, Camilla suddenly bent down over the

baby, pointed at me, and whispered, "That's a wicked uncle, Petie Baby."
She looked at me, her eyes flashing with rage and disappointment. I almost
had to laugh. She really was still very immature, even if she had turned
twenty in the meantime.

I told myself at least my son seemed well cared for. That's lucky, I
thought, she doesn't scrimp on clothes or food for the little one. I gave her
a hundred marks extra so she could buy my son a few bananas.

*　　*　　*

For a few months I heard nothing from her. I talked myself into being
glad of that. Nevertheless, I was startled every time I saw a woman on the
street who looked like Camilla.

I was surprised to see her in one place I never would have expected her—
in the doctors' lounge in our hospital. That is where we held our Christmas
party, or year's end party, as it's called now.

Camilla turned up escorted by a colleague I didn't like. She didn't walk
beside him across the hall, she strutted. Her skin glowed through the thin
black fabric of her dress. I noticed a few of my colleagues shifting back
and forth nervously in their chairs. To me, the fabric looked like a scaly
snakeskin. It may sound very old-fashioned, but I prefer women who wear
white cotton underclothes. It looks clean and decent. Provocative underwear makes me suspicious. Maybe especially now, because I'd had such a
bad experience with Camilla.

Anyway, they started whispering at the next table, and I saw one colleague punch the other as they both smirked. Camilla was at the other end
of the dance floor with Dr. Carlo. Of course she had seen me right away;
she flirted conspicuously with Carlo and smiled in my direction now and
then. I had the feeling she wanted to make me jealous. But it all seemed so
disingenuous that I found it revolting. She's primitive, I thought.

I waited until the mood had lightened and I could move to another table
unnoticed. The colleagues who had been talking about Camilla a moment
before had come without dates and had already had a few glasses of cognac.
First we talked about our medical director, then about complex cases in our
practice. Our work is so demanding that we can't forget it after hours either.
As a result our conversations are one-dimensional—how rarely can one of
us tell about a new play or a film!

"Who's the young woman Carlo brought along?" I began, pretending
ignorance.

"Oh, you like her?" grinned the colleague meaningfully. "Ask Richard, he knows her better."

The man being referred to blushed a little and made an embarrassed gesture of denial. "Used to know her, you should say." After a while he added, "It's been quite a while, at least a year and a half. She wanted me to get a divorce. But it's not that simple when you've got three kids . . ." Then he was silent.

It sounded passionless. I had the feeling he was suffering little regret over breaking up with Camilla. I listened to all this with remarkable detachment, like someone who has been hardened by too much suffering. I didn't need to do much arithmetic, it was obvious! We changed the subject very quickly. About ten o'clock I got up without explanation and went home. No one noticed particularly, since they were all quite drunk.

In the cabinet at home I found a bottle of Hennessy that a patient had brought me recently. For a second, I seriously considered getting drunk, but instead forced myself to work through Hegel's *Science of Logic*. Of course, it was a fruitless effort.

The next morning I went to see a lawyer and, without emotion, disputed the paternity claim. I had to undergo the usual tests so the reports could be prepared. The blood tests took valuable work time, and besides I felt I was treated without respect. My rage against Camilla grew.

*   *   *

The court date was set for three months later. Even today it makes me uncomfortable to think of the tall gray staircase of the county courthouse. Camilla was already there, waiting on a bench by the door. She got up and came over to shake hands. I ignored her and walked over to the other side. What did she expect of me now?

I did not get to look at her unobserved until the proceeding had begun. She wore her hair straight and parted like a madonna. She kept her lips tightly closed, which gave her an ascetic look. Oh, did I know better!

The reports were read aloud, one from Professor M., the other from the famous Professor P. Both concluded definitively that I could not be the father.

What a liar, I shuddered. Sure, he has your straight nose and your eyes . . . I wanted to cry, I was so insulted. Only now did I realize that I had secretly hoped I was the father after all. I am sure no one noticed my disappointment. But what a scene Camilla made!

"That's impossible!" she exclaimed, sobbing. Then she sank into her chair whispering, "This is the only man I love or have ever loved, him and only him." Tears filled her eyes.

"The woman is convincing," I heard a man behind me in the audience say.

The court was obviously of the same opinion, for both the judge and the two jurors looked, moved and fascinated, first at Camilla, then at me, as if the whole thing were a play by Arthur Schnitzler and not a court proceeding. But maybe it only seemed that way to me because I was so furious.

"What do you have to say about the matter?" the judge turned to me with a mild but austere voice.

"What am I supposed to say?" was my unintentionally curt reply. "The medical reports document that I am not the father."

"Yes, that is true," responded the judge after a while, with emphasis. "The facts speak against it, and our task is to judge the facts alone. But you're still young. Maybe this woman really does love you, and you ought to give her and yourself a chance . . ."

I didn't answer but suppressed my temper. What was the judge thinking? After all, I was thirty years old and knew what to do and what not to. Still, I often think of his comment, even now. The older I get, the more often I think of it. Maybe her son could have become my son after all, I think, when I put new mothers' newborns into their arms. The thought that Camilla's child could grow up without a father disturbs me. Sometimes I follow a woman on the street because she resembles Camilla. But then I realize that everything was over ten years ago, and we probably wouldn't even recognize each other. The older I get, the more often I wonder whether I did the right thing back then. But whatever the outcome, there are mistakes that can never be corrected.

Translated by Nancy Lukens

Maja Wiens

Photo by Dieter Andree, Berlin, courtesy of Verlag Neues Leben.

Maja Wiens was born in 1952, the daughter of a celebrated poet. She grew up in a suburb of Berlin, finished high school in 1970, and worked as a statistician for three years. She entered the university in 1973, majoring in mathematics and economics, but left at the end of her sophomore year and spent the next six years working as a waitress and barmaid. Since 1981 she has earned her living as a writer. In addition to her novel she has written several radio plays and a film script, and a number of her short stories have appeared in anthologies and journals.

Wiens has described herself as a member of the first generation that experienced the GDR as a given rather than an alternative experiment or dynamically changing society. Her stated intention is to provoke a response with her prose, from the powers-that-be as well as from her readers. As a long-term volunteer in her district's social welfare commission, she is particularly concerned with the problems of children and troubled families.

The following selection is the first chapter of her novel, *Traumgrenzen*.

Traumgrenzen (Dream limits). Berlin: Neues Leben, 1983.

Dream Limits (1983)

IT'S TIME, says the nurse and pushes a gurney next to her bed. She gets up and lies down on it, barely managing to cover her naked body with the scrap of cloth they had given her. It has only one frayed tie at the back to close it.

You'd only ruin your own nightgown afterward, the nurse had said.

She's afraid in spite of the sedative. She's cold. She can't see the face of the nurse who is pushing her down the corridor. She looks at her feet sticking out below the short cover and sees the doors of the elevator coming toward her. The nurse opens them without a word and pushes the gurney through. They ride down to the basement. Once again, she is pushed down hallways, feet first. Heating ducts run along the gray walls. She feels sick.

Nurse, I feel sick, she says.

So, now you feel sick, but you didn't feel sick while you were doing it.

The nurse parks the gurney against the wall next to a door marked Operating Room I. The woman looks up at the door. The nurse's retreating footsteps echo through the basement. It isn't long before she is back, pushing another gurney in front of her. Soon, six of the rolling raised beds are standing next to each other.

One of the women is crying.

Shut up, another one yells at her.

It gets quiet. The one who's been crying sits up, slips down to the floor, and walks away down the hall barefoot. Nina watches her go. They all watch her go.

She's crazy, says the woman lying closest to Nina, but her voice sounds uncertain.

The door of the operating room opens, and a woman in a surgical gown comes over to the women.

Mrs. Nina Rothe? she asks.

Nina raises her hand.

Well, we talked everything over yesterday, now please give me your arm.

The anesthesiologist takes her blood pressure. Then her practiced fingers search for a vein. She inserts the needle.

Please hold your arm still, she says, and immediately asks for Katherine Salkow.

Nina looks at her arm. The IV swings back and forth.

There's still time, she thinks, I can still get up and leave just like that other woman left. There's still time.

She hardly feels the slight jerk of the gurney. The operating room door is open, and someone pushes her in and lifts her onto the table.

It's curare, Nina thinks, the Indians poisoned their arrows with it, it works instantly.

The anesthesiologist opens an ampule, then Nina hears one of the doctors: You're lucky, you're the first one today, the bucket's still empty.

She hears laughter, then it fades, silence.

*   *   *

Nina wakes up. The clean-smelling hand of an orderly pats her face.

I'm not a horse, Nina thinks, almost amused.

Mrs. Rothe, Mrs. Rothe, open your eyes. Open your eyes!

She tries to. A narrow strip of light appears.

Well, everything OK? The orderly seems truly concerned. He strokes Nina's face. She recognizes the hallway.

Yes, yes, she says in a stranger's voice.

The orderly pushes her into the room and lifts her onto her bed.

It's over, she thinks. Everything is decided.

Then she falls asleep.

She wakes up at noon. The women are laughing raucously. They are sitting at the table in the middle of the room, eating. Nina sits up and looks at them. She doesn't feel any pain. She looks over at Christine, who is back in the bed next to her again. Christine is still asleep. Nina is afraid of the moment when Christine will wake up; she doesn't know how she can comfort the girl.

Nina gets up; she wants to go to the bathroom and smoke a cigarette. Then she notices that she is still wearing the short white surgical gown. It is damp and bloody. Nina sees that there is a large stain in the bed too. She feels nauseated. Her toilet bag is on the lower shelf of the nightstand with a clean nightgown next to it. Nina takes both with her, wanting to go wash herself, when she realizes that the only place in the room to wash is a small sink directly across from the table where the women are eating lunch. They are having spaghetti with tomato sauce. They keep laughing at the jokes that Carmen, the youngest one, is telling. Nina takes a stack of gauze pads from the nightstand, carefully lays them out on the edge of the bed, sits down and weeps.

When the nurse comes into the room to collect the dishes, Nina calls her over.

My bed's so dirty. Nina points to the stain.

We don't change until evening, now you'd just get it filthy again anyway. We don't have that much linen.

Nina lies down again. She soon falls asleep.

*   *   *

She had gone to her gynecologist after six weeks.

Yes, you're right, you're pregnant. The doctor smiled. Well, Mrs. Rothe, I'm sure you're pleased. We managed it once, we're sure to manage it again. Of course we'll have to insert a ring as soon as we can, next week. But you already know all about it. I'll do it outpatient.

No, no, I don't want the baby. I don't want another child. I want to terminate it.

It's called an interruption, Mrs. Rothe.

But the pregnancy isn't interrupted, it's terminated.

You don't need to lecture me about it, Mrs. Rothe. The doctor's face froze. You should have thought a bit sooner about contraception, if you don't like children. Just what did you do with the . . .

I like children. And you know it. And now please write me the referral.

No, I'd like you to think it over carefully. We have time. Come back in a week. If you still want it then, I'll give you the referral.

*   *   *

Get up, Mrs. Rothe, it's almost time for visiting hours, we have to make your bed.

Oh, Nurse Helga. Nina is glad that Nurse Helga is on duty. Even when she's busy she always has a moment.

Nurse Helga, can I please go out with my friend, later?

Of course, Mrs. Rothe, if you feel up to it, you can go out to the day room. You look just fine. Just a little pale.

The nurse changes Nina's bed with a few quick motions. When Nina tries to help, she pushes her away.

No, no, don't bother, it's easier alone.

Nina takes her toilet kit, cigarettes and matches, the nurse smiles, and then she walks down the hallway past promenading mothers-to-be and the old woman who keeps crying for her mama. Even the bathroom has only a small washbasin. It is dirty. She dampens her washcloth and locks herself into a toilet stall. She pulls the gown up over her head, drops it on the floor, and looks at her naked body. For the first time since she's been awake, she wonders why she doesn't feel any pain. Nina looks at her naked, shaved pubis. After she had been shaved, it had reminded her of a little girl's; now she thinks of a man's badly shaved face.

Groans come from the next stall. Nina suddenly realizes that she isn't alone. A trembling voice pleads: Hello, you there, somebody is there, please, please help me, get the nurse. I've lost blood again, so much blood, where does it all come from.

It sounds unreal, broken. Nina picks up the surgical gown off the tiles. It is cold and unpleasantly clammy. The latch sticks.

I'll get somebody right away, Nina says, but the voice is silent.

Nurse Helga comes quickly down the long hallway. It's the first time Nina has seen her upset; the nurse needs no further explanation. The woman is unconscious.

It's only shock, Mrs. Rothe, can you please help me. They carry her to a bench standing against the wall in the corridor. Nina is shocked by how young the patient's face looks. Her voice had sounded so old.

It's a good thing she hadn't locked the door, it would have taken us longer, you have no idea how much trouble the patients' foolishness causes us.

But sometimes you just want to be alone for a few minutes, somewhere, at least when you're peeing, Nina says.

Nina doesn't wash after all. After wiping herself between the legs once with the washcloth, she throws it into a huge plastic sack; a narrow strip of adhesive tape announces its purpose: napkins. She remembers that there had been a bag just like it in the ward where she had Aron. Except this one isn't transparent, it's dyed a yellowish color. There's progress everywhere. Nina smiles as she finally lights her cigarette and smokes hastily.

Actually, it isn't really over until now.

*   *   *

Christine. Christine, the beauty, the sad, slender beauty. When Christine had walked into the women's ward, everyone had fallen silent. Maybe it happened whenever someone new came, but Nina had been struck by it.

Christine's pale wrists stood out in contrast to the harsh red of her sweater. Somehow, it sounded like goodbye when she said hello. Christine was given the bed next to Nina's, it was the only one still empty.

Christine doesn't say anything more for a long time. She doesn't ask any questions, doesn't cry, and doesn't say anything about herself either. Sometimes she stands at the window and smiles. She watches as the pigeons fight over thrown breadcrumbs. Even her smile is sad.

Nina and Christine spend the days before the operation next to one another. There is just enough space between their beds for their shoes.

The room, which holds up to twelve women, is crowded. The beds are arranged in pairs separated by portable screens. Sometimes, Christine and Nina watch the shadows play across the screens. At those moments the women behind them seem like strangers again. The hours turn into small eternities. It seems like a punishment to Nina when her temperature rises and the operation is postponed so that she has to stay here two days longer. Why me, she asks herself. The first night she hears Christine crying. She speaks to her, but Christine doesn't answer. She just cries more quietly. So Nina is silent too.

The next morning Christine is called for a consultation with the senior surgeon. When she comes back—she doesn't come back until lunchtime—she has shadows under her reddened eyes. Everyone is nice to Christine. Nina's a little jealous of the niceness, but then is ashamed of herself and wants to be nice to her too, gentle. Christine is so lovely. Around her, Nina is much less aware of her own physical inadequacy or what she thinks or has been taught to think were her flaws. There is something about Christine, something special that makes it a pleasure just to look at her. She herself doesn't seem to notice it. Nina tries to decide whether it is her eyes or her mouth or the way she walks, but it's probably a bit of each. It is probably because Christine looks like such a real person, she decides.

Nina is standing by the window in the day room smoking a cigarette when Christine walks over to her.

I'm Christine, she says.

I'm Nina, says Nina.

Then they're both silent. Nina, cheerful, sad, lively Nina, is silent. She would have asked anyone else everything she could think of. Nina is forthrightly curious. With Christine, she doesn't say a word. At first.

The next day, when the two women are standing at the window again, Christine speaks.

I'm married, I love my husband, and I want a child. We want a child. We've been hoping for a child for five years. I've been pregnant four times. Three miscarriages in the first trimester. One stillbirth. This is my fifth pregnancy. I didn't realize it right away. I had two X-rays. The pregnancy is normal this time, but the baby might not be.

Yes. Yes, says Nina. She thinks now would be the time to say something comforting, that Christine is still young and can still have lots of children or something like that. But she doesn't say anything. Just: Yes, Christine.

When she's lying in bed again listening to the other women's laughter, she wonders why Christine doesn't get up and slap them in the mouth. It isn't happy laughter, it sounds forced and tinny.

Carmen, the seventeen-year-old who's already been here twice, is telling stories about men again. She's one of the ones who already have "it" behind them.

The women on the ward fall into those who have "it" ahead of them and the others who already have "it" over with. Having "it" ahead of them together creates a common bond. Fear makes the women seem quieter than they usually are. They seldom talk about the termination and even less often about their reasons for it. Most of them feel guilty. They hide the abortion just as they hid the pregnancy. Often, when it's all over, they quickly pick up their lives where they had left off. They don't forget.

Carmen is laughing about the doctors trying to explain to her that she has to take the pill regularly.

I'm too lazy, she laughs. And if I always have to think about the pill, I don't have any fun fucking.

The women laugh again.

If I were Christine, thinks Nina, I'd get up and slap her in the face. I'd really do it. But Christine doesn't say anything and smiles at Carmen.

*   *   *

Thomas is on time, as usual. As usual, Thomas doesn't bring flowers. Thomas sets three books down on Nina's nightstand.

Well, Nina, how was it, did everything go okay? Thomas asks because he doesn't know what he ought to say.

Yes, yes, said Nina. What else is he supposed to say, she thinks. She gets up and puts on her bathrobe.

Come on, let's get out of here.

Thomas is surprised that Nina is allowed to get up so soon. It almost frightens him. It's as if nothing had happened, and although that's exactly what Thomas had wanted, now it's too easy for him. He wants to ask her if it had hurt, but then the question seems embarrassing, and Nina, standing beside him, is further away from him now than she was before.

Nina looks over at Christine's bed again before they leave, but Christine is sound asleep. They're all trying not to disturb her because they know that

Christine's husband isn't coming. He's a journalism student in Leipzig and has an important final exam today. That's the only thing that Christine had told everyone.

It's better for her to sleep. Nina looks quizzically at Thomas, although he doesn't know Christine at all.

There were three old armchairs in the day room. The chair Thomas sits down in begins to wobble threateningly. So they move over to the window. Thomas pulls a fairly crumpled pack of cigarettes out of his hip pocket.

Me too, says Nina.

Can't you even quit while you're here? Thomas asks. The look he gives her annoys Nina.

No, she says, and I don't want to either. It can't do me any more harm now than any other time.

So Thomas gives her a light. He thinks she's pale.

Everything's fine at the kindergarten, he reports. Aron is really sweet, and the two of them are getting along fine. The only place there had been any trouble was at Nina's job when he dropped off her sick-leave form. They had recognized the diagnosis code, and Nina's boss had made a piggish remark in front of all of her co-workers: He, Thomas, apparently wasn't capable of supporting his own child, but this way things were better for the company in any case; Nina was already out sick all the time anyway.

Nina's furious.

I'll show him. I'll go to the union representative, to the Party secretary.

But Nina. Thomas smiles. Haven't you figured out yet that it wouldn't do any good?

No, I haven't. And I'll do it, he'd better start feeling sorry for himself, even if his brother-in-law is the chair of the grievance committee ten times over and the union representative is his next-door neighbor.

Translated by Dorothy Rosenberg

Katja Lange-Müller

Born in Berlin in 1951, Katja Lange-Müller grew up in the Berlin area. She worked briefly as a printer and photo editor after finishing high school but soon left journalism and worked as a nurse's aide in Berlin hospitals for five years. Lange-Müller attended the Becher Creative Writing Institute in Leipzig from 1979 to 1982, then received a stipend to spend a research year in Mongolia. Thereafter, she worked as a literary editor in Berlin until she left the GDR to move to West Berlin in 1984.

Lange-Müller's work has been published in a number of journals and anthologies. This story first appeared in a 1978 anthology of East German short stories; it was reprinted in West Germany in Lange-Müller's 1986 collection of short stories, *Wehleid wie im Leben,* her first independent publication.

Wehleid wie im Leben (Self-pity). Frankfurt am Main: Fischer, 1986.

Kaspar Mauser: Die Feigheit vorm Freund (Kaspar Mauser: Cowardice in the face of a friend). Frankfurt am Main: Fischer, 1988.

Sometimes Death Comes in Slippers (1978)

Senile, demented, and schizoid grannies, formerly of the female sex, haunt the long dark hallways of the locked geriatric-psychiatric women's ward. In worn-out felt slippers, or barefoot when they can't find them, they shuffle drunk with sleep to the toilet. Past the tub room where the gurney, freshly covered with a clean hospital sheet, is waiting behind the door left ajar, between the bathtub and the washing machine, IV stands, buckets, diapers, nail clippers in shoe cartons, cupboards full of cockroaches. The fear of wetting themselves again so soon drives them out of their crowded rows of beds. They set off by the roomful in loose single file, groping awkwardly at walls fingered raw or grabbing blindly at the hem of a friend's nightgown, nothing but the driving sensation of a full bladder in brains clogged with psychoactive drugs. Shreds of dreams cling to their tangled braids like drunken trainbearers.

Suddenly they stop in front of the tub room, where the electric light falling through the crack in the door frame blinds them for a moment. But then they lurch on in their worn-out slippers like a conquered navy on its last battleships. Hardly a single one will manage to wear out her last pair. Most will have to cede them to later admissions. The slippers are the property of the clinic, and when one patient no longer needs them, the pair provided for her use will be put on the next candidate for death. When one of these pairs of brown and yellow checkered size eight slippers has been left for the sixth or seventh time beside that resting place from which no one ever rises again, it is withdrawn from circulation. Whenever someone dies, all of the patients' slippers are redistributed. They don't die so often that the trading around seriously disturbs the ward's normal routine.

What does it matter, they find the toilet, and if someone is already on it there's always the potty chair, they sit down and listen as best they can, to the flow of events: light next door but dead silence, the roaches wait timidly in the cupboard corners. It's easy to guess what's going to happen. Cross yourself and hope it's not you.

They're faster on the way back to their nests, even though they don't have to pee so badly any more, and surer. "Whoever makes it through till Spring will eat for another year . . ." It's engraved on a wooden wall plaque that Susie made earlier in occupational therapy, burned into it with a red-hot knitting needle. It's the refrain of a song that was her favorite.

     *   *   *

Susie, Susanna-Magdalena Dombrowski, from somewhere in Poland on the Vistula river, the schizophrenic, the heavy dosage, the old washer-woman, the former laundress who rhymed sayings, collected dead flies, hit nurses, fired doctors, and claimed that a long-lost twin brother who was a structural engineer somewhere in America was paying for the hospital and everything else, who died unobserved, eighty-four years old, with a bed sore the size of a fist in the small of her back, of acute heart failure during the midnight potty rounds.

The veteran night-shift nurse who had defined the four geriatric key words—fussing, farting, nose-picking, and peeing—didn't notice the exact moment of her passing. It must have happened just as she was lifting a real dream of a granny out of her wet diapers and putting her on the potty, whis-tling her north German "Let's make a tinkle, now" through the gap between her teeth.

Bending over the bed, she's a little amazed that there's a corpse lying there. She had just gotten a half-cup of cold Ovaltine down Susie at 11:00 P.M., and now she's dead.

"Heaven knows if she even heard the little nightingale sing before she died, it's singing like crazy again tonight."

Completely lost in thought, the bird-loving night-shift Nurse Barbie listens for the sweet sounds of the nightingale's fluting through Granny Bauer's constant ". . . yes Daddy, yes Daddy," blind Trudy's ". . . my Mamma says . . . ," and all the other snoring, moaning, and delirium. Now she can take time to set the point where the line between dying and being dead had been crossed: at exactly ten minutes after midnight.

"Dead is dead, and the dead don't care since when. Funny, most of them join the angels at night. Probably because they stand out so nice, the little white souls against the black sky. They steer by the stars, like the old mariners. So it's easier for them at night. And that sad character, the Fisher-man, with the big key around his neck—he's no youngster either, he can keep an eye on them better, the poor, skinny little souls, they always fly up, like thin air, just when I'm on duty, nights. She's done suffering, our Susie."

Barbie stares absentmindedly at Susie's left eye, which flashes up at her from the bottom of its deep tear-filled hollow, silvery, like a dime in a bucket.

The veteran night nurse doesn't really feel like crying after all, but she shares the depth of her emotional range with her handkerchief out loud: "Every night a little fuss."

Quietly, she goes into the nurse's station.

"Don't let's wake sleeping dogs."

She has to notify the doctor on duty now, so that he can establish the already obvious death, as well as its perfectly clear immediate cause. Then pull the chart and lay it neatly on a gauze-covered tray along with a death certificate, stethoscope, and tongue depressor, a tray which, following protocol, she will hold ready in front of her stomach, wordless and humble, like the Chocolate Girl on the wall in the nurse's station holding her stupid, forgotten, useless porcelain cup.

The file folder with the death certificates also contains the "Instructions for Nursing Assistants Employed as Substitutes and Other Non-ward Temporary Help in the Event of a Death to Be Confirmed by a Doctor." Night nurse Barbie has nothing to do now but wait until some bleary-eyed doctor comes wandering over to the station with his lab coat buttoned wrong. So she reads, maybe for the hundredth time, the head nurse's instructions, which she had neatly copied down years ago and had the former Granny Amanda sew into a plastic folder with lovely scallop stitches.

The Preparation of a Corpse

First, place wet cotton pads on the corpse's eyelids after pulling them down over the eyeballs. This is to be done immediately after the onset of death, as it cannot later be accomplished by natural means. It is definitely in the interest of the person performing the preparation to pay strict attention that their hands show no injuries or wounds of any kind. Should even a minor break in the skin be present, the use of rubber gloves is strongly indicated.

Between as well as during the necessary manipulations, emotional responses are to be suppressed. If this cannot be accomplished, because of inexperience, etc., care should at least be taken that this not unnecessarily delay the prompt completion of these tasks.

Frequently, too little force is applied in the important cosmetic task of binding the jaw, especially by young and inexperienced staff. Loosely tied chin straps rarely withstand rigor mortis, with the result that the usually toothless mouth is soon gaping again.

At this point, the corpse, especially those areas which may have been affected by the process of death, is to be thoroughly washed in lukewarm water.

When all the required procedures have been carried out in the order described above, the corpse need only be dressed in a fresh nightgown, open at the back, and placed on the gurney.

The death certificate (preferably completed by a doctor) is not to be attached with a piece of string to one of the big toes, as is the frequent practice elsewhere, but attached to the shin with a piece of adhesive tape.

Finally, the corpse is to be completely covered with another fresh sheet and taken to as cool and secluded a place as possible (bath) until morning.

Everything else is the responsibility of the morning shift.

Night nurse Barbie has gotten the corpse clean. She looks as she had in life. The hair like always, the hands folded, and all in white. Now the nurse pulls the two corners of the sheet out from under the mattress, lays them over poor Susie and takes her gently in her arms. The carefulness is a conditioned reflex, from the potty rounds. Because they always wail so terribly, the emaciated fly weights, if you straighten them out a bit while you're moving them, so they'll fit on the potty.

But Susie, thin as a rail, is much heavier now than she was alive, and stiff. She lies on Sister Barbie's fleshy forearms like the floating Virgin. "Always afraid of letting them fall, because of that sneaky saying: 'If you bed others badly you'll lie badly yourself.' They used to hammer quality nursing into us with threats like that in the old days."

Sister Barbie goose-steps the stiff, heavy Susie to the gurney, rolls her out of the sheet onto her left side, smooths the two corners of the open gown over her bottom and lets her fall onto her back. "Well then, 'bye sweetie," she says again before spreading another fresh sheet over the dead woman. Her nose and the tips of her toes draw it up in the middle like two tent poles. She'd had a strong personality.

"That snob on-call doctor who came by before, they all wanna be psychiatrists now and hypnotize their bleached-blonde girlfriends. He pinched together both tiny assholes of his little snub nose as if we were a cage of mountain lions here. Almost all of them are so disgusted they can hardly breathe when they get lost and end up here or have to come because it's their turn. Better they should thank their old mothers for turning something with a nose like that loose on the world, perfume dispensers with moustaches."

Poor Susie is finished, and Sister Barbie gives her the last push.

"There should be a drink for this, on the clinic or the devil knows who. A nice cold double shot. The traveling undertakers always used to get at least one, usually more. But then, the corpses might have been a lot older pretty often."

Sister Barbie has pushed the gurney back into the bath again. Now she can open the windows, turn out the light, wash her hands several times with ethanol and once with soap, and finally warm up the large bowl of potato soup, saved for her from lunchtime.

She has to hurry. In less than an hour she'll wake up "the girls," three fiftyish idiots who perform simple chores and dirty work. Between 3:30 and 4:00 A.M. the girls can wash and dress themselves. In the meantime, Sister Barbie takes care of the last potty-round on her shift. After that the four of them will start washing the stationary patients. At the moment, there are thirty-two out of the forty-six. Night sister Barbie greedily gulps the soup out of the pan. A cigarette stub burns down in her left hand.

The cockroaches in the bath can finally start rustling around and eating toilet paper again for two or three more hours at most. Then the night will be over.

*   *   *

The morning begins a Thursday. That's the day they get cake. The four workers—they're kept busy with a bit of crocheting in the hospital sewing room—and the girls get to have baths and clean underwear today.

"Our Susie died," says the first-shift nurse while passing out two pieces of bread each, one with sausage and one with marmalade. They chew silently. For most of them it's not news. They had already suspected that something was up before midnight, in a dream, when they went to pee. And it's almost a miracle, Susie was only the third oldest. But then again, it's also just as they expected. She was always like that, so stubborn. They're really very quiet at breakfast this morning, not complaining, not poking each other. Some of them who otherwise avoid it are actually looking at one another.

Before the workers and the girls bathe, the music therapist comes with his accordion, just in time for cake and coffee. He plays for forty-five minutes and gets paid for a full hour. He reels off a well-tested repertoire: "The Men Are All Crooks," "Down in the Valley," "The Gardener's Wife," "The Waltz of the Fleas," "My Parent's Grave," and the last half-hour "Long May She Live," over and over. They sing to that. Too slow, too fast, off key, and of course loud.

When the therapist is packing up, the first-shift nurse whispers to him: "We lost one last night." The therapist looks at the clock, puts on a patronizing expression, straps his instrument back on, and plays something by Lehar. Everyone is pleased by the encore and keep on singing their favorite song, "Long May She Live," without paying any attention to the new melody.

They really love birthdays. A birthday means weak coffee, a treat paid for by whoever's birthday it is. That is, the one who's beaming because you can't do anything but be happy when you can't do anything else anymore. And it does make you happy to see something so nice, a happy birthday girl. It lets you hope, encourages you to stay in the running for the most years. Birthdays count. Nobody collects death days. What counts, counts. What doesn't count, doesn't count. Eighty-seven summers to one winter.

"Whoever sees the next spring will eat for another year."

Lack of appetite upsets them the most, and it's also the only thing they tattle on. "Nurse, she doesn't want her soup."

The music man is long gone, and they're still singing. Singing Susie's death dead. "Long may she live."

These things heal quickly for them. A broken hip or leg doesn't heal. Not for them. The penalty for clumsiness: whoever falls goes down. Whoever is down falls into what falls over them, if they're on the bottom. But the loveliest song on earth covers it all. Long may she live.

*   *   *

After four o'clock, the head nurse clears out the night-stand next to Susie's former bed. Tomorrow she won't have time; tomorrow is Friday and she wants to get home early. Besides, they may still have to be moved around today. The head nurse can't decide who goes where until after she has seen what the new admission looks like. Either straight into the infirmary or everyone has to change beds. You have to be prepared for surprises. Some of them hardly survive the day they're admitted.

Susie's property consisted of a blue-framed pocket mirror, a hairpiece worn as thin and dull as a mouse tail by the years of lying down, three photographs, and a beaded chemise the pattern of which can no longer be determined. The muslin, the soft lining of the rotted embroidery, must have been eaten by moths. Only a hopelessly matted, snarled tangle of metal threads still holds the tiny black beads together. Who knows, maybe none of it ever originally belonged to Susanna, and these were just gifts from other patients who had also only received this or that object as a gift. They are always quite generous with their friends on the ward when they notice that the end is near. Sometimes one of them makes a mistake and recovers. Then, no matter how much fuss she makes, what she has given away is gone. No one steals here, but everyone guards her belongings. Neither insanity nor forgetfulness is an excuse.

Susie's personal belongings go to the girls. They can hardly find a use for any of it but are pleased anyway and express their gratitude in work. The girls are needed on the ward, so they should get it.

Everything else in the nightstand is state property. Pullover, skirt, apron, underwear, stockings, and the oldest pair of slippers on the ward. An unopened sample jar of Nivea lotion, which a student nurse had brought Susanna for the dry patches on her face, goes to the nurse's station.

"These are finished," says the frugal ward nurse, putting her finger through a hole in the left slipper. "You don't need to patch it again, the new admission can have new ones. Goodbye."

At five o'clock the bell on the safety-glass door rings. The second-shift nurse opens it, surrounded by the curious girls. The others are uninterested in the new admission. An opening is always filled on the same day.

The new admission looks around her, bewildered and confused. The two ambulance attendants have linked their arms in hers as if they were about to swing into a waltz.

"Well, come on over here, nice and easy. Now who's afraid, we're just going to take a little bath."

The nurse sits the new admission on the plastic-covered examination chair in the nurse's station, undresses her, and hangs a bath towel around her shoulders. So that she doesn't feel completely naked. Old people are often very modest.

Admissions Form

Schneider, Hildegard
Born 7/3/1900 in Ottendorf-Okrilla
Preliminary diagnosis: senile dementia
Property at admission:
    1 summer coat
    1 dress (cotton, green)
    1 undershirt
    1 pair underpants
    1 pr. pantyhose
    1 pr. street shoes (old)
    identification papers
    3 photographs
    1 silver ring (without stone)
    1 pocket mirror
    1 letter opener (genuine tortoiseshell)
    1 imitation leather purse (old)

The nurse puts everything into a cambric bag, writes "Schneider, Hildegard" on a piece of adhesive tape and sticks it to the bag, and crosses the same name off a list with the heading "Cases to be admitted as soon as possible by order of the Medical Officer." Schneider, Hildegard, had been in the second row from the top but was marked with a red "Urgent" stamp. In the meantime, the tub is half full.

"Just lift your leg. Don't be afraid. I'll hold on to you. Now, don't go all stiff. And now for a dash of rose oil, and everything will be lovely."

The rose oil is a strong disinfectant. The new admission is trembling but can wash herself. A good sign. "The girls will show you your bed. It's in room four, the sixth one on the left side. The one by the window."

The girls stand behind the sister, giggling. They are still full of joy at their recently received inheritance.

"Quick, take this stuff up to the attic with the other bags. But Hilda should put it away, at least she knows the alphabet, more or less. So, and now here are your things to get dressed." The nurse counts the standard assortment into the new admission's lap: underpants, undershirt, stockings, garters, skirt, pullover, apron. But she still stares fixedly at the floor. Toward where the brown and yellow checkered slippers are. She stares at them without a word, like a four-year-old who has won a deluxe edition of Goethe in the lottery. Until she finally gropes at one of the teddy-bear yellow pompons with a wet toe. "Mine?" she asks. "Well, we'll have to cut the fuzzballs off again," answers the nurse and helps the awkward, trembling, crippled feet twisted with Parkinson's disease into the pair of slippers assigned to them, for the time being.

Translated by Dorothy Rosenberg

Doris Paschiller

Doris Paschiller was born in 1953 and grew up in Berlin. After finishing high school, she worked at a number of different jobs and also began writing. The novel excerpted here is her only independent publication. Paschiller left the GDR to move to West Berlin in 1984.

Die Würde (Dignity). Berlin: Buchverlag der Morgen, 1980.

Dignity (1980)

ROBERT AND JOHANNA were married on July 2 at ten in the morning in the Tangermünde registry office. The city was the home of the Strand family, whose name Johanna and the child in her belly would henceforth bear.

The day was mild; it had rained the day before and during the night. The puddles in the street steamed in the sun, and drops of water fell on Johanna's hands from branches hanging over the garden fences. They were cold. She would forget nothing that happened that day, none of the sounds or smells, her thoughts or feelings. The long procession marched through the streets, with Johanna in the lead and Robert beside her. It was quiet at first and then became noisier. It was an endless, tiring, and sobering walk. Johanna was conscious of the seriousness of her action. She was about to marry. And all around her, in this city that she hardly knew the gardens were in bloom. But Robert had always been here, everything seemed to point to Robert and everything gave him a different face, these frugal gardens and the luxuriantly clean facades of the medium-sized buildings and narrow streets. It all belonged to Robert and was strange to her.

The sun disappeared behind a cloud, and the day became unpleasantly overcast and cool; everyone began talking at once, urging one another to hurry for fear that it might begin to rain again, but nothing happened.

Johanna was in her fifth month. She had not been accepted but was now tolerated. Johanna hadn't wanted to parade her belly through the streets in a white bridal gown, followed to the city hall by a colorfully dressed entourage. She had wanted to go there with Robert, unseen and unaccompanied. But it had to be this way, because there were a lot of people who needed this, a wedding, a white, white wedding.

Robert's mother had spent a lot of money, had had people cook and bake.

Everything is lovely, she said, but her thoughts had been far away.

Yes, time passes so quickly, and every cake marks its passage.

And Robert's mother smiled and set them on the tables and said they were lovely, very lovely. She looked at the stately row of bottles and the steaming coffeepots and bowls and was satisfied.

As Johanna walked along beside Robert, a phrase kept running through her head in rhythm with her steps. A drop upon the stone, a drop upon the stone. A strange thought for an important day when everything felt so un-real. And then she began to worry that she might stumble or make herself ridiculous some other way, and life seemed very dangerous to her.

Robert's arm felt like a piece of wood covered with fabric.

They entered the city hall and then the registry office and walked to the front. Three couples followed behind them and stood in two rows during the ceremony. The other guests seated themselves on the benches.

Johanna held a large bouquet in her arms. It was purple orchids, held together with tulle and florist's wire. They sat on a bench and listened to a speech that you would have had to laugh at or be outraged by if it hadn't been part of a sort of sacred event that involved Johanna herself.

The baby moved, and Johanna felt for it inconspicuously. She wore white gloves, which made her fingers seem longer. The dress was a white bridal gown that was neither pretty nor elegant nor simple but simply uncomfort-able. Everyone could see it. It was a punishment. A stiff artificial something with a flounce and a short veil that stuck out from her head instead of draping softly around her body.

If this is what you look like at your wedding, you probably won't get over it for the rest of your life, Johanna thought. As if you were torn off and thrown away on the day when you were supposed to blossom. Beauty is gone forever, just when you are obliged to be beautiful.

The young men stood on the left. One of them was Christoph, Johanna's friend and colleague. Across from him stood Dyomee. She wore a tight dress of pale raw silk, and a beam of sunlight falling through the window touched her short, black hair. Sometimes people shook their heads when they saw her or threw her hostile looks. Most of the time she slipped away from them; she showed no sign of guilt. Her skin was white and she had a touch of rouge on her cheeks. No one saw the two girls standing next to her with their eyes lowered to their bouquets. The bride looked toward the window, and in heaven the little angels sang a short, painless song.

Then Johanna had to stand up. Someone took the flowers from her. But everything was too far removed from what she had imagined a wedding to be—glowing and full of music that made you feel important and appreci-ated.

It was embarrassing, and the image one had held of a wedding shouldn't have been destroyed like this. This wedding had fallen upon her like a judgment.

When the ceremony was over, Robert and Johanna turned around slowly and walked arm in arm to the exit. They were stiff. The three couples joined in a circle behind them and followed them out. Then the guests got up from the benches and followed after them.

Robert and Johanna stopped at the door to accept congratulations. Everything went according to plan, and Johanna was glad for the blankness that had spread through her mind and saved her from showing any strong emotion.

But then her mother reached the front of the line. Her hair had turned gray in the past year, she had gotten old. She must have accidentally ended up in the last row, and Johanna felt ashamed. Her mother looked at Johanna's belly and patted it. And that was the end for Johanna. Her face crumpled and began to tremble. She couldn't hold back the tears. It was humiliating not to be able to control herself, and she had a dreadful feeling for the second time that day, as if she were wearing a little girl's dress that was much too short. And the more clearly she felt unable to control herself, the worse and more hysterical her tears became. Her throat burned and her face turned red. She wore this face for hours, everything that it had been supposed to conceal had broken through, and it now looked like a battlefield. Johanna was ashamed, and two black tears ran down her cheeks and smeared the face that had been so radiant. Her suffering seemed endless, and people wondered where this young person could have gathered so much sorrow or if she wasn't just overstrung. She didn't calm down again until evening. She wasn't sure whether she had forced Robert into this marriage or whether he had talked her into it, if she had wanted a child so soon or at all (she admitted to herself that she did, otherwise she could have gotten rid of it). Robert sat next to her at the head of the table and watched his friends and relatives. The party had gotten lively; they danced, ate, smoked, and drank. Robert had pulled his hair back into a braid, which he normally did only before he went to work.

Robert's hair was exactly the same length as Johanna's, and she loved it and was proud of it because no one had hair as thick and as long as he did. He wore a dark green satin tie and a black suit. Now and then he drank half a glass of wine and then poured more. He had pushed himself back from the table a bit and laid his arm on the back of Johanna's chair. At that moment, it seemed to Johanna that he was protecting her, and she felt very deeply connected to him.

Now she felt sorry that she was just sitting there watching the others celebrate her wedding. She took off her veil and got herself something to eat.

When the others saw that she had recovered, they began to celebrate even more gaily and noisily. They became a wave of exuberance and behaved as if they all loved one another. There were no more distinctions between them; the effort to have a good time had reconciled them. And the alcohol had lightened their hearts.

*   *   *

Johanna's parents drove home early the next morning. They had probably celebrated enough. They usually preferred quiet and enjoyed being alone in their apartment.

The summer ripened and the fall drew nearer. Johanna had never felt so peaceful in her entire life. She observed how she changed, almost abruptly, from one week to the next. She also began to experience her body more consciously. Now and then a whitish liquid oozed from her breast. She tried as much as possible to conceal it from anyone else; after all it only concerned her.

So that's how it works, the breast expels something, like a cow. Who would have thought.

Only Robert saw it sometimes and got used to the idea that something was happening to her body.

Toward the end he became impatient and kept thinking that the baby must be dead or would die at birth. He was afraid, and Johanna was afraid too. It seemed to them as if they had waited for this baby for years.

In September they renovated their apartment. Robert had found it with the help of some buddies, guys he knew from home who had moved to Berlin before he had. It consisted of one room, a small kitchen, and a toilet. It was dark and located in the second courtyard. Now Robert stood on a ladder and nailed up wallpaper molding. They'd carried the furniture up to the attic. Only the bed was left in the apartment.

Freshly painted and empty, the apartment didn't look bad if you ignored the kitchen, where dry rot spread under the sink. You can probably get used to anything if you try, Johanna thought. That way one day you'll see a medium-sized revelation in every piece of dust, something lovely, as Mrs. S—— would say, that has just as much right to exist.

The kitchen was going to be the nursery, and Johanna pondered whether it was a good idea to stick the baby in the kitchen, since it didn't have double-glazed windows. But she couldn't think of a better solution.

Robert folded the ladder and went up to the attic. He brought the furniture back down again. He set up the kitchen cabinet in the hallway so that there was room in the kitchen for a kind of changing table. The kitchen cabinet had been left for Robert by the previous tenant, who had painted it bright orange; the paint was peeling off again. The cabinet was very large and took up a lot of space, so that only thin people could get through the hall into the apartment.

Johanna stood at the window and held her belly. She felt safe watching Robert setting up the table, cabinet, and chairs. They had also bought another single bed because they had thought that you can't spend your whole life sleeping together in one single bed. Now each of them had their own, everything was orderly, and their life didn't look any different from that of other people who all were joined together in the same or a similar way.

Of course, Johanna could have decided to raise the baby by herself; she had often considered it as a way of avoiding a certain kind of subordination that you didn't talk about and that you constantly tried to wiggle your way out of.

But the other alternative was probably complete self-sacrifice. To be nothing but a mother in every opinion that you expressed. Your struggle is mother, above all else mother. To earn your bread only as the mother of your child. To meet a man only as a mother. To have only mothers as friends and to raise another mother. The whole world is a mother. Hold on, mother. Your child is as lonely as you are. Its religion is mother, its life is mother.

When Robert was finished, he looked at Johanna and laughed. We've done it, he said.

Even if what they had created was very modest in comparison with their parents' apartments, it still filled them with a certain satisfaction, for they thought, as long as we have each other for support, we can put up with living in this cave.

Johanna went into the kitchen and warmed up some lentils. She carried the meal into their room and set it carefully on the table. Dishes, linens, and books lay spread across the carpet. Johanna took two spoons out of an enameled pot. Then she put a candle on the table and turned on the television set. They already felt at home again in the apartment.

After they had eaten they went to bed, cuddled up together, and fell asleep.

*   *   *

In October a baby girl was born and named Henriette. Johanna built a fire in the kitchen boiler every morning and every evening now, and wiped the ashy dust from the table, chairs, and cupboard.

In the mornings when she washed diapers in the kitchen, Henriette was moved into the living room, and in the evening Henriette was put back into the kitchen.

Robert looked at the baby for a long time before he could bring himself to touch it or hold it. Johanna didn't put the child into his arms because she didn't want to bother him. Just once, when she wanted to visit her friend Christoph in the evening, she asked him to give the baby its bottle and change its diaper. She explained everything to him very carefully and, while doing so, realized for the first time that she had cared for the baby like a mother animal for weeks now as if she were following an instinct. So it had worked. She thought, that's Henriette, and was amazed. She lived in a cloud and couldn't really see beyond it. Her job and everything that had surrounded her seemed very far away and was recalled only now and then when one of her friends came to bring her a baby jacket or playsuit, which was always too big for the tiny baby. By now, everyone had been there and had looked at Henriette and hadn't wanted to disturb them. They saw that everything had gotten more crowded and that there was no room left to sit together and no time to talk.

Only Johanna's mother sometimes came and looked around the apartment with concern, held the baby for a while, rocked it and talked to it. She brought juice, fruit, and toys. Johanna's father was also very touching and sometimes wrote her a letter giving her all kinds of advice.

After doing the laundry in the morning, Johanna would go out with the baby to do the shopping. She had spent a long time wrapping it up warmly and then laid a red wool blanket over the baby carriage, which was lined with red fabric. It had been a gift from a friend of her mother.

The street smelled strongly of exhaust fumes, which she had never noticed before. Now she was afraid that it might do some harm to the baby. She had an intense longing for calm and walks in the woods.

Johanna usually took a nap with the baby in the afternoon and then only got up to fix meals. She lived isolated in a silent unity with the child. When Robert came home, he tried to be quiet so as not to disturb them. He would sit down in the kitchen next to the crib, drink a beer, and watch the baby, unable to imagine that it was his. It had only cried the first night and now hardly ever made a sound. Robert took a cloth and wiped the drool from its chin. It looked as if it were smiling. Robert was glad to be all alone with the baby where no one could see him. So he could watch it, pat it, and try to make contact with it. It lay there and seemed to be looking at him. Its mouth was open, and sometimes it wiggled a little and moved its head. Johanna had said that the baby had to be turned over from one side to the other so that its head would be properly formed.

Robert drank his beer and breathed on the baby. He had been oddly moved when Johanna had nursed the baby, and at the same time it had made him happy that there was something that belonged only to the two of them. Now she didn't do it any more. She had gotten an inflammation and had had to stop.

While Robert sat there lost in thought, Johanna came into the kitchen and took the bottle left from that afternoon out of the refrigerator to warm it up. She put the bottle in a pot of water on the stove. Then she knelt in front of Robert and put her head in his lap. Later, while Johanna took care of the baby, Robert carried dinner into the living room and sat down. After a while he got up again and went to Johanna. She was squatting in front of a dishpan on the floor, putting laundry to soak.

My god, said Robert and groaned, aren't you ever going to be finished? Are you going to wash that too? I'm only putting it to soak, answered Johanna.

When she was finished, she had trouble standing up. She made a face.

Shall we open a bottle of wine? she asked.

Robert nodded and got a bottle out of the refrigerator. They sat down in the living room and drank a toast to having made it.

The time when Johanna would have to return to work and put Henriette into a day-care center was still many months away.

Robert and Johanna both worked in Schoeneweide at the power station. He was a truck driver, and she worked in the drafting office. She and Christoph sat together under a ficus plant across from another draftsperson, one you really couldn't look at very long without a certain feeling of disgust. The office had an incredibly high ceiling beneath which you felt lost. If you opened the door, you could hear a distant clatter from the cable works.

*   *   *

It was summer again and already warm and light in the early morning. Through the open window you could hear that life had already begun.

Robert and Johanna lay covered with sweat in their bed, even their hands were wet and felt sticky. The covers and a pillow had fallen on the floor. Robert and Johanna lay facing away from each other without touching, and Johanna tried to dry herself off with a corner of the sheet. The alarm clock rang, it was 4:00 A.M. Johanna sat up, reached for the alarm and shut it off.

Robert turned over toward her and put his arms around her. He spread her legs and laid himself on top of her. Johanna was finally fully recovered from her pregnancy. They had spent the whole night making love and were both exhausted; they would have given anything not to have to get up. On the other hand, Henriette was awake immediately and made herself heard.

After a while Johanna got up, pulled on a nightgown, and went into the kitchen. She put on water for coffee and wrapped sandwiches.

She washed herself with cold water but still couldn't wake up. She wondered whether she shouldn't just go back to bed, but then she thought that Henriette wouldn't let her go back to sleep anyway. She was just ready to put her head down on the table for a moment when Robert came into the kitchen and said that she had better pull herself together. Johanna stood up and got dressed. Then she picked Henriette up out of her crib, washed and dressed her too. Then they drank their coffee and ate a little.

The day was already unbearably hot. Johanna's upper lip and forehead were covered with sweat.

If you could only take a bath or at least had enough room to wash properly, said Johanna. This shitty apartment, this rotten, shitty apartment.

Stop it. We can't do anything about it right now anyway, said Robert. He had just finally managed to get a rental agreement for the apartment; at the time, he had simply moved in without one. It seemed to Robert that it made absolutely no difference whether you filed an application for an apartment or not. You could count on waiting two, three, four, five, or more years. There are much, much worse cases, people who need an apartment far more urgently. And you have to go to the district housing office every Tuesday and listen to the ladies telling you that they can't do anything for you. They say it in a certain condescending tone. They'll teach you to have patience. You shouldn't keep bothering them. They just gave you a rental agreement. They didn't have to do that, the way you had behaved. And then they lost your file. And the next time: Oh yes, you have a child. How old is the child? You won't get more than two rooms anyway, and if you're lucky, an indoor toilet. But at the moment there's nothing they can do. Why don't you try to get into a cooperative apartment project through your workplace? That was the first thing you should have done. You haven't put enough effort into it yourself. We have certified to your workplace that we are making an effort, but we can't pull apartments out of a hat. Besides, you're still young and just starting out.

Robert had to leave first. He began at work 6:00 A.M. when he was on first shift. Johanna started at seven. He said goodbye to Johanna and his daughter and left. Johanna sat on her chair and nodded off. After a while Henriette woke her up. Johanna held her face under the cold water again. She silently begged Robert for help. She looked at the clock and saw that she had to leave immediately, picked up her bag and the baby and rushed out, but her train had already left and she would be late.

She took the elevated train. She looked out at bricks, elderberry bushes, train stations, train stations. And she realized that she couldn't let herself relax. Everything that she saw, at the same time every day for years, was a handhold to pull herself along by. And something always welled up inside her that overcame all the pain; then she pressed her lips together and stared into some face in front of her. You can't let yourself go, if you do you will never be safe. People with no skin cannot breathe, and besides you have to know why you obey.

Translated by Dorothy Rosenberg

Afterword

Nancy Lukens

> Candida, my daughter, Maria spoke to her. It's no use shutting
> yourself off. If you don't like the world you'll have to change it. You're
> right that it is impossible to live in. So drink. You have to grow strong.
> And open your eyes.
> Maria decided to raise Candida to bear pain and fight for happiness.
> —Christa Müller, "Candida" (1979)

THE SHORT PROSE in this collection bears witness to the fact that, far from
erupting suddenly in 1989, pressure for change in the German Democratic
Republic was part of the fabric of life in that society. That these texts were
published despite censorship constraints indicates the state's increasing tolerance, even encouragement, of literature that exposed contradictions, in-
justices, and ambivalence about its acknowledged accomplishments, especially those related to equality of opportunity for women. Daniela Dahn
ironically suggests in "The Contemporary Feminine," for example, that even
the most unenthusiastic participants in the Marxist system, if they were
beneficiaries of the myth of exclusive male strength, were willing to col-
laborate in the social culture of dominance. It becomes apparent that the
issues were more complex than a Cold War mentality allowed us to perceive, and that the demise of the GDR regime has by no means brought
about a resolution of the issues addressed by its critics.

This volume presents a cross section from the mid-1970s to the mid-
1980s, a dynamic decade in GDR women's writing that reflects their commitment to what Christa Wolf earlier called "authentic subjectivity."[1] Wolf
wrote in 1968 of the power of literature to create more honest images of
fully human life: "Prose creates human beings, in a dual sense. It deconstructs deadly oversimplifications by introducing possibilities for existing
humanely. It serves as a storehouse of experience and judges the structures of human social relationships by their productivity. Prose can speed
up time or save it, simply by playing out the experiments humanity is confronted with."[2]

Similarly, novelist Irmtraud Morgner, known for her extraordinarily imaginative and rich montage novels, asserts that "prose requires many individual experiences; there must be huge treasure troves of experience in large segments of a population before the Word breaks forth as Literature. Even if public discourse about certain experiences is not deemed desirable, the experiences are nevertheless registered."[3]

The twenty-five women included here represent diverse generational, ethnic, social, and educational experiences, political orientations, and approaches to writing within the GDR context, from documentary, reportage, and essay to fantasy and satire. All our selections address questions relating to *women at work, women in personal relationships,* and *women's self-consciousness.* Because these gender issues are present across cultures, the reader is more likely to notice the aspects of each text that refer to the specific GDR milieu and to ask what was different or similar about the cultural assumptions of writers and their characters in that society. We have consciously chosen to bring to American readers the voices of women whose ideas and perceptions were shaped primarily in the context of the socialist German state, since they differ significantly from their Western counterparts and from older generations of East German women who began writing before the founding of the GDR in 1949.[4]

These texts, deliberately located within GDR socialism, contain references to both welcome and unwelcome features that have been dismantled in the process of unification, along with the Wall and the former German-German border. First and foremost, readers will have encountered numerous indications of the fact that women took for granted their participation in the labor force with extensive state supports. These benefits are described quite precisely in the four interviews from Irene Böhme's documentary volume. The filmmaker and single mother in Christa Müller's "Candida" relies on a boarding nursery, as well as an understanding collaborator, in order to pursue her work. Daniela Dahn appropriately criticizes the day of paid leave for women to do housework as a patronizing gesture that ensures gender-role stereotyping in family management. Maja Wiens's description of women's experiences in the gynecological ward of a hospital reflects the fact of legalized abortion (since 1972), as well as the complexity of the issue for all concerned.

The division of Germany, the experience of the border, and travel restrictions also figure in a number of texts, breaking one social taboo of prerevolutionary polite conversation. Helga Schütz's Anna goes to the Friedrichstraße checkpoint in East Berlin at midnight, the visitors' curfew, to "see the show" of Western visitors' goodbyes—in this case playing voyeur to her former lover's parting from his new Western girlfriend. She watches the pension-ers—the only general class of GDR citizens to enjoy unrestricted travel before the opening of the Wall—returning from "over there," an everyday expression in Cold War Germany, East and West alike, with which Böhme signifies the alienation it connotes. Anna's nocturnal wandering over the fields from the train station takes her along a border road closed to through traffic, an apt setting for the scene in which we see Anna huddled asleep beside a ghostly threshing machine. Not unlike Anna's fascination with the impossible unknown at Friedrichstraße is that of the young child Candida in Christa Müller's story: when her father, who has emigrated to the West and visits periodically, disappears across the bridge to West Berlin, he is as utterly "gone" in her perception as the doll she drops over the bridge into the river.

Our texts also reflect the socialist economic system, its terminology and its structures. Work is often referred to in terms of brigades and collectives; Party members are "comrades"; the centralized economy's emphasis on pro-duction quotas results in stress on employees, whether in a mathematical research institute, in factory work, or in agricultural production. Two texts mention the indoctrination sessions (*Parteilehrjahr*) that were mandatory for Party members. In Morgner's "Tightrope," the nuclear physics institute de-pends on hard currency from the government to buy Western high-tech equipment. The scarcity of goods and equipment for home repair and con-struction, and the practice of solidaric sharing that often resulted, is seen when Christine Wolter's protagonist in "Early Summer" wonders if her neighbor knows "when the electric saw is coming" and sighs that there are no vacuum cleaner bags to be had. Though housing was a social pri-ority in the GDR and there were virtually no homeless prior to the advent of the market economy, the fact that many families were cramped into too little living space while waiting for better accommodations is reflected in, for example, "The Bridge Builder," "Dignity," "The Other Side of the Boule-vard," and "Lies Have Bright Wings," where a corner of the kitchen serves as bedroom or nursery. Gabriele Eckart's interview with Ilse G., director of an agricultural production cooperative (LPG), offers an insider's view of the economics and the decision-making processes in that form of farm labor organization. We see an occasional Trabant, the most common GDR passen-ger car. Apitz's Manny goes to the Soviet Union to study Marxism, and Elsa to Leningrad as part of a factory employees' tour.

Likewise, there are markers in these texts that indicate how the political culture and policy of a stagnant and fear-ridden one-party system did or did not affect individuals. For example, the fact that personal contacts with Westerners were seen as a corrupting influence and strictly prohibited in many contexts does not keep Ute G. (in Maxie Wander's documentary narrative) from describing how much she enjoyed conversing with her Dutch lover in Leningrad about their very different concepts of freedom.

Such markers place characters and situations in a political context that no longer exists; however, they are rarely the primary ingredients in women's experience of their work, their relationships, and their self-perception. In a few instances, such as Angela Stachowa's "Talking about My Girlfriend Resa," the narrator could be describing the dynamics of any love triangle. There is nothing specifically socialist about Resa's affair; the issues are common to women the world over. What marks this text as more characteristic of GDR women authors than of many Western counterparts is the ironic detachment of the narrator.

Women and Work

Readers accustomed to a service-oriented economy may have been surprised by the value women in these texts place on production and collective work. Wander's Ute G. registers her dismay at the discrimination inherent in banning pregnant women from night-shift jobs. Krauß's depiction of Felicity Haendschel and her tired, reproachful mother Marianne suggests that Marianne's unhappiness stems from having sacrificed her meaningful work in the coal briquette factory in order to care for her grandson. On the other hand, Gerti Tetzner's Karen W., working in a textile mill at half her former lawyer's pay (in defiance of her husband), has a "hesitant sense of demonstrably useful work" on the production line—which disappears as she contemplates the "impenetrable web of motions." She looks back on the time when, as a lawyer, she had sent people into production for disciplinary purposes, now realizing that was no solution. Tetzner's implicit criticism addresses two forms of alienation. One is the class bias Karen W. encounters in the workplace: when her supervisor learns she is a lawyer, he stops saying "Sweetie" and "Karen, do this, do that," and begins addressing her with proprietary and surreptitious glances. But what most alienates Karen W. in her experience of her own and her husband's work lives is "this closed circle of life and work." Tetzner's image of the "visible track, as if you reached a certain goal by way of certain stations," is indicative of the critique of linear, instrumental thinking that we find also in Morgner, Wolf, and Königsdorf. These four, all belonging to the generation born before the war, articulate this critique poignantly and consistently in a social context, while their younger peers often situate the problem in the personal sphere.

The perennial theme of the double or triple burden of women's work in the workplace and in caring for men and/or children is centrally problematized in Charlotte Worgitzky's "I Quit" and Morgner's "The Tightrope," and is implied in "Candida," "The Bridge Builder," "The Contemporary Feminine," and several of the documentary interviews. Most striking about the depiction of work-related conflicts in these stories is that the women are portrayed as competent and consciously interactive with their male counterparts, who may or may not know how to handle women's independence or their different approaches to the notion of productivity. In "Third Fruit of Bitterfeld: The Tightrope," Vera Hill puts her colleague (and lover) Gurnemann on the spot by her honesty: when he claims that her "absurd" and "unreal" actions (walking on air) are threatening the institute and giving "the competition" an edge, she asks whether he regards her as competition.

In "The Tightrope," the central issue seems no longer to be the double burden but rather the need to broaden the scope of society's conceptions of the rational and the real in both public and private spheres to include women's ways of working and perceiving, so that the "balancing act"— which is fatal when it tips in favor of the boss's or the system's definition of reality—will become unnecessary. In different ways, Worgitzky, Morgner, and Königsdorf all thematize the syndrome of professional men who seem to be driven to define and control their women associates, whether in professional matters or in the personal sphere. Helga Königsdorf's prize nominee mathematician, Cornelia Froehlich, is finally called a "shameless hussy" by "His Eminence," once his purposes have been thoroughly thwarted, precisely because of her imperviousness to his attempts at revenge and for the added insult of being happy following her divorce. Implicit in these authors' writings, as in the younger Christiane Grosz's "The Trick," is that behind the achievement ethic is male fear of loss of control, whether that control is illusory or real. In this literature, admissions of weakness or perceived discrepancies often figure in the picture of human productivity, challenging traditional views of power and implying the inclusion of a feminine dimension to productivity.

Women and Men, Women and Other Women, Women and Family

What about the role of men in these women's texts? The collection spans a broad spectrum. In Tetzner's semiautobiographical "Karen W.," the dissolution of the first-person narrator's amicable relationship with her husband stems more from a sense of social alienation than from any hostility toward her husband or men in general. Rosemarie Zeplin's "Shadow of a Lover" deconstructs the "miracle" of Pilgram and Annette's courtship by showing the pattern of traditional gender roles as unworkable. Pilgram's patronizing and conventional opportunism and Annette's codependence lead inexorably to her painful and unceremonious departure from the city she loved. Similarly, Doris Paschiller's "Dignity" deconstructs the myth of the perfect "white, white wedding" from the perspective of a five-months pregnant bride who feels that this wedding has "fallen upon her like a judgment." Paschiller's matter-of-fact description of Johanna and Robert's marriage and young parenthood reflects all the classic emotional ambivalences. Presented from Johanna's perspective, the narrative's laconic observations about life as a mother, lover, and worker suggest that there is both alienation and affirmation. In Maya Wiens's "Dream Limits," it is also without hostility that Nina encounters her lover Thomas after the abortion of their second pregnancy, though her thoughts reflect a profound sense of pain and alienation at his inability to relate to the many levels of experience that the first seven-eighths of the narrative before Thomas's entrance have conveyed.

The documentary selections in Böhme's "Women and Socialism" provide a symptomatic mix of women's experiences with men and partnership. Regine R., single and a successful manager with three children, at thirty-seven marries a truck driver younger than she. Karin A. recounts how, after marrying too young and being miserable at first, she learned to live by her own expectations rather than her husband's. Ingeborg T.'s divorce results in a GDR "equal rights" ruling that the professional woman pay alimony to support her son, who lives with her ex-husband's mother. Marianne E., who married naive and inexperienced at eighteen, goes through a stage of competing with her ex-husband to get her revenge for his behavior (but also to give her daughter a role model of a competent mother), then arrives at an amicable collegial relationship with him. That she creates a "woman's household" with a friend and no longer expects to find the "man of her life" is a fact she attributes to skepticism toward herself, not toward men.

Positive relationships with men are also depicted without marriage, and with inherent ambivalences. In Maria Seidemann's "Bridge Builder" the relationship described is a contractually temporary one between a woman with a background of parental abuse and neglect, who understands a lot about vulnerability and the necessity of arming oneself against it, and a worker who expects to leave town when his job is finished. Seidemann begins the story from the perspective of the lonely man in search of a woman, revealing Benita's perspective only through dialogue and, eventually, the inserted monologue in which she tells her life story. Gregor is portrayed as sincere, and aware that as a temporary lover he cannot expect Benita to give up her "armor" and, by extension, her emotional distance.

Wander's Ute G. respects her partner Ralph as a man who thinks the prevalent stereotypes of tough men and submissive women are "gross, dishonest, and unnatural." Renate Apitz's narrator keeps trying to find men for Elsa in all her incarnations: Charlie is likable but hopelessly self-absorbed; his successors drink too much and are boring; the husband of the last fantasy is nameless and not further described.

Narratives about women's relationships with or reflections on other women, such as we find in Morgenstern, Helmecke, Wander, Wolter, Krauß, Stachowa, and Paschiller often suggest ambiguities in the narrators' or protagonists' evolving self-perception as well. In Beate Morgenstern, the older woman's low self-esteem becomes more and more evident as she tries to enter the personal world of her younger colleague on the "other side of the boulevard." In Wolter's story of attempted rape, we become acutely aware of the loss experienced by both the victim-protagonist and the perpetrator's wife, whose relationship is disrupted when the wife refuses to acknowledge the breach of trust that has occurred among three friends. By choosing to depict a self-respecting, mature, and confident widow who seeks approval for her garden as for her own appearance, Wolter makes her story all the more strikingly understated. In Monika Helmecke's day-in-the-life-of-a-mother story, the mother tries to signal her loneliness to the friends she has gone out with by suggesting they stay out a while longer for a walk, but she knows to expect the "friendly pirouettes" that she hears as blunt rejection. A similar sense of isolation is experienced by Johanna in Paschiller's "Dignity," when her friends come to visit and find there is no longer time or space in Johanna's life just to sit around and talk. In Stachowa's "Resa" the narrator's reflection about her friend challenges the reader—partly by communicating her own mystified fascination—to look beyond the stereotypes of the "young, single woman" at the layers of paradox in Resa's life, particularly in her "stuck" position with a lover whose unalterable devotion to his "Mommy" Resa refuses to see.

It is striking that of these twenty-five texts, very few specifically thematize friendship between women. Other than the intergenerational attempt at friendship in Morgenstern's story, only Wander's interview implies a comfortable difference of taste and opinion between Ute G. and Erni and the prospect for a workable extended family living situation among the two couples.

Women appear as mothers—and daughters—in many different circumstances in this volume but exhibit similar perspectives and experiences. Helga Schubert's "Breathing Room" traces the consciousness of a mother from her pregnancy at nineteen to the day her soldier son returns from basic training eager to see his girlfriend and for the first time calls her "mum." Krauß's Felicity Haendschel, a teenage single mother living with her parents, defines herself in large part in terms of the adolescent conflict with her mother.

Women and Self-Image

If "prose creates human beings," as Wolf believes, it is fair to ask what models and images of women these writers have created. We see women learning to express awareness of their bodies and the emotions they experience in relation to their bodies, as in Schubert's nineteen-year-old new mother, or Paschiller's Annette ("So that's how it works, the breast expels something, like a cow. Who would have thought"). We see identity conflicts, as in Grosz, Morgner, and Tetzner, which arise out of an unwillingness to compromise one's sense of the integrity of life and work, or, as in the case of Schütz's Anna, are caused by a ruptured love relationship. Wolf's own narrative voice in the tomcat tale, hidden beneath the figure of the fictitious editor and ironically informing even the tomcat's words, places the identity conflict at the heart of the male culture itself.

One index of the vitality of this literature, and of the multiplicity of voices exploring women's identity, is the variety of prose forms and individual styles that have evolved. We have focused on short prose forms in the interest of exposing readers to the diversity of women's experiences and analyses typical of the 1970s and 1980s. Moreover, the genre of *Kurzprosa* (short prose) as an open form is particularly characteristic of the decade represented here and of the aesthetics of women's writing. An important new short prose form that developed in the 1970s as a vehicle for women's voices was the taped interview pioneered by Sarah Kirsch with *Die Pantherfrau* (1974), now available in English,[5] and followed by Maxie Wander's *Guten Morgen, du Schöne* (1977) and others, including the volumes by Eckart and Böhme excerpted here. In Wander, one senses the caring and involved presence of the interviewer behind the first-person narratives of her subjects. Here, the function of the writer-interviewer is neither to speak in her own voice nor to gather information to support a thesis but rather to facilitate a relationship of trust and intimacy which results in the mutual creation of an open-ended, authentic life story without violating her subject's privacy. Eckart followed Wander with her oral histories of the Havelland fruit growers, which appear in the 1984 volume from which "Ilse" is taken. In the same year, Böhme introduced the narratives of representative women from different generations of GDR history with *Die da drüben* (literally, "those people over there"). However, unlike Wander and Eckart, Böhme framed her taped first-person accounts in a series of her own interpretive essays (not included here), thus assuming an authorial voice and objectifying her subjects to some extent.

Another form that women began to appropriate in this period, the *feuilleton*, a short essay or commentary, is illustrated by the selection from Daniela Dahn in this volume. Technically a journalistic form, *feuilletons* have begun to be collected in independent single-author volumes with a life of their own. Most often lighthearted but serious in intent, they seem especially suited to public reading, a form that was crucial to the process of communication between writers and the public in the GDR.

The short stories included here comprise a wide range of narrative styles and techniques, from Helmecke's laconic, almost monosyllabic moment-by-moment description of a single day in the life of the mother of two young children to Morgner's highly allusive language, symbolic imagery, and intricate structure. Whether the reader associates the image of the ropewalker-superwoman with Nietzsche's rope-dancer and *Übermensch*[6] or simply experiences it, the tightrope is a powerful metaphor for the creative balancing act required of those with career, parenting, and household responsibilities. Morgner's montage combining a detailed technical description of nuclear scattering experiments with the story of Vera Hill's public "offense" may appear arbitrary and alienating, until one notices formulations in Professor Gurnemann's description of the experiment that, unknown to him, draw attention to the subtext of the main narrative and explain the otherwise abrupt demise of Vera Hill: "violation of the momentum and energy balance"; "she is dealing with two-armed events"; "the elastic interactions can be distinguished from the inelastic ones"; "individual reaction channels are studied . . . with regard to the excitation of mesons by nucleons."[7] By alternating interpretive material about conflicts experienced by the protagonist with passages spoken by her "opposite," Morgner creates the interconnection between the two worlds, which the female physicist perceives, but the professor in his one-track orientation does not.

Similarly complex and multilayered is Wolf's "Revised Philosophy of a Tomcat." This tale resonates with motifs from the German Romantics, Ludwig Tieck's *Puss 'n Boots* (1797), and E.T.A. Hoffmann's *Lebensansichten eines Katers* (1819–21), as well as from the Faustian tradition in that Mikhail Bulgakov's *The Master and Margarita* is alluded to in the first line of the story as the tomcat finds inspiration from a novel.[8] Another ironic allusion, in the context of the tomcat's condescending comment about humans' wish to "be helpful and good," is to Goethe's poem "Das Göttliche" (The divine), with its opening line, "Edel sei der Mensch, hilfreich und gut" (Noble let man be, helpful and good). Above all, through the persona of the literate tomcat, Wolf ridicules the highly technical jargon and rationality fetish of the GDR's "scientific-technological revolution" in the 1960s. By creating a feline male narrator who has become totally accommodated to the instrumental thinking and gender stereotypes of this technological culture, and a fictitious editor of his writings whose perspective more nearly resembles that of the author, Wolf provides a subtext that critiques the male-dominated world, its blind servitude to "progress," its demeaning of women, and its engendering of emotional cripples.

The collection also offers a wide variety of narrator figures and narrative stances, which involve the reader in different ways. A first-person narrative such as Tetzner's interior monologue "Karen W." consciously undermines the authority of the "I," focusing all attention on the protagonist's intense will to leave her husband—who is submerged in his own sensitivities and has become accommodated to the system—while letting the narrator's need for warmth and affection present a real conflict in her resolve to leave him. Third-person narratives that are descriptive in style, such as Krauß's "Work," create a whole panorama of "still-life" images set off by sparse dialogue. Katja Lange-Müller and Maja Wiens, both born in the 1950s and hence among the youngest of our authors, create narrators who are not present to the reader but step aside to allow us to experience the full shock of the blunt instrument of their narrative. Both describe with relentless and intimate detail the dehumanizing experiences of women in institutional "care" situations. Lange-Müller's "Sometimes Death Comes in Slippers" reproduces the idiom of a geriatric ward down to the verbatim instructions for preparing a corpse; Wiens's "Dream Limits" achieves a similar effect through the static rhythm of clipped, cold sentences as she recounts the abortion experience of her protagonist.

Helga Schütz's "In Anna's Name" is the only text included here in which the narrative perspective shifts from third to first person and back again, reflecting Anna's trying on of faces and identities, like masks, and her inability to separate herself from Rolf. It is an excellent illustration of the recognition among women writers of the complexities involved in learning to say "I."[9]

Interestingly, there are only two male narrator figures among these twenty-five pieces by women authors: Christa Wolf's tomcat, and the male gynecologist of Petra Werner's "Lies Have Bright Wings," who tells the story of the single mother desperately in search of a father for her children. The author uses a subtle narrative trick to create this lonely workaholic's character: each time he recounts his interactions with Camilla/Ilona, the narrator glibly attributes traditionally "feminine" sensitivity to his own behavior ("I replied gently"; "I asked patiently"; "I asked innocently"; "I sighed"; "Honest, I tried to judge her fairly") and reproaches Camilla for traditionally "masculine" acts of defiance, contempt, and duplicity. Werner's male narrator identifies not with the helplessness of the teenager desperate for an identity but with the policeman whom the fourteen-year-old Camilla/Ilona begs to change the name on her ID. He refers to the space they share as "my apartment" and the progeny of their relationship as "my son," while Camilla's discourse reflects her own perspective with "our apartment" and "our son." The author thus creates an ironic subtext of sympathetic understanding for the behavior of "Camilla," behavior that is outrageous to the narrator himself and, by extension, to the world in which he is accustomed to dominating.

Another group of stories relies heavily on elements of the fantastic, on magic and fantasy. In Apitz's "Harmonious Elsa," the narrator, a graduate student fantasizing during a university lecture about how her professor manages to integrate her multiple roles, literally "creates" a series of possible life stories for her mentor, including men, jobs, and children. Werner's Camilla devises multiple identities in the attempt to forge a real one. In Grosz's "The Trick" the female magician protagonist has become physically ill from suppressing her own strength and talent and from watching her husband, the performer, attempt to remain credible without actually knowing any magic. In this context, the motif of magic becomes a metaphor for the power relationship in a marriage; the issue becomes one of veracity versus complicity with a whole system of lies: "I could not compromise. I could either be alone and do magic or be married." And in the end, illness forces the larger question: "What would happen if, for the sake of truth, someone [that is one of her husband's "subjects" in the circus audience, who "plays along" with his trick] remained silent?" Seidemann's "Bridge Builder" turns on the ancient motif of the invisible magic hood that disguises its wearer and makes him or her invulnerable. In Charlotte Worgitzky's "I Quit," it is a blue-stockinged angel who enables the school principal to maintain her multiple roles in career, marriage, parenting, and household.

Beyond their exploration of new forms and genres, perhaps the most important contribution of these writers has been to question the basic values at the root of their own society and, by extension, all of industrial society—and, in some cases, to offer imaginative alternatives. Christa Wolf in particular—as part of the generation that experienced fascism as young women and then, as mature adults, the major social changes that occurred in the GDR and the industrial world—has become known for depicting the quality of authenticity that derives from facing head on the conflicts and contradictions inherent in one's culture and oneself. Like Irmtraud Morgner, Wolf has articulated a feminist critique of Western civilization in a context different from that of her Western counterparts. She has contributed, especially since her Frankfurt Lectures on Poetics (1983) and her novel *Cassandra* (the English version of which also contains the Frankfurt Lectures), to the growing international discourse about *weibliches Schreiben* (feminine writing and, by extension, feminist aesthetics), as well as to that about the connection between patriarchy and the threat to survival of the species. Both Wolf and Morgner have made the connection as well between the discounting of imagination and creative thinking in Western thought and industrial culture's tendency toward aggression.

Christa Wolf observed in "Berührung" (In touch), her introduction to Maxie Wander's 1977 interview collection from which "Ute G." is taken,[10] that it was precisely the legal emancipation of women in the GDR, "the opportunity our society gave them to do what the men do," that predictably led them to ask, "What *do* the men do, anyway? And is that what I want, really?" Daniela Dahn took the question further when she asserted in 1980 that "by now word has gotten around that emancipation doesn't mean turning into a man or doing away with difference" but that it was not yet quite clear just what the "contemporary feminine" does imply. The self-examination of whole generations of women, their probing into the nature of authority structures in themselves, in relationships, and in institutions has, according to Wolf, extended far beyond the quest for individual identity and power in male terms to the "radical claim to life as whole persons, capable of using all their senses and abilities."[11] This claim determines both one's ability to think and act collectively, in identification with a group, and one's ability to say "I," to experience personal responsibility, as Helga Königsdorf expressed it at the Tenth Writers' Congress of the GDR in 1987.[12] But whole persons who have not lost the human inclination toward mutuality and cooperation cannot live fully if they are isolated from others who have lost that gift or who are victimized by the culture of dominance. Dahn concludes her humorous reflection about the desire of emancipated women to be allowed to be weak by noting very soberly that "this desire for weakness within strength" is not only the "contemporary feminine" but the "essentially human." Masculine weakness within strength has been buried under masculine vanity for so many centuries that it is "barely able to acknowledge itself." In a similar vein, Wolf renders her technology critique gender-specific when in her tomcat story she creates an ironic variation on the classic definition of love in 1 Corinthians 13—"*Ratio*, the force that knows all things, explains all things, and controls all things"—implying that the traditionally male dependence on reason as control has devalued the creative force of love.

Thus the literary legacy of this representative group of writers is not women's empowerment based on an essentialist definition of female difference or superiority but a reintegration of "feminine" values into all human life. What one critic wrote of Christine Wolter is true for many of these writers, who in very different ways "carefully, but utterly unsentimentally, [forge] into areas of conflict that can no longer be resolved through individual compromise."[13]

Notes

1. Christa Wolf, "Subjektive Authentizität," interview with Hans Kaufmann in *Weimarer Beiträge* 6 (1974): 90–112.

2. Christa Wolf, *The Reader and the Writer: Essays, Sketches, Memories* (New York: International Publishers, 1977), p. 212.

3. Irmtraud Morgner, "Frauenstaat," interview with Harrie Lemmens in *Konkret*, September 1984, p. 59.

4. Of the twenty-five authors in the anthology, one is deceased, and three left the GDR prior to the mass exodus of 1989–90.

5. Sarah Kirsch, *The Panther Woman*, trans. Marion Faber (Lincoln: University of Nebraska Press, 1989).

6. Friedrich Nietzsche, *Thus Spake Zarathustra*, trans. Marianne Cowan (Chicago: Gateway, 1957), pp. 11–12. In the rope-dancer's act (Zarathustra's Prologue, Part 6), he loses his footing and hurtles to the depths when a rival overtakes him.

7. Professor John Dawson of the University of New Hampshire's Nuclear Physics Group comments that though bubble chambers are no longer used for nuclear scattering experiments, they were current at the time Morgner's story was written, and the descriptions she puts in the mouth of Professor Gurnemann are amazingly accurate.

8. The quotation is from the last paragraph of chap. 6 of Mikhail Bulgakov, *The*

Master and Margarita (New York: Penguin, 1985), p. 75, and is a literal rendition of the Russian sentence. The novel was first published serially in Russian and not translated into German until after Wolf wrote this story.

9. Wolf's *The Quest for Christa T.* sparked this discussion, which has continued since its first appearance in the GDR in 1968.

10. Maxie Wander, *Guten Morgen, du Schöne* (Berlin: Buchverlag der Morgen, 1977).

11. Christa Wolf, "In Touch" (my translation, from *Die Dimension des Autors* [Darmstadt/Neuwied: Luchterhand, 1987], p. 207).

12. Writers' Union of the GDR, *Zehnter Schriftstellerkongreß der DDR, 1987*, vol. 1, *Plenum* (Berlin/Weimar: Aufbau, 1988), p. 96.

13. Eduard Zak, Afterword to *Wie ich meine Unschuld verlor* (Berlin: Aufbau, 1976), p. 128.

Sources

Gerti Tetzner's "Karen W." is translated from the introductory scene of her novel *Karen W.* (Halle/Leipzig: Mitteldeutscher Verlag, 1974). © Mitteldeutscher Verlag, Halle (Saale), 1974.

Renate Apitz's "Harmonious Elsa" ("Die harmonische Else") is a short story translated from her *Evastöchter* (Rostock: Hinstorff, 1981), pp. 92–99. © VEB Hinstorff Verlag, Rostock, 1981.

Maxie Wander's "Ute G., 24, Skilled Worker, Single, One Child" ("Ute G., 24, Facharbeiterin, ledig, ein Kind") is an interview narrative translated from the collection *Guten Morgen, du Schöne: Frauen in der DDR* (Berlin: Buchverlag der Morgen, 1977), pp. 36–47. © Buchverlag der Morgen, Berlin/DDR, 1977.

Charlotte Worgitzky's "I Quit" ("Karriere abgesagt") is a short story translated from her *Vieräugig oder blind,* (Berlin: Buchverlag der Morgen, 1978), pp. 77–91. © Buchverlag der Morgen, Berlin/DDR, 1978.

Christa Müller's "Candida" is a short story translated from her *Vertreibung aus dem Paradies* (Berlin: Aufbau, 1979), pp. 7–56. © Aufbau-Verlag, Berlin and Weimar, 1979.

Christine Wolter's "Early Summer" ("Frühsommer") is a short story translated from her *Wie ich meine Unschuld verlor* (Berlin: Aufbau, 1976), pp. 36–45. © Aufbau-Verlag Berlin and Weimar, 1976.

Helga Schütz's "In Anna's Name" ("In Annas Namen") is an excerpt translated from her novel *In Annas Namen* (Berlin: Aufbau, 1986), pp. 128–35. © Aufbau-Verlag, Berlin and Weimar, 1986.

Christa Wolf's "Revised Philosophy of a Tomcat" ("Neue Lebensansichten eines Katers") is translated from one of a trilogy of short stories, *Unter den Linden: Drei unwahrscheinliche Geschichten* (Berlin: Aufbau, 1974), pp. 97–123. © Aufbau-Verlag, Berlin and Weimar, 1974.

Irmtraud Morgner's "Third Fruit of Bitterfeld: The Tightrope" (Dritte Bitterfelder Frucht: Das Seit) is a short story translated from her novel *Leben und Abenteuer der Trobadora Beatriz nach Zeugnissen ihrer Spielfrau Laura* (Berlin: Aufbau, 1974), pp. 388–94. © Aufbau-Verlag, Berlin and Weimar, 1974.

Helga Königsdorf's "The Surefire Tip" ("Der todsichere Tip") is a short story translated from her *Der Lauf der Dinge* (Berlin: Aufbau, 1982), pp. 139–50. © Aufbau-Verlag, Berlin and Weimar, 1982.

Rosemarie Zeplin's "The Shadow of a Lover" ("Schattenriß eines Lieb-habers"), is an excerpt translated from her novella *Schattenriß eines Liebhabers* (Berlin: Aufbau, 1980), pp. 5–19. © Aufbau-Verlag, Berlin and Weimar, 1980.

Daniela Dahn's "The Contemporary Feminine" ("Das heutig Weibliche") is an essay translated from her *Spitzenzeit* (Halle/Leipzig: Mitteldeutscher, 1980), pp. 121–23. © Mitteldeutscher Verlag, Halle (Saale), 1980.

Irene Böhme's "Women and Socialism: Four Interviews" is a series of autobiographical narratives translated from her essay collection, *Die da drüben* (Berlin: Rotbuchverlag, 1982), pp. 83–102. © Irene Böhme.

Christiane Grosz's "The Trick" ("Der Trick") is a short story translated from the anthology *Das Kostüm* (Berlin: Aufbau, 1982), pp. 162–65. © Aufbau-Verlag, Berlin and Weimar, 1982.

Monika Helmecke's "September 30th" ("Der 30. September") is a short story translated from her *Klopfzeichen* (Berlin: Neues Leben, 1979), pp. 91–97. © Verlag Neues Leben, Berlin/DDR, 1979.

Helga Schubert's "Breathing Room" ("Luft zum Leben") is a short story translated from her *Blickwinkel* (Berlin: Aufbau, 1984), pp. 28–36. © Aufbau-Verlag, Berlin and Weimar, 1984.

Beate Morgenstern's "The Other Side of the Boulevard" ("Jenseits der Allee") is the title short story of her *Jenseits der Allee* (Berlin: Aufbau, 1979), pp. 31–51. © Aufbau-Verlag, Berlin and Weimar, 1979.

Maria Seideman's "The Bridge Builder" ("Der Brückenbauer") is a short story translated from *Der Tag an dem Sir Henry starb* (Berlin: Eulenspiegel, 1980), pp. 36–49. © Eulenspiegel Verlag, Berlin/DDR, 1980.

Angela Stachowa's "Talking about My Girlfriend Resa" ("Plauderei über meine Freundin Resi") is a short story translated from her *Kleine Verführung* (Halle/Leipzig: Mitteldeutscher Verlag, 1983), pp. 64–76. © Mitteldeutscher Verlag, Halle-Leipzig, 1983.

Angela Krauß's "Work" ("Arbeit") is translated from the first chapter of her novella *Das Vergnügen* (Berlin: Aufbau, 1984), pp. 7–24. © Aufbau-Verlag, Berlin and Weimar, 1984.

Gabriele Eckart's "Ilse, 56, Chair of an Agricultural Cooperative" is an interview narrative translated from her *So sehe ick die Sache: Protokolle aus der DDR* (Cologne: Kiepenheuer & Witsch, 1984), pp. 119–36. © Gabriele Eckart, 1984.

Petra Werner's "Lies Have Bright Wings" ("Die Lüge hat bunte Flügel") is the title story translated from her *Die Lüge hat bunte Flügel* (Berlin: Neues Leben, 1986), pp. 130–59. © Verlag Neues Leben, Berlin/DDR, 1986.

Maja Wiens's "Dream Limits" ("Traumgrenzen") is translated from the first chapter of her novel *Traumgrenzen* (Berlin: Neues Leben, 1983), pp. 5–13. © Verlag Neues Leben, Berlin/DDR, 1983.

Katja Lange-Müller's "Sometimes Death Comes in Slippers" ("Manchmal kommt der Dot auf Latschen") is a short story reprinted in her *Wehleid wie im Leben* (Frankfurt am Main: Fischer, 1988), pp. 26–38. It was first published in *AUSKUNFT 2: Neue Prosa aus der DDR,* edited by Stefan Heym. © Katja Lange-Müller, 1978.

Doris Paschiller's "Dignity" ("Die Würde") is an excerpt translated from her novel *Die Würde* (Berlin: Buchverlag der Morgen, 1980), pp. 7–19. © Buchverlag der Morgen, Berlin/DDR, 1980.

Other Volumes in the European Women Writers Series

Artemisia
By Anna Banti
Translated by Shirley D'Ardia Caracciolo

Bitter Healing
German Women Writers from 1700 to 1830
An Anthology
Edited by Jeannine Blackwell and Susanne Zantop

The Maravillas District
By Rosa Chacel
Translated by d. a. démers

The Book of Promethea
By Hélène Cixous
Translated by Betsy Wing

Maria Zef
By Paola Drigo
Translated by Blossom Steinberg Kirschenbaum

Woman to Woman
By Marguerite Duras and Xavière Gauthier
Translated by Katherine A. Jensen

Hitchhiking
Twelve German Tales
By Gabriele Eckart
Translated by Wayne Kvam

The Tongue Snatchers
By Claudine Herrmann
Translated by Nancy Kline

Mother Death
By Jeanne Hyvrard
Translated by Laurie Edson

The House of Childhood
By Marie Luise Kaschnitz
Translated by Anni Whissen

The Panther Woman
Five Tales from the Cassette Recorder
By Sarah Kirsch
Translated by Marion Faber

On Our Own Behalf
Women's Tales from Catalonia
Edited by Kathleen McNerney

Absent Love
A Chronicle
By Rosa Montero
Translated by Cristina de la Torre and Diana Glad

The Delta Function
By Rosa Montero
Translated by Kari A. Easton and Yolanda Molina Gavilan

Music from a Blue Well
By Torborg Nedreaas
Translated by Bibbi Lee

Nothing Grows by Moonlight
By Torborg Nedreaas
Translated by Bibbi Lee

Why Is There Salt in the Sea?
By Brigitte Schwaiger
Translated by Sieglinde Lug

The Same Sea as Every Summer
By Esther Tusquets
Translated by Margaret E. W. Jones